VINEYARDS TO VICTORY

BY TED HART

Vineyards To Victory

A French Soldier, Yorktown,
and the Making of an American Family

By Ted Hart

DEDICATION

*To my fifth-great-grandfather Siméon Gaugien,
and to every member of our family, past and present, whose labor,
faith, and hope built the path that led to me. And to my children,
Sarah Grace and Alexander Michael, may you always remember
where you come from and the strength that lives within you.*

TABLE OF CONTENTS

PART I
ROOTS & REVELATION

PART II
THE SOUND OF DRUMS

ACKNOWLEDGMENTS

This book rests upon the archival work of historians and researchers in France and the United States who preserved the records that made Siméon Gaugien's story recoverable after more than two centuries.

In France, I am especially indebted to Jean-Marie Guillaume of Saint-Marcel for his genealogical expertise and guidance in local archives. This work also draws on extensive French scholarship and archival research reflected in the bibliography.

In the United States, I benefited from foundational scholarship, including edited journals of French officers and English translations of primary accounts.

All translations and interpretations from eighteenth-century French sources have been undertaken with reference to primary documents and archival paleography guides and informed by consultation with French researchers when additional interpretation was required. Any errors are my own.

I thank my family, friends, and colleagues for their unwavering support.

ABOUT THE AUTHOR

Ted Hart is the fifth-great-grandson of Siméon Gaugien, a French artilleryman who served with Rochambeau's expeditionary forces in America. His multi-year research across French and American archives confirmed Gaugien's service and became *Vineyards to Victory*.

Hart is a global philanthropy executive and the author of eight books on leadership, management, and social impact. His professional career informs his approach to historical narrative, with a focus on service, sacrifice, and the enduring consequences of ordinary lives shaped by extraordinary events. He lives in the Washington, D.C. area.

MUSICAL COMPANION

To accompany this narrative, I have composed and produced a nine-song original album inspired by the events and lives depicted in Vineyards to Victory. The America 250 Companion Album traces the emotional arc of the Franco-American alliance, from the vineyards of France to the siege at Yorktown.

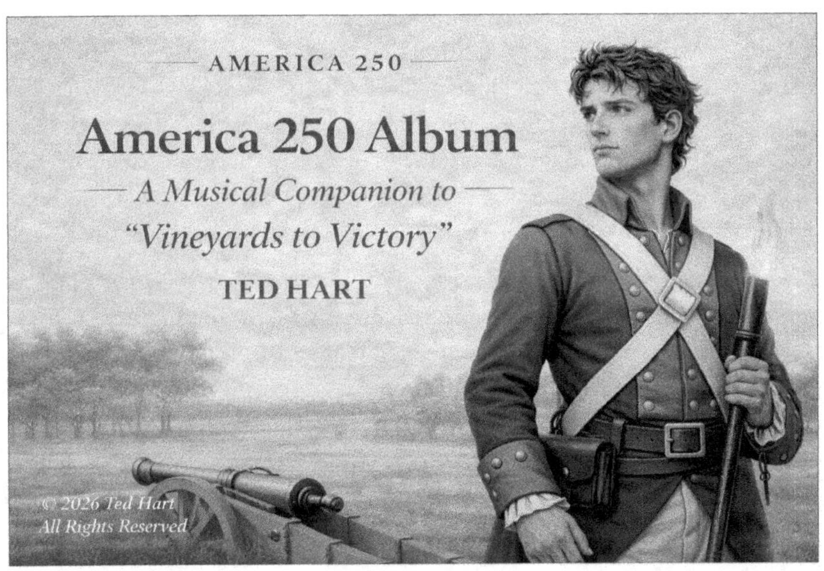

Readers may listen by scanning the QR code below.

A NOTE TO THE READER

This book begins in the present but soon carries you back to a time and place now distant. The story that follows is grounded in the true life of my ancestor, Siméon Gaugien, who left the vineyards of eastern France at seventeen to fight for American independence.

Throughout this book, I use the term War of American Independence to refer to the conflict as it was known in France (la Guerre d'Indépendance) during Siméon's lifetime.

This work is grounded in archival and genealogical research across two continents. Primary sources include military rolls of the Régiment d'Auxonne, parish registers from Franche-Comté, immigration records, letters, regimental orders, and firsthand accounts from the French expeditionary forces of 1780 to 1783. Every soldier named in these pages is a documented historical individual, drawn directly from the regimental rosters.

Dates, battles, ships, regiments, and locations have been verified. Siméon's entry into the Régiment d'Auxonne artillery, a selective branch requiring literacy and mathematical skill, is confirmed by records in the French Ministry of War and the U.S. National Archives. His voyage with Admiral de Ternay's fleet and his service at Yorktown are equally attested.

Where the historical record falls silent, I have drawn on period customs, documented soldier experiences, and informed historical judgment. The goal has been fidelity to historical context and to the spirit of those who lived this story.

This book does not retell the war through its famous commanders; it follows the conflict as experienced by those who lived within its uncertainty, marked by waiting, illness, endurance, alliance, and loss. Victory, when it came, was neither inevitable nor evenly shared.

Though centered on one man, this narrative echoes the lives of many whose service shaped events and whose stories seldom survive. It follows Siméon beyond the battlefield, into the transformations that swept France in its wake.

This is an effort to reclaim a fragment of historical memory. May these pages restore some of the courage and humanity of those whom history nearly forgot.

PROLOGUE

Two moments, separated by centuries, frame my family's story.

The first unfolded in the winter of 1779. Seventeen-year-old Siméon Gaugien stood in the cold of rural France, shouldered his satchel, and kissed his mother goodbye. He was leaving the vineyard that had sustained his family for generations to enter a war in a land he could not picture, in service of an ideal he could not yet fully name.

The second arrived more than two centuries later. I opened a drawer in an old cabinet inherited from my grandmother and found a bundle of documents, folded and refolded, their paper brittle. The words carried voices across time, turning a name on a genealogical chart into a living presence. A son. A brother. A soldier. A father. A man.

Siméon's journey toward war began in a vineyard; mine into his life began with fragile paper and unanswered questions. This book traces the line between those two moments and the lives they set in motion.

INTRODUCTION

The victory at Yorktown, the siege that secured American independence, was a Franco-American triumph. George Washington commanded the allied armies, and the outcome depended on French military power, technical mastery of siege warfare, and sustained financial support from Spain and the Netherlands. Rochambeau's expeditionary force reduced British defenses, while Admiral de Grasse's fleet enforced the naval blockade that sealed Britain's defeat. At the moment of surrender, French and American soldiers stood shoulder to shoulder in nearly equal numbers, their victory forged through alliance, coordination, and sacrifice.

I grew up in the shadow of that alliance long before I understood it. My childhood unfolded near Rosiere, New York, a hamlet within Cape Vincent in Jefferson County, founded by French settlers and named for their village of origin. Like most American families, we celebrated the Fourth of July. Each summer, however, we also observed Bastille Day at the local French festival. The crackle of July fireworks honored both the fourth and the fourteenth. Only when I left home for university did I recognize that this was not a universal experience, but the living inheritance of a shared past.

That inheritance came into focus after my grandmother's death, when I received a cherrywood cabinet she called the sideboard. In the family, she was known simply as Granny. The cabinet had anchored family meals for decades, as solid and dignified as she was. As a child, determined to reach a candy dish placed beyond my grasp, I once climbed it and slipped, dislodging a strip of decorative molding. She delighted in retelling the story and often said it was the moment she decided the sideboard would one day be mine. Years later, when it came into my possession, the faint scar of that mischief remained.

Inside one of its drawers, tied with a faded ribbon, I found a bundle of aged documents. The pages were yellowed and brittle, some written in French, many bearing unfamiliar names. One stood out. Siméon Gaugien.

As the fragments came together, I learned that Siméon was my fifth-great-grandfather, a young artilleryman in the Régiment d'Auxonne who left his family's vineyard in Rosières-sur-Mance, Franche-Comté, to fight for American independence as part of Rochambeau's expeditionary force. The ideals of liberté I had celebrated at summer festivals were no longer abstract. They were the convictions that carried one young man across an ocean to risk his life for a cause not his by birth.

That discovery led me into archives in France and the United States and, ultimately, to the formal verification of Siméon's service through the Sons of the American Revolution, recognition I later shared with my son, Alexander Michael. My daughter, Sarah Grace, joined the Daughters of the American Revolution, extending that recognition across another generation. What began as a family inheritance became a recovery of history. It revealed how easily individual lives recede within great events, even when their contributions are essential.

Lafayette, Rochambeau, and Washington rightly dominate the historical record, but behind them stood thousands of soldiers, engineers, and artillerymen whose labor made the alliance decisive. Their experiences are rarely told at ground level, where endurance mattered as much as strategy and where liberty was lived not as rhetoric, but as hardship, waiting, and loss.

This book follows one of those soldiers. Siméon Gaugien fought for France, serving his king and the alliance his nation had forged. He could not have known that his service would carry his descendants across an ocean to settle in the nation he helped bring into being. The story is American by consequence. Siméon's journey reveals the Franco-American alliance not as diplomatic legend but as lived experience, the improbable beginning of an American family.

This is an American story, shaped by shared sacrifice and sustained by cooperation across borders. It begins in a French vineyard, passes through the smoke of Yorktown, and ends in the nation Siméon helped bring into being: The United States of America.

<u>Vineyards to Victory Family Tree</u>

Nicolas Gaugien (1716–1793)
m. Jeanne Richard (1722–1794)
Children: Four children, including Siméon Gaugien (1761–1831)

Siméon Gaugien (1761–1831)
m. Laurence "Laure" Hudel (1761–1847)
Children: Three children, including Siméon Gaugien, Jr. (1794–1865)

Siméon Gaugien Jr. (1794–1865)
m. Jeanne Baptiste Thierat (1792–1878)
Children: Six children, including Charles André Gosier (1818–1898)

Charles André Gaugien dit Gosier (1818–1898)
m. Geneviève Branche (1828–1901)
Children: Seven children, including Mary Gosier (1858–1933)

Mary Gosier (1858–1933)
m. Nicholas Aubertine (1857–1926)
Children: Two children, including Grace Sarah Aubertine (1891–1983)

Grace Sarah Aubertine (1891–1983)
m. Walter Andrus Hollenbeck (1887–1964)
Children: Three children, including Mary Elizabeth Hollenbeck (1917–2007)

Mary Elizabeth Hollenbeck (1917–2007)
m. Kenneth Ransier (1919–1983)
Children: Four children, including Shirley A. Ransier (1944–)

Shirley A. Ransier (1944–)
m. Theodore I. Hart (1939–2018)
Children: Seven children, including Theodore R. Hart (1964–)

Theodore R. Hart (1964–)
m. Tracy L. Smith (1962–)
Children: Sarah Grace Hart (1991–) and Alexander Michael Hart (1993–)

PART I
ROOTS & REVELATION

Chapter One:
Le Début: Sons of the Vineyard

Siméon Gaugien was born into a world at war. Yet he never saw a British soldier, never heard a cannon fired in anger on French soil. He grew up in its wreckage: a kingdom bled dry by defeat, a countryside crushed under taxes to pay for a lost empire, and a village where men spoke of the humiliation as if the wound were fresh.

His grandfather often said, "Strong roots make a sturdy vine, and a sturdy vine weathers any storm." He spoke these words with the weight of scripture, and for generations, the Gaugiens had lived by them. Yet for a second son, mere endurance would not suffice. Siméon would need to draw upon those roots to withstand challenges his grandfather could never have foreseen.

To know the boy who would one day leave his father's vineyard for a distant war, one must first understand the France that forged him.

The Seven Years' War (1756 – 1763) reshaped the global order and shattered France's colonial and maritime power. What began as a European struggle for supremacy soon ignited across continents: the forests of

North America, the sugar islands of the Caribbean, and the trade routes of India. Ambitious yet overstretched, France confronted its old rival, Britain, in a worldwide contest for empire. Although French armies secured victories on the continent, Britain's command of the seas proved decisive.

France lost valuable Caribbean islands, and its influence in India crumbled to a handful of trading posts. When the Treaty of Paris was signed in 1763[1], France ceded all its North American territories east of the Mississippi to Britain, while secretly transferring the vast Louisiana colony to Spain.[2] These losses were staggering. Although France remained a preeminent European land power, its army was constrained by a bankrupt treasury and a diminished global empire.

The humiliation would haunt the kingdom for a generation, fueling aspirations that would shape French imperial policy for decades.

While declared the victor, Britain also drowned in debt. Within the year, it began imposing new taxes on its American colonies to recoup its losses. These levies sparked protest, rebellion, and ultimately, a war that would bring France back into the fight.

The global conflict exposed the French army's deficiencies in expeditionary warfare and emptied the royal treasury. To address the staggering debt, the crown relentlessly raised taxes, imposing a crushing burden on peasant farmers. Paying the *taille* on their land was mandatory; even more resented was the *gabelle* on salt. On top of that, they owed the Church the *dîme* (tithe), and their *seigneur* demanded feudal fees for use of his mill, oven, and wine press. With each visit from the tax collector, fear and resentment grew, intensifying year after year toward Versailles.

Hatred of Britain united the people. In taverns and marketplaces, curses and gossip flared. The war touched Rosières-sur-Mance not with

---

[1] **The Treaty of Paris** (1763), ended the Seven Years' War and redrew the map of North America. France ceded its North American territories, including Canada and all its claims east of the Mississippi River, to Britain. For the French, the loss was a humiliation that would not be forgotten. Sources: *Fred Anderson, Crucible of War (2000); Colin G. Calloway, The Scratch of a Pen (2006).*
[2] **Treaty of Fontainebleau** (1762), France secretly transferred Louisiana to Spain to prevent it from falling into British hands. The transfer was kept hidden for over a year; even as France ceded its eastern territories to Britain in the Treaty of Paris (1763), it did not reveal that Louisiana west of the Mississippi already belonged to Spain. The secret was not made public until April 1764. Spain held the territory until 1800 – 1801, when Napoleon reclaimed it under the secret Treaty of San Ildefonso, then sold it to the United States in 1803 as the Louisiana Purchase, a transaction that doubled the size of the young republic. Sources: *Fred Anderson, Crucible of War (2000); Colin G. Calloway, The Scratch of a Pen (2006).*

cannon smoke, but with slow, suffocating debt. In the tavern, men spoke softly about crushing levies and the corvée, the forced labor owed to the King, stealing them from their fields at crucial times. The village endured in weary resignation. Amid hardship, the Church remained its anchor.

By the time the church bell rang at six, the family was in motion. Nicolas pulled on his boots for the vineyard. Jeanne handed Siméon, now a boy of ten, a cloth-wrapped loaf of dark bread. "For Père Charles," she said, smoothing his hair. "Mind your manners. And listen to the scripture."

At the church door, Père Charles waited in his white surplice. He accepted the bread with a nod. "Thank you, my son. Your father's kindness is a daily sacrament." His hand rested briefly on Siméon's head. "*Benedicat te Deus,*" he murmured. "God bless you. Come, let us give thanks."

Inside, the church breathed cold and incense. The small congregation knelt on hard wooden benches. Père Charles's Latin chant rose and fell, a familiar melody. Its rhythm was the heartbeat of Rosières. Religion served as the loom upon which each day was woven.

Père Charles preached that sacrifice was a duty to both King and God, as he worked quietly to steady his flock. He offered counsel, gathered alms, and led processions that bound the village to something greater than war and taxes. Faith, as much as bread or wine, held them together.

A thoughtful man who saw discipline and learning as devotion, he sometimes spoke of ideas that unsettled the old order, not to provoke, but because he believed them true: that knowledge served justice, that a man's worth could be measured by effort as much as birth. He spoke of a modern army that sought young men who could read, calculate, and lead, where talent might earn a commoner honor, if not command. Siméon Gaugien was born in 1761, the third child of Nicolas[3] and Jeanne[4]

---

[3] **Nicolas Gaugien**, vigneron of Rosières-sur-Mance, Haute-Saône, France; born November 29, 1716; married Jeanne Richard on April 22, 1755; died February 9, 1793; father of Siméon Gaugien and sixth great-grandfather of the author. Sources: *Registres paroissiaux et d'état civil, Rosières-sur-Mance and Lécourt, Archives départementales de la Haute-Saône.*

[4] **Jeanne Richard**, born August 5, 1722, in Saint-Marcel-lès-Jussey, Haute-Saône, France; married Nicolas Gaugien on April 22, 1755; died September 22, 1794; wife of Nicolas Gaugien and mother of Siméon Gaugien. Sources: *Registres paroissiaux et d'état civil, Saint-Marcel-lès-Jussey and Rosières-sur-Mance, Archives départementales de la Haute-Saône.*

Gaugien, modest vintners who worked a small parcel of vineyard and owned some dairy cows, a pig, and several chickens on the outskirts of Rosières-sur-Mance.

Their firstborn, a daughter named Adrienne,[5] was born on January 20, 1757, but survived only twenty-three days. Her father, Nicolas, along with the village schoolmaster, Joseph Rets[6], signed the parish register attesting to this sad moment. A year later, they welcomed a son, Nicolas[7], known affectionately as Colas, a sturdy and spirited boy whose laughter soon filled the house.

Église Saint-Siméon-Stylites,
Rosières-sur-Mance

HISTORICAL NOTE: CHARLES HENRI THÉRION, PARISH PRIEST OF ROSIÈRES

Charles Henri Thérion, born 1722, led the parish of Saint-Siméon in Rosières-sur-Mance from 1767 to 1791. Like most rural curés, he came from modest origins and lived among his parishioners. When the revolutionary government required clergy to swear loyalty to the Civil Constitution of the Clergy, Thérion refused. Branded a prêtre réfractaire, he followed his archbishop into exile across the border to Soleure (Solothurn), Switzerland, where he died on June 5, 1796. Sources: *Jean-Marie Guillaume; Archives Diocésaines de Besançon; FamilySearch: Carolus Heinricus Therion.*

---

[5] **Adrienne Gaugien**, born January 20, 1757, in Rosières-sur-Mance, Haute-Saône, France; died February 12, 1757; daughter of Nicolas Gaugien and Jeanne Richard and elder sister of Siméon Gaugien. Sources: *Registres paroissiaux et d'état civil, Rosières-sur-Mance, Archives départementales de la Haute-Saône.*

[6] **Joseph Rets**, born 1731; served as schoolmaster, recteur d'école, of Rosières-sur-Mance, Haute-Saône, France, during the mid-eighteenth century, the period in which Siméon Gaugien and his brother Nicolas Gaugien would have attended instruction. Sources: *Parish and communal records, Rosières-sur-Mance, Archives départementales de la Haute-Saône.*

[7] **Nicolas Gaugien Jr.**, (referred to as Colas in this book); born June 21, 1758, in Rosières-sur-Mance, Haute-Saône, France; elder brother of Siméon Gaugien and son of Nicolas Gaugien and Jeanne Richard. Sources: *Registres paroissiaux et d'état civil, Rosières-sur-Mance, Archives départementales de la Haute-Saône.*

When Siméon[8] arrived, Jeanne sensed something different, a bright, alert infant, quick to fix his gaze. They named their second son after Saint Siméon le Stylites, the pillar-dwelling ascetic who symbolized steadfast faith, and in honor of the village church that bore his name just beyond the vineyards.

The stone church of Saint-Siméon was built on a narrow rise. It was one of the few churches in France oriented north to south instead of the customary west to east. This choice was shaped by the land. Some in town were superstitious: they said a church facing north cast a shadow rather than light. Yet others believed faith needed no compass to be true.

On feast days, the community gathered in procession and prayer, and by 1773, the newly built bell tower summoned them with its steady call, candles flickering in the dusk, a reminder that faith endures even when kingdoms falter.

The Gaugien vineyard[9] lay on the hillside at the edge of Rosières. Below, the communal herd grazed near the millstream. The mill wheel turned to the steady fall of water from a man-made pond, its sound both the village's heartbeat and a reminder of the compulsory tax.

Three years later, in 1764, Jeanne bore another daughter, Jeanne Françoise[10], who survived only a day. Loss settled over the house. Yet Siméon's laughter and Colas's mischief became their parents' solace, a reminder that life, like the vines, could wither and still bloom again.

The area was alive with constant activity, fascinating to a growing boy. Men with sacks of wheat trudged in from the fields, their grain destined by the *seigneur's* decree for his mill. Women herded geese or goats along the road. The town lay a few minutes' walk away. Its tavern and square

---

[8] **Siméon Gaugien**, born September 6, 1761, in Rosières-sur-Mance, Haute-Saône, France; married Laurence, known as Laure, Hudel on January 29, 1788; enlisted January 12, 1779, in the Régiment d'Artillerie d'Auxonne; and was assigned to the Compagnie Bonnay de la Rouvrelle, he served with the French Expédition Particulière under the command of Jean-Baptiste Donatien de Vimeur, comte de Rochambeau; fought in the Siege of Yorktown; died May 30, 1831. Sources: *Registres paroissiaux et d'état civil, Rosières-sur-Mance and Lécourt, Archives départementales de la Haute-Saône; and Les combattants français de la guerre américaine, 1778 – 1783 (Service historique de la Défense).*

[9] **The Gaugien vineyard** and mill site, powered by a millpond fed by a weak tributary, survive only as foundation traces in a field currently owned by the family of local historian Jean-Marie Guillaume. Source: *Correspondence and research of Jean-Marie Guillaume, Saint-Marcel.*

[10] **Jeanne Françoise Gaugien**, born and died August 25, 1764, in Rosières-sur-Mance, Haute-Saône, France; younger sister of Siméon Gaugien and daughter of Nicolas Gaugien and Jeanne Richard. Sources: *Registres paroissiaux et d'état civil, Rosières-sur-Mance, Archives départementales de la Haute-Saône.*

were the place where news from the wider world arrived, carried by traders and travelers. Siméon absorbed it all, his young mind quick to wonder.

His older brother Colas had little patience for such musings. He was a blend of tormentor, companion, and protector. When Siméon lingered too long listening to the miller's tales, Colas would cuff his shoulder and tease him for thinking too much. He preferred to drag his brother into the vines to gather kindling, drive geese from the grapes, or mend fencing. There, between tasks, they might race dragonflies or wrestle in the dust until their father called them back. Even in teasing, there was affection. But if anyone else mocked Siméon's curiosity, Colas's temper rose like summer thunder.

Each morning began with chores. In winter, when the vines slept, the boys walked to the parish school, where Maître Joseph Rets drilled them in letters, numbers, and catechism. In summer, when chores and lessons were done, moments of freedom appeared: a stolen swim, a climb up the haystack, a race between the fruit trees. Evenings were always spent near the hearth, listening to Grand-père Jean's stories.

The Gaugiens believed the small school fee was worth every sou. For Siméon, these hours were a delight. Colas endured them as an interruption to his true schooling, the honest education of work, mud, and open air.

In the one-room schoolhouse beside the rectory, their hours were shared between Père Charles and Maître Rets. Maître Rets was a wiry man with a patient manner and a sharp eye, a figure who smelled of chalk dust and beeswax. Where Père Charles guided with warmth, Maître Rets demanded precision. Yet the two men worked in easy partnership: the *père* overseeing religious instruction, the *maître* ensuring the boys could navigate the written world.

The true shift came the year Colas turned twelve. As the eldest son, the mantle of the vineyard settled on his shoulders. His schooling now ended; his days were claimed by the rhythm of his father's footsteps and the weight of the pruning hook. Nicolas now spoke to him of more than soil; he spoke of the *banalité,* the crushing weight of the *seigneur's* fees, and the necessity of a cart sturdy enough to carry their grapes to the *seigneur's* press.

Siméon felt the absence of his brother's companionship. The chapter of their shared childhood had closed.

For the Gaugiens, the land was modest but sufficient. The vines yielded enough wine to drink and trade, the cows gave milk, and the garden provided vegetables. Chickens and a pig helped keep the family fed, and though they remained peasants, they preserved enough food to carry them through the long winter. Jeanne and Nicolas counted their blessings often, mindful that many folk lived with far less, and they were careful never to squander what the Lord had placed in their hands.

Nicolas watched every cask and every cow with measured care. "The *seigneur's* agent takes his share at the press before the wine is even made," he would grumble, "and the tax man comes for what's left."

Jeanne eased the burdens. She stretched meals, kept a wary eye on prices, and tended the family's vegetable garden and orchard. From these she fed her household without a sou changing hands.

Colas, as the eldest son, was treated with special regard, though the Gaugien family held no title or wealth to speak of. In eighteenth-century France, custom and law still bowed to the system of *primogéniture masculine*, male-preference inheritance, where the firstborn son, whether noble or farmer, was seen as the natural heir and the future head of the household. Younger sons learned to carve their own path, often in the army, the church, or a trade.

Thus, while Colas would one day manage the vines, it was understood that Siméon's future lay elsewhere. His would be a life of strength and discipline rather than soil and grapes. Jeanne prayed his path would be kind.

Siméon was shaped by all that surrounded him: the weary village, the rising taxes, the murmured regrets. He knew from an early age that his fortune lay elsewhere. As the second son, the earth beneath his feet was not his to inherit. While his parents instilled faith and family duty, his thoughts wandered beyond the parish fields. The artillery fascinated him: the meeting point of mathematics and courage.

Nicolas's parents lived under their roof, a custom that filled the house with stories and warmth, with generations sharing the same table and fire. Siméon loved it. After his grand-mère passed when he was eleven, he grew especially close to his Grand-père, the family patriarch, whose presence still carried quiet authority even as age thinned his voice and slowed his step.

Each evening by the hearth, Grand-père shared lessons wrapped in stories: tales of vines and seasons, of the clay-and-limestone earth that yielded its best only to patience. He spoke of pruning by the waning moon and pressing grapes before the first frost. Every story ended with a saying about the land, simple truths shaped by decades of toil.

Yet Grand-père was more than a farmer with proverbs; he was the bridge between the old world and the new. After *souper*[11], with a cup of wine in hand, his stories lengthened. He would speak of how "our grand-parents once belonged to Spain," recalling the Treaty of Nijmegen nearly a century earlier, when Franche-Comté passed from Spanish to French rule. To him, borders were fragile; lines drawn and redrawn as kings quarreled. "The only constant," he would sigh, "is the *seigneur's* press. Spanish king, French king, the tax on our grapes remains." Siméon and Colas listened and often wondered what their lives might have been like if Spain still ruled their corner of France.

Grand-père spoke, too, of soldiers: men who had gone to war and returned as heroes, and others who never came home. His tales kindled something deep in the boy. Whenever Siméon saw a soldier in uniform in nearby Jussey, he felt a magnetic pull toward that life of purpose.

Nicolas, however, had no patience for such talk. To him, the world was simple: a man's duty was to his family, to the land, to God, and to the King. He believed in staying rooted where one was planted and finding pride in one's station, no matter how modest.

The tension between father and son sometimes surfaced when Grand-père's stories turned toward war. Nicolas would mutter that soldiers

---

[11] *Souper* (French): the evening meal, typically lighter than the midday *dîner* in eighteenth-century rural France; in many provincial communities it was taken after sunset and often consisted of bread, soup, vegetables, or leftovers from the main meal earlier in the day.

were fools who traded one master for another. "Let the boy learn the land," he would say. "That's where his future lies."

But Grand-père saw something different. He loved Colas, dutiful, steady Colas, the heir who would keep the vineyard and the lineage intact. Yet he held a quiet affection for Siméon that ran deeper than duty.

In private moments, Siméon would whisper his questions about battles and destiny. The old man would nod, his eyes bright in the firelight. "Every man has his calling, boy. Some belong to the plow. Some to the sword. You'll know which claims you soon enough."

His father's plans pressed him toward the vineyard, but Grand-père's words kindled another vision. When talk spread that local boys were leaving to join the military, Siméon began to sense the shape of his own future.

Early March 1778

By early March, the vineyard showed its first signs of waking. Men and boys worked the slopes with ploughs and pruning hooks, loosening the earth so it could breathe. Careful hands inspected each vine. They cut back what the frost had spared and reset stakes, retied bindings, and restored rows. The work unfolded with the familiarity of prayer: deliberate, patient, each vine tended as if counted bead by bead.

Before the pâtre's horn sounded each morning, Jeanne made certain the cows were milked and ready. Throughout the day, Jeanne worked near the vineyard, listening for familiar sounds and keeping watch on the road. By afternoon, she anticipated Pâtre Antoine's return with the herd; their bells grew louder, and Jeanne recognized each animal by its tone. Evening brought her the steady rhythm of milking, the bucket filling with warm, grass-scented milk. For Jeanne, the land had resumed its order: dependable, unyielding.

Yet that spring, one rhythm was missing.

CULTURAL NOTE: THE SHEPHERD OF ROSIÈRES-SUR-MANCE

In eighteenth-century villages like Rosières, most families owned only one or two cows. Meadows were unfenced. The village's cattle were gathered into a communal herd entrusted to a professional *pâtre* (shepherd). Each morning, the shepherd walked through the village blowing his *trompe* (signal horn). Families brought their cows to join the procession to the common grazing land. Each evening, he returned every animal to its owner's door. He was compensated in kind and kept a large mastiff to protect against wolves. In parts of rural France, this system continued until the mid-1950s. Sources: *Contract of the communal herdsman of Chaignay, Burgundy, 1791; correspondence with Jean-Marie Guillaume, December 2025.*

Colas had been gone nearly a month. He left before winter loosened its hold, summoned with other men from Rosières to labor at the Château d'Oricourt. Winter storms had torn shingles from the roof and fractured the stone of the outer gate. The *seigneur's* steward demanded repairs before the thaw. It was the old *corvée*[12] obligation, familiar and unavoidable.

For families like the Gaugiens, the burden was not danger but injustice. Colas's absence was felt in quiet ways: one fewer pair of hands at the plough, one more reminder of how the labor of common men served the wealth of others.

The road to Oricourt lay some thirteen *lieues* to the southeast, nearly fifty kilometers. Colas traveled on foot with the others, carrying a small bundle of bread and dried pork. He carried the tools of repair: a mallet, a chisel, and a patched leather apron. It was the same journey his father had made many times before.

As the vines stirred and pruning gave way to planning, Jeanne counted the days until his return. She knew he would be home before Saint Joseph's

---

[12] **The** *corvée* (French): a system of compulsory unpaid labor imposed on peasants under the ancien régime. It took two principal forms: the *corvée royale,* requiring labor on royal roads and infrastructure, and the *corvée seigneuriale,* obligating peasants to maintain seigneurial estates, mills, and harvests. Peasants could be required to serve several weeks annually, often during planting or harvest seasons, contributing to growing resentment toward feudal inequality. The institution was formally abolished during the French Revolution. Sources: *William Doyle, Origins of the French Revolution (Oxford: Oxford University Press, 1980); and Peter McPhee, Liberty or Death: The French Revolution (New Haven: Yale University Press, 2016).*

Day, March 19th. When there would be the baking of special breads and the family meal after Mass.

Siméon felt that restlessness like a second pulse.

That morning in the village church, Père Charles stood before the congregation holding a letter from the archbishopric. His voice, solemn beneath the stone vaults, carried news that rippled through the pews: His Eminence, Archbishop Raymond de Durfort, confirmed that France had entered into alliance with the American colonies. Two treaties had been signed, one of commerce and one of arms. France now stood openly against Britain.

The pews stirred with murmurs. Some crossed themselves. Others shook their heads. A woman near the front clutched her rosary tightly. The news struck Siméon with the force of revelation.

He knew his traditional parents, especially his father, would not share his excitement. At sixteen, his tall, lanky frame hinted at strength still forming. His eyes carried the fire of untapped ambition.

Word spread quickly. Outside the church, Siméon heard that recruiters had already arrived in Jussey, banners flying, drums sounding, calling young men to enlist. They promised pay, honor, and a place in history.

He thought about Antoine Porcherot[13] of Fouchécourt, four years his senior, now serving with the Auxonne artillery. Antoine trained in mathematics and gunnery, part of the king's scientific arm. Siméon remembered delivering wine to Antoine's family and the confidence with which Antoine departed. There was also Jacques Crevoisier[14] from Jussey, scarcely older than Siméon when he enlisted. If they could go, why not him?

He hurried home, heart pounding faster than his feet.

---

[13] **Antoine Porcherot**, born in Fouchécourt, Franche-Comté; entered military service June 30, 1777, enlisting in the Régiment d'Artillerie d'Auxonne, Compagnie de Neurisse. Source: *Les combattants français de la guerre américaine, 1778 – 1783 (Washington: Imprimerie Nationale, 1905), 350.*

[14] **Jacques Crevoisier**, born 1761 in Jussey, Franche-Comté; entered military service July 13, 1777, at age fifteen, enlisting in the Régiment de Gâtinais of the French Royal Army. The regiment, commanded during the American campaign by the Marquis de Rostaing and serving under Major General the Marquis de Saint-Simon, sailed north from the West Indies with Admiral de Grasse in 1781. It fought at the Siege of Yorktown, participating in the assault on British Redoubt 9 on October 14, 1781, and later resumed its former title, Royal Auvergne. Source: *Les combattants français de la guerre américaine, 1778 – 1783 (Washington: Imprimerie Nationale, 1905), 313.*

The Gaugien farm stretched across the hillside in front of him like a quilt of brown and green. Around it, other families' small vineyards formed a patchwork on the slopes surrounding Rosières-sur-Mance. The Saint-Marcel path ran past the mill beside their home and continued toward Jussey, the market town where fairs were held and justice was meted out. There, merchants struck bargains and boys dreamed of larger worlds. It was from Jussey that Antoine and Jacques had departed, answering a recruiters' call.

Archbishop of Besancon.
His Eminence Raymond De Durfort

HISTORICAL NOTE: RAYMOND DE DURFORT, ARCHBISHOP OF BESANÇON

Raymond de Durfort served as Archbishop of Besançon from 1774 until his death in exile in 1792, previously holding the sees of Avranches and Montpellier. When the revolutionary government required clergy to swear loyalty to the Civil Constitution of the Clergy, de Durfort refused. Rather than submit, he led his diocesan clergy across the border to Soleure (Solothurn), Switzerland, where he died on March 19, 1792. His refusal gave canonical weight to the decisions of parish priests like Thérion throughout the diocese. Sources: *Catholic-Hierarchy.org; Archives Diocésaines de Besançon.*

Near the vineyard's heart, his father Nicolas stooped low, inspecting a vine for mildew. His hat tipped forward over his sun-weathered face. His hands moved with practiced precision among the new leaves, checking each one for signs of disease. His mother, Jeanne, worked close by, humming softly as she tied back stray shoots with measured grace. Now and then, she paused to touch the rosary that hung from her neck. The rosary was a wedding gift from Nicolas's mother, who had prayed over the same vineyard decades before.

Leaning on his cane, overseeing it all with sharp, steady eyes, Grand-père Jean was as much a part of the vineyard as the vines themselves. Widowed five summers earlier, he still missed Siméon's Grandmère, Jeanne, and the soft hum of her songs drifting through the rows as they worked side by side. At times, when the sun struck the leaves just right, he almost saw her there again, basket in hand.

Grand-père knew he did not have many summers left before he joined her. Seeing his son and grandsons at work filled him with quiet pride. Nicolas carried himself with the same surety Grand-père once had. He was a man of action, decisive, with a temper that flared and cooled quickly, like summer storms.

Siméon was different. A little like his father in spirit, but more like his mother, he possessed a gentler heart and a mind that seemed always to be turning. Where Colas saw what was, Siméon pondered what could be. He moved around the farm with a quiet curiosity, noticing the angle of the sun, the hum of the bees, and how the soil crumbled differently in the shade.

When they walked together between the rows in the soft light of evening, Grand-père would rest a weathered hand on his grandson's shoulder and murmur, "Remember, strong roots make a sturdy vine, and a sturdy vine weathers any storm."

To Siméon, those words were the rhythm of their lives. He carried them not as inheritance but as understanding.

Siméon ran to his father, breathless with excitement. "Papa! Have you heard? France has joined the Americans! The recruiters are in Jussey; there are drums, songs, and banners, the whole square alive with it. They're calling for new men to enlist. It could be my chance."

Nicolas straightened, already knowing the names that would come next. "Do not think about following them," he said sharply. "Antoine's family has connections. His father and brothers will manage without him. And Jacques's family? His people think differently. They see opportunity where we see risk. Your duty is here, to this soil. The artillery is for sons of noblemen, not sons of the vineyard."

The words struck deep. It was not the work Siméon resented but the certainty, the wall his father built with a sentence.

"But Papa," Siméon said, his voice quick with urgency, "this is my chance!"

He hesitated, searching his father's face. "I want to fight the British. I want Grand-père to see that I'm ready."

Siméon Racing Through The Vineyard

His mother was not surprised by his words. She remembered the way he lingered on Grand-père Jean's stories, not for the battles themselves but for the men in them, their courage, their purpose, the way they had been tested and proved worthy. As the second son, he would have to forge his own path. But was he suited for the artillery?

Anxiety pressed upon her.

Grand-père Jean's lips curled faintly, a blend of pride and warning. "The boy is nearly a man, Nicolas. We cannot keep him tied to the vines forever."

For Siméon, his grandfather's voice carried both comfort and command; a living echo of generations who had coaxed life from the soil of Rosières-sur-Mance.

Nicolas's tone cut like a blade. "He's just a boy. There's no place for him on a battlefield." He turned away and spat on the ground.

"I am nearly seventeen," Siméon said. "Old enough to work from dawn to dusk."

Nicolas shook his head. "Ideas do not tend vines."

Siméon's voice dropped, steady but fierce. "Colas inherits everything. What is left for me?"

Silence settled between them.

Nicolas's jaw tightened. "That's the way it's always been. The eldest takes the land, the others find their path in the Church, or in a trade. You've been given a home, a place, and food on your plate. Be grateful for it."

Siméon held his father's gaze.

Nicolas turned away. "I will not hear more of it."

The tension hung thick between the two men, like smoke that refused to lift. Siméon stood between them, fists clenched at his sides, his pulse loud in his ears.

A startled blackbird burst from the branches of a nearby tree, winging high into the pale sky. To the family, such a bird was a soul-bird. No one let the moment pass without meaning, though no one spoke it aloud.

Siméon followed the bird's flight as it disappeared beyond the ridge. The bird was free, owing nothing to land or name. Why, then, should his father decide that he could not be?

The small farm was the family's pride. It was modest but steady, yielding enough to sustain them through good years and bad. Their red wine was known in the nearby taverns, and the milk, churned into fresh butter and soft curds, was welcomed at the village market.

Almost every day at their main meal, they would raise their mugs, one calling out, "The vines root us," the other answering, "and the farm sustains us." Jeanne would often chime in with a gentle, "And our Heavenly Father protects us."

The ritual shaped Siméon and Colas in ways they did not yet understand. These words shaped his understanding of resilience, responsibility, and faith, lessons that extended beyond the farm.

Siméon was expected not only to master the work that sustained the family's land but also to learn the discipline his father prized. Nicolas had taught him to shoot when he was barely old enough to hold the musket steady. "Hunting requires more than good aim," his father often reminded him. "It is about patience and knowing when to take the shot."

Siméon learned those lessons well. The forest of Bois du Voisey lay nine kilometers to the north. The nearer woods belonged to the seigneur, and the penalties for poaching were not worth the risk. In the Bois du Voisey, dense with undergrowth and game, he could hunt freely. Since turning fifteen, he had often made the journey, returning with a hare or pheasant for the family table. The forest became his proving ground, where patience mattered more than powder and a steady hand meant supper.

But Grand-père Jean had taught him other lessons in those woods, years before he'd learned to shoot. One autumn afternoon when Siméon was perhaps twelve, the old man had stopped mid-stride and pointed to a patch of slender green shoots near the base of an oak. "Come here, boy," he'd said, kneeling down with a soft grunt. He'd pulled his pocket knife from his coat and carefully dug around the cluster. "Wild onions. See these?" He pulled one up and held it to Siméon's nose. "Smell."

Siméon inhaled. Sharp, unmistakable.

"If it smells like onion, it is onion," Grand-père said firmly. "Nothing dangerous smells like this. Remember that." He showed Siméon how to dig carefully, loosening the soil around the bulbs. "Always leave some behind so they grow again next year. The forest gives, but only if we're wise." Siméon watched his grandfather's gnarled hands work with surprising delicacy, felt the weight of the knife when Grand-père pressed it into his palm to try. "Like this?" he asked. Grand-père smiled. "Exactly like that. You're learning."

Nicolas and Jeanne focused on the vines and the household, relying on trusted help for the day's many tasks. Claude Meugnier, a steady presence from Rosières, and his nephews Michel and Henri worked alongside them, tending the vineyard, caring for the pig, feeding the chickens, and keeping the household running. When Jeanne was unable, they helped milk the cows before Pâtre Antoine gathered them in the morning and again after their return in the evening, settling them fed and secure for the night. Their voices and laughter carried across the fields, proof that the Gaugiens did not work alone, and that survival, like harvest, was shared.

Nicolas took his responsibility to his workers seriously. The vineyard depended on their labor. They were welcomed for hearty meals and the camaraderie that marked each season. The shared meals left behind stories that became as much a part of the farm as the soil itself.

That Sunday morning after mass, the square filled with voices. The smell of fresh bread and pine smoke drifted from the ovens. Men spoke of taxes. Women worried aloud. Younger men gathered, eyes bright.

Down the road, a small crowd began to gather. Someone shouted, "They're back from the château!" Heads turned.

A line of men came into view, boots caked with dust, tools slung over their shoulders. Among them was Colas.

"Colas," Siméon called, breaking free.

His brother dropped his pack and caught him in a quick embrace, lifting him clear off the ground. "I leave for a month, and you grow like a weed," he said, laughing.

Jeanne crossed herself, murmuring thanks. Nicolas and Grand-père Jean followed more slowly, both smiling despite themselves.

"The roof is patched," Colas said. "The walls will hold. They paid us in bread and wine. Better than expected."

"You have your father's hands for the work," Grand-père said, clapping his shoulder.

Nicolas nodded, glancing at Siméon. "Hands for building. Not fighting."

Colas glanced between them. "Again with this?"

Jean-Claude, a neighbor, joined them, grinning. "Your brother talks. Wants to settle scores with the British."

Nicolas folded his arms. "He's sixteen. We have trouble enough."

Colas raised an eyebrow, exchanging a look with Siméon. "Dreams, is it?"

"It's not just dreams," Siméon said. "It's our chance to fight back for what's been taken and maybe help restore France's honor. That's worth something."

Grand-père nodded thoughtfully. "France and Britain at each other's throats again. Some things never change."

Colas's smile faded. "Still, a man might learn something beyond the land," he said quietly. The bell tolled the hour, a somber reminder of time's march. The family stood a moment longer. One son returned. Another strained toward departure.

That evening, *souper* passed in uneasy quiet. The table felt smaller beneath the candle's light. Nicolas spoke little. Jeanne moved steadily, ladling stew, refilling mugs. Grand-père hummed under his breath, watching his grandsons.

When the meal was finished, Nicolas rose and went out to check the stable. Grand-père followed, complaining about the chill.

As Jeanne began clearing the table, she reached across and laid her hand over Siméon's. Her voice was soft, meant only for him. "Your father fears losing you, not only for love, but for the land. This small farm has carried our family through storms you cannot imagine."

She bent to kiss his forehead, then turned to the dishes.

Colas paused in the doorway, watching her. When Siméon looked up, their eyes met.

"If you go," Colas said, "don't waste it. Don't throw yourself away."

Then he followed their father into the dark, the door closing softly behind him.

Later, in the loft, Siméon stared at the moonlit rows below, picturing distant roads. Convincing a recruiter, or his father, seemed more daunting than facing battle.

Below, he heard his parents' low voices through the floorboards, the soft click of his mother's knitting needles, the steady cadence of Colas recounting his days at the château, Grand-père's gentle snoring, and Nicolas's murmured skepticism. His father's words still echoed in his mind.

He heard the distant bell of curfew.[15] Eventually, Colas climbed into the loft as well.

Siméon listened to the night, imagining distant places where even his father's doubts might fade. At last, sleep came.

The next morning, Siméon woke early as usual and tended to the animals and gathered the day's supply of firewood for his mother's cooking while Jeanne stoked the embers, coaxing the fire back to life.

In the yard, Pâtre Antoine was already collecting the cows, their low bells clanking softly in the still air as he set them in motion toward the pasture. Colas emerged from the stable with his sleeves rolled to the elbow, the scent of hay and leather clinging to him. He had been up since before dawn as well, wanting to make up for the time he was away, checking the plow harness and preparing to cut a drainage trench along the lower vineyard rows.

When the morning chores were done, the family gathered at the table, their movements practiced, each gesture part of a rhythm as old as the land itself. For generations, the vines had been their anchor, their labor, their faith. Yet this morning, tension rippled beneath the calm routine, an undercurrent that no one named.

---

[15] *Curfew* comes from the Old French *couvre-feu,* "cover the fire." For centuries, towns and villages rang a nightly bell reminding residents to extinguish or bank their hearth fires before sleep, a safeguard against accidental blazes in timbered homes. By the late eighteenth century, the practice had become more custom than law, but the bell still marked the close of day in rural France.

By the time they stepped inside, the kitchen breathed warmth into their bones. The hearth fire snapped and glowed, its heat rising into the rafters as bowls of steaming *gruau* (oatmeal porridge) waited on the aged wooden table. Jeanne moved with practiced ease, and the air around her carried the faint, honeyed aroma of *tilleul* (linden tea) warming near the hearth. Beneath it lingered the honest, natural aroma of soil and smoke, clinging to their clothes after the morning's work.

Morning in the Gaugien Cottage

"Siméon," Nicolas said. "You and your grandfather will start with the south rows today. The vines need tending."

"Yes, Papa."

The words came out flat, dutiful. Nicolas seemed satisfied.

Grand-père Jean, who had been eating in silence, set down his spoon and regarded his grandson with eyes that missed little. "We'll walk the rows together," he said. "A man may find many kinds of strength in the soil."

Siméon nodded, not trusting his voice.

Grand-père rose slowly, leaning on his cane. "Come," he said. "The vines are waiting."

They worked in silence for a time. Then Grand-père Jean straightened and leaned on his cane.

"You held your tongue," he said.

"There was nothing left to say."

"Perhaps not yet," the old man replied. "But a man who governs his voice may yet reach another's ears."

He rested a hand on Siméon's shoulder. "This land is not only soil. It is our life. If you leave it, do not expect your father to yield easily. Speak plainly. Show him you see the burden he carries."

Siméon met his gaze. "Do you think I am wrong?"

"Mistake or not," Grand-père said, "it is your path. Just remember that those who remain will live with its cost."

He squeezed Siméon's arm. "Strong roots make a sturdy vine."

They returned to their rows. The future remained unwritten, but for the first time, Siméon saw a path that did not require breaking what he loved in order to leave it.

Chapter Two:
No One Heard The Casks Fall

March 1778

Boots sounded in the yard. Nicolas came first, his face unreadable. Colas followed, shoulders damp from the trough, swinging his jacket with easy confidence, searching for cheer as afternoon faded.

"The cows were restless," Colas called with a grin. "The brown one kicked twice to remind me who runs this farm."

Grand-père chuckled. Nicolas did not look up. "You talk too much. If you worked as fast, the south rows would be finished."

Colas winked at Siméon. "I leave the clever work to papa. Someone must charm the cows while you charm the vines."

"Enough," Nicolas said, the word clipped. "The soil is soft. Loose bindings cost us time."

When the final row was tied, the sun had slipped behind the hills. The four Gaugien men walked back toward the cottage in silence.

As they entered the cottage, the kitchen filled with the scent of roasted meat and winter vegetables. Firelight glowed against the stone. Jeanne moved between hearth and table, ladling stew, slicing bread, pouring wine. Her motions were steady, but her eyes betrayed a tension she could not conceal.

They took their places. Spoons scraped bowls. No one spoke.

Colas tried first to lift the air. "If the vines work half as hard as we did, we will drown in wine by harvest."

Siméon smiled. Nicolas did not. "Vines need care, not jokes."

Colas's grin faltered. "Even vines rest, Papa."

"There is talk," Nicolas replied, "and there is nonsense."

Grand-père watched them quietly. "Laughter does not spoil a crop."

Nicolas turned to Siméon. "You worked well today. I am pleased."

"Thank you, Papa."

Grand-père nodded. "When your father was your age, he thought dreams alone would make him a man. The land taught him otherwise."

"Dreams don't fill a cellar," Nicolas said. "Prove yourself here first, then we'll speak of wars."

"I have," Siméon said, his jaw set. "Every season."

"He pulls his weight," Colas said. "Seeing past these hills won't ruin him."

"And if it takes him?" Nicolas said. "If he never returns?"

Jeanne's hand trembled at the pitcher. "Please."

Grand-père spoke quietly. "To serve well is no shame. Whether a man ploughs a field or mans a cannon."

Colas nodded. "Maybe Siméon's right. You always said a man must prove himself, maybe this is his way."

Nicolas's fist touched the table, firm. "He will prove himself here."

Colas and Siméon exchanged a glance, Grand-père cleared his throat but said nothing.

At last, Nicolas said, "I will not bury my son across the sea."

After *souper*, Nicolas reached for his coat. "I am going for a walk. Maybe the tavern."

He glanced at his father. "Papa?"

Grand-père shook his head. "Not tonight. I'll check the cows and make sure the stable doors are set. Wolves have been bold." Nicolas turned to Colas. "You?"

Colas shook his head. "A cow's near calving. If there are wolves, I'd best stay close."

Siméon stood. "The boys will be at the square. Papa, may I go?"

Nicolas hesitated, then nodded. "Come on then."

Jeanne caught Siméon's sleeve. "Be safe."

They stepped out into the cool night. Smoke drifted from the chimneys, and the road into Rosières-sur-Mance lay still beneath the moon. At the crossroads, Siméon turned toward the square while Nicolas continued.

"Don't be long," Nicolas called.

"I won't, Papa," Siméon replied.

Nicolas kept on toward Le Coq Hardy, the local tavern that had been a gathering place for generations. The sign above the door, weathered but proud, bore the image of a rooster mid-crow.

As he pushed open the heavy wooden door, his thoughts were heavy too, dwelling on Siméon's longing to leave and how far-reaching that choice would be for the family and the farm.

Inside, the tavern smelled of ale, smoke, and wood. Nicolas nodded to Martin, the owner, who poured beer without a word.

"Busy night," Martin said, leaning an elbow on the counter.

"The King's proclamation… France stands with the Americans."

"More taxes," Nicolas replied.

"More than that."

Nicolas frowned into his mug. The cost would be real enough. Complaining too loudly felt dangerous, even here. "The King knows what France needs," he said carefully. "We may not see the wisdom of it from Rosières, but Versailles sees more than we do." He believed it, mostly. Or needed to.

Martin wiped the counter, smirking. "Aye, they see our coin."

Nicolas grunted, lifted his mug, and turned toward the tables. In the corner, he spotted the smithy, Nicolas Bresson, seated with three other farmers, their shoulders hunched close in the firelight. Bresson caught Nicolas's eye and gestured toward an empty stool. Nicolas joined them.

Bresson said, "No one wants France weak. But when recruiters come, it's our sons they're recruiting. When loans come due, it's our harvests."

"Aye," Nicolas admitted quietly, thinking of Siméon. "That's true enough."

"And the artillery regiments," another added, "that is no common infantry. After the last war, they say it is where the clever boys go. You need a steady hand and enough letters to read orders and fire cannons. That is where honor lies."

"Aye, but also danger," someone muttered. "The boy who goes may never come home."

"But what glory," a third said, his tone reverent. "To fight for the King, and man the guns alongside Washington himself. The chance of a lifetime."

Martin arrived with drinks. "Aye, and half will line up to join. Your Siméon among them, I wager."

Nicolas drank. "The farm needs him." He left the rest unsaid.

Bresson's hand rested briefly on his shoulder. "We do what we must and call it what we can."

Nicolas said nothing. He listened as the talk around him swelled again.

"And that young marquis Lafayette has gone to fight in America," said another, leaning forward. "You know the King told him not to go? He paid for his own ship and named her *La Victoire*, and now they say Washington trusts him like a son."

Nicolas frowned. "Lafayette defied the King. That's not the example to praise."

But as the words left his mouth, he heard how they would sound to Siméon, like fear dressed up as loyalty. The boy would call it courage, not disobedience. Perhaps, Nicolas thought bitterly, that was the difference between a second son with nothing to inherit and a father watching his labor walk away.

Nicolas finished his ale slowly, the warmth of it doing nothing to ease the cold in his gut. Gradually, he considered the possibility. If Siméon truly meant to leave, he would need to be well placed. Would he be good enough for an artillery regiment? Nicolas would ask Père Charles for his thoughts.

And yet, he could not shake the thought of what might happen to the farm in Siméon's absence, the burden that would fall heavier on Colas and on his own aging shoulders.

Meanwhile, Siméon strode through the village square. At the fountain, he found his friends gathered in torchlight: Pierre, Louis, and Baptiste, friends who had once knelt with him as altar boys at Père Charles's Masses. Their bond ran deep: boys who had shared Latin chants, nervous laughter in the sacristy, and now the restless edge of manhood.

"There he is!" Pierre clapped Siméon on the back. "Ready for the *école de pièce*?"

Louis leaned in, his face etched with a mix of admiration and envy. "You've heard… France and America united against the British!" He took a breath and asked with mock seriousness, "So you'll be off to follow Antoine and Jacques? Will you win glory, or at least win the ladies?"

"Bah, he doesn't need to win them," Pierre added, unable to hide his jealousy. "Half the girls already sigh when Siméon walks past."

Siméon flushed, shaking his head. "Papa thinks it's foolish. He says it's only for aristocrats, not farmers. He says I have work here."

"He's not wrong," Louis said with a shrug, his cynicism rising. "You can fight, but you'll still be taking orders from some marquis's son. You won't be leading any parades."

"Aye," Baptiste chimed in, his anxiety shifting to a more practical fear. "The promise of good pay can sway a heart. But my father tells me stories from his time in the army… he didn't speak much of glory. Just the mud and the fever."

"But you're made for more than mud, Simi," Pierre said, cutting through the doubt with his characteristic certainty. "Everyone knows it." He took a sweeping bow, "the next artilleryman, Siméon Gaugien."

Beneath the laughter, unease lingered.

"And fearless," Louis added. "Remember when they were building the new bell tower, and we climbed to the top? He was the first to step out on the beam and didn't even tremble."

"Not like you!" Baptiste ribbed him. "You said we'd all die and wanted to climb back down!"

Louis gave an embarrassed grin. "Aye, but Siméon didn't laugh at me."

"There's no shame in taking your time," Siméon reassured him. "Sometimes you just need to know where your feet are going." Then, smirking, he added, "If I recall, it was you, Baptiste, who froze on the way down…"

Baptiste groaned as the others roared with laughter.

As they talked, the church bell tolled faintly from across the square; it was the hour before curfew.

Baptiste, ever restless, added with a grin, "Still, no village girl to keep you here? Not even Margot?"

Siméon smiled faintly. "Aye, she's lovely. But if I'm to find someone, it won't be here. Not yet."

Soon their talk turned back to America. Rumors of liberty and the names of Washington and the young Lafayette slipped into their banter as easily as saints' stories once had.

The others fell quiet again. Then Pierre clapped him on the shoulder. "You were born restless, my friend. Whatever happens, you won't be here long."

Siméon again smiled. "Maybe not."

When Nicolas left the tavern, the conversations lingered as he turned towards the square. He spotted Siméon across the square and slowed his pace, pausing in the shadow of a building to watch.

It was not the boy he saw, but the man emerging. Siméon stood not just among his friends, but slightly apart, his gaze turned toward the dark road that led south to Jussey and the wider world. Torchlight caught his jaw, set not with youthful stubbornness but with resolve. The other boys looked to him, their postures loose with the comfort of the familiar, while Siméon seemed to hum with a restrained energy, like a bowstring pulled taut.

In that unguarded moment, Nicolas saw it clearly: this was not a son of the vineyard yearning for adventure. This was a soldier, born in his own home, waiting for his war to begin.

"Papa!" Siméon called when he saw him. Nicolas waited at the edge of the square as Siméon quickly said his goodbyes and jogged to catch up.

The Walk Home

They fell into step together, their footsteps crunching softly on the uneven dirt road. The moon bathed the village in silver light, casting the sleeping countryside in long shadows.

Clearing his throat, Nicolas said quietly, "I see how much slower Grand-père is moving these days. You should help him in the mornings while you can. Those hours won't come again. Time with him. Well, it's something you'll never regret."

Siméon nodded. "I will."

Neither spoke the rest of the walk home, but the silence between them was not uncomfortable.

Once home, Nicolas removed his coat and headed for bed. "*Bonne nuit, mon fils*," he said softly, warmth tempered by unspoken fear.

"*Bonne nuit, Papa,*" Siméon replied.

The fire had burned low, its glow soft against the stone. The rest of the house was already asleep.

As he climbed the narrow ladder to the loft, each wooden rung marked the distance between obedience and departure. His father had called the land duty, soil and sweat binding a man to place. Beyond the hills, war might take everything. Yet his feet, even now, pointed south.

Later March 1778

Early the next morning, Grand-père Jean was already in the stables, moving through his chores before the church bell sounded. Jeanne moved from cow to cow, finishing the milking. Siméon soon joined them, cheeks flushed with cold and purpose after bringing in the wood. When Pâtre Antoine arrived with his great *chien mâtin* (mastiff dog), they knew the road and pasture would be guarded.

"The cows know their way," Grand-père murmured as their cows joined the herd. "Still, it is no small charge Antoine carries. He takes them out and brings them home, and every bell must answer at dusk."

By the time they returned to the kitchen, Nicolas was already seated at the table, tearing his bread in thought. "We need to finish the vines as soon as we can," he said, breaking the morning calm. "The buds will finish bursting before long, if this warmth keeps up. There's no time to lose."

Colas, who had been mending a harness by the hearth, looked up.

"If the buds continue this quickly, the pruning will have to be twice as careful," he said, thinking before continuing, "The younger vines still look weak near the slope."

Nicolas nodded approvingly. "You've got a good eye, son. We'll start with those today. Their roots haven't taken deep hold yet; they'll need more care and steady, consistent trimming."

Grand-père gave a short laugh. "Aye, and don't count on the vines waiting politely for a blessing to bloom. The calendar means nothing to nature."

"That's true," Nicolas agreed. "Easter falls late this year, mid-April."

Everyone knew a late frost could still undo the season.

As the family prepared to leave the warmth of the kitchen, Siméon lingered, glancing at his grandfather. "What happens," he asked quietly, "if the roots don't take hold, if they never grow strong?"

Grand-père rested a weathered hand on his shoulder, his gaze steady. "Then we help them along, lad. We guide them until they're ready to stand on their own. That's our duty, as farmers, as family. Remember, strong roots make a sturdy vine, and a sturdy vine weathers any storm."

Colas stood by the door, fastening his coat. "Then we'd best get to work before the day warms. If the vines won't wait for the calendar, neither should we."

Nicolas gave a faint smile as they stepped out into the chill.

The frost still sparkled on the grass as they crossed the yard together, a family bound by the land, by faith, and by the work that would carry them toward the long-awaited growing season.

As they reached the courtyard, Grand-père could see Michel, Claude's youngest nephew, unloading a pile of wood for the kitchen. His hands trembled slightly as he reached to adjust the collar of his coat. Siméon noticed but quickly turned back to the task at hand, unwilling to dwell on the subtle signs of age taking over his grand-père.

Grand-père Jean called to Michel, "Stack it tighter, boy," his voice steady despite the strain in his posture. "The wind's not done with us yet.

We don't need the stack coming down on someone."

Michel nodded, adjusting the pile without a word. Behind him, over-hearing the exchange, Claude and Grand-père shared a glance and a nod, the unspoken understanding between them as old as the vines themselves.

As the men left, Siméon glanced back and saw his mother's silhouette at the window, her gaze following them into the fields. She watched Grand-père pause to adjust his cane, and her hand went to the cross at her throat. *Take care of each other,* she said softly to herself.

Back in the kitchen, the chill of the yard lingered near the door, but the hearth held its warmth. Jeanne settled at the butter churn. She poured in the morning's cream, still faintly warm from the cows, and began the slow push and pull of the plunger. Swoosh… swoosh… swoosh.

Her arms began to burn, a familiar ache. She hummed softly to the rhythm, an old hymn for the feast of Saint Joseph, a tune about labor and providence. But her thoughts, like cream separating from milk, drifted from prayer.

Swoosh… swoosh… swoosh… The men moved through the rows differently now. Colas with his father's sure stride. Siméon restless, his eyes lifting again and again toward the road to Jussey.

Swoosh… swoosh… swoosh… Nicolas had changed as well. The gruff instruction had given way to silence, to a watchfulness that felt like a man holding his breath.

A deeper, final sound resonated through the churn. The butter had "come." She stopped, panting, and wiped sweat from her brow with her wrist. She peered inside. Pale golden clots floated in the buttermilk. With practiced hands, she gathered the butter, pressing and squeezing it against the wooden bowl to work out the remaining liquid. Each press was a small act of preservation, turning the fleeting bounty of morning into something that would sustain them.

She shaped the final pound, her thumb pressing a smooth cross into its surface. As she set it on the cold slate shelf, her gaze drifted again to the window, to the distant figures moving among the vines.

When Siméon came in from the rows, she handed him the pail. "The cistern is low. Fetch water from the fountain."

Siméon approached the fountain just as the women's gossip turned to the *seigneur's* gamekeeper. Their voices lowered to a thread.

"...paraded through town for snaring rabbits... the stocks for a day..."

"Best not to speak of it too loudly," one muttered. The others fell silent, eyes sweeping the square before fixing on him. Siméon filled his pail without looking up.

Such murmurs were part of the landscape as much as the fields themselves. Everyone knew the deer that came down at dusk to nibble young shoots were untouchable, belonging to the *seigneur*, and it was the same for the other game that crossed their land.

Even hunger granted no exception. Only the small creatures taken from the designated common grounds, the truly public game, were theirs to hunt without fear of punishment.

Siméon, slipping quietly along woodland paths later to fetch kindling, knew how to place his weight on soft earth, how to breathe with the wind so as not to snap a twig. He sometimes considered slipping off the path into the nobleman's land to gather wood or catch a meal, and he knew he would not be caught.

But he did not. The punishment would fall on his family.

HISTORICAL NOTE: THE LAST SEIGNEUR OF ROSIÈRES-SUR-MANCE

François-Gabriel de Chappuis, Marquis de Chappuis and President of the Parlement of Besançon, held seigneurial authority over Rosières-sur-Mance during the late eighteenth century. In 1761 he married Jeanne-Claude de Cordemoy, Dame d'Oricourt, uniting two lines of landed power within a single household. After 1789, the abolition of feudal privileges stripped the Marquis of his seigneurial rights, though he remained in the region as a private landowner until his death in 1814. No successor assumed the role of seigneur in Rosières-sur-Mance; the château passed into private hands. Sources: *Rosières-sur-Mance (Haute-Saône, France). Registres d'état civil (1790 – 1814). Accessed via Geneanet Family Archives.*

Nicolas completed the inventory of quarter casks. With five sound empties on hand and one cherished barrel kept full from the last vintage his late mother had helped prepare, they would still need eleven new casks to meet this year's expected harvest.

He hitched the donkey to the cart and set out for Jussey to collect the order placed the year before. Siméon had argued to come; Nicolas had refused. The new growth needed tending and Colas needed his brother's hands, not his absence. These were true enough reasons. They were not the only ones. Nicolas Gaugien had no intention of delivering his son to a recruiter's table.

The road to Jussey was familiar, a gentle descent through fields and hedgerows already greening with spring. By midmorning, he reached the cooper's yard on the edge of town, crowded with carts and stacked timber.

The *tonnelier's* workshop smelled of sawn oak and damp earth. Inside, the cooper, a broad-shouldered man named Girard, stood over a half-finished cask, tightening an iron hoop with careful blows of his hammer.

"You're early, Gaugien. That's a good sign."

"A man who waits leaves his wine to chance," Nicolas replied. This year, he would not stand at the back of the queue at the *seigneur's* press, watching his grapes spoil in the sun. His eyes were already on the row of new quarter-casks aligned against the far wall.

"Nor should he." Girard gave a final *thonk* and straightened, wiping his hands on his leather apron. "And the family? Your boys keeping you busy on the slope?"

"They are. Colas has the measure of the vines. Siméon… his mind is on other things."

Girard nodded, a knowing look in his eye. Many sons' minds were on other things these days. "Well, give Madame Gaugien my respects." He gestured to the casks. "Your… eleven was it? are ready. The oak cut three autumns past. Seasoned slow, like my father taught me."

Nicolas approached. He ran a palm over the surface of the first cask. The wood was smooth, cool, and dry, the grain tight and straight. He crouched, pressing his thumb against the seams where the staves met the head. Perfect. He thumped the side with his knuckle, a solid, resonant *tok*, then leaned close to a bunghole, inhaling. No hint of green sap, just the clean, vanilla promise of seasoned oak.

Nicolas traced a finger over the iron band. "They'll bite and hold," Girard said, watching him inspect.

Nicolas moved down the line, inspecting each cask with methodical care. This was no mere purchase. A poorly seasoned stave could taint a year's labor; a weak hoop could mean a catastrophic loss. Finally, he nodded. "They'll do."

A faint smile touched Girard's lips. "They'll do for a century, if you treat them well. The price is as we agreed."

"Agreed." Nicolas pulled a worn leather pouch from his coat.

Girard called to his son, a strong, handsome youth who appeared from behind the stacks. Together, the three of them rolled the casks across the yard and hefted them onto the cart. As they worked, Nicolas's attention was caught by a distant, rhythmic thudding from the market square.

Girard noted his glance. "Recruiters. They've been at it all week. Promising the moon and a new coat to every boy who signs."

Nicolas grunted, tying the last rope himself and testing the knot. "A man's work is here. In soil. In wood. Not in that noise."

"Perhaps." Girard's tone was noncommittal. "But the world makes its own noise. Sometimes a man must answer."

The drums still hung in the air as he guided the cart from the yard. In the square, a crowd had gathered. Nicolas kept his eyes on the road ahead. When he returned home, he said little of the town, but his brow was furrowed. Later, Colas told Siméon what their father had seen in Jussey: the recruiters, their drums and banners, a vibrant, threatening pulse in the spring air.

By the time Nicolas returned and the brothers had rolled the barrels into the courtyard, it was late afternoon, and the sky was thick with gathering clouds. Nicolas lingered in the yard after they'd unloaded and stacked them in the barn, taking a moment to wipe the sweat from his brow.

The barrels stood neatly aligned, waiting for their turn in the vineyard's long cycle.

He paused, unsettled, and turned back to the stack, checking the balance of the barrels as if certainty could be forced from wood and iron.

Grand-père called Siméon back into the house for a whetstone, while Colas left to tend to the pig and chickens behind the cottage. Alone now, Nicolas saw a better way to stack the casks, so that those to be used next would be closer to the front. It would only take a few minutes.

No one heard the casks fall.

When Siméon returned, his heart froze. Quarter casks lay scattered across the ground. Among them, Nicolas lay sprawled on the ground, one hand clutching his leg, his face pale and streaked with dirt.

"Papa!" Siméon cried, dropping the whetstone with a clatter as he sprinted forward, heart hammering.

Nicolas's face was drawn with pain, but his eyes were open. "It's nothing. Help me up," he muttered, holding out his other hand, though his voice trembled with effort.

"It's more than nothing, Papa," Siméon said sharply, kneeling beside him. His breath caught as he saw the torn breeches, the deep cut, and the leg bent at an angle.

"What happened?"

Nicolas grimaced, trying to shift himself upright. "I was rolling the old barrel stack and it rolled out too fast. I couldn't stop it in time." He exhaled shakily; his pride stung as much as his leg. "I've done it a hundred times before."

"Colas!" Siméon shouted over his shoulder, his voice breaking. "Come quick!"

From the far side of the yard, Colas came running. Something in Siméon's voice told him it was serious. He wiped his hands on his work shirt, his face stricken as he saw their father. "What happened?" he gasped.

"The casks rolled out, his leg's hurt badly," Siméon said, already slipping his arms beneath Nicolas's shoulders. "Help me get him up."

Together, the two brothers lifted their father to his feet, Nicolas groaning as the movement jarred his injury. He leaned heavily between them as they half-carried, half-walked him toward the cottage.

Jeanne, seeing them from the window, dropped the bowl she'd been holding and rushed outside, her apron flying. Her face went pale at the sight of the blood soaking through Nicolas's breeches. *"Mon Dieu*, what happened?" she cried, holding open the door wide.

"The casks fell," Siméon panted, his shoulder aching under his father's weight. "It's his leg, he needs a doctor." He looked at Nicolas, forcing his voice level. "Papa, you'll be all right. We'll get you help."

"The casks rolled out too fast."

Jeanne's hands trembled as she helped ease her husband into a chair by the hearth. "Siméon, Doctor Marcel Mairet[16] is away visiting family. Fetch Madame Lemaire. She has helped before. She will know what to do."

---

[16] **Doctor Marcel Mairet** (1748 – 1820), approximately three kilometers from c, is identified in parish and civil records as a praticien de santé and chirurgien, and appears as physician to the Gaugien family. Source: *Research and correspondence of French genealogist Jean-Marie Guillaume of Saint-Marcel.*

She met his eyes. "Go now. Quickly."

Behind her, Grand-père had been roused by the commotion and was rummaging for cloth to make bandages, his weathered hands steady despite the worry etched on his face.

Siméon nodded, "Stay with him. I'll bring Madame Lemaire."

Outside, the cold air hit his face. He broke into a run down the lane, the echo of his mother's words and his father's groan driving him faster toward the village.

He ran at a steady pace to the home of Madame Lemaire, Rosières-sur-Mance's guérisseuse and *rebo*uteuse,[17] less than a mile away. Madame Lemaire cultivated the herbs and flowers she used to make the salves and ointments she applied in treating her patients.

A brisk, no-nonsense woman, she and her sister lived together in their family home.

Madame Lemaire saw Siméon running to her house and met him outside. He told her what happened, and to his relief, she agreed she could come immediately. Siméon helped her harness her mare to the cart before climbing into the back for the bumpy ride to the farm.

The creak of wooden wheels announced the old barn cart long before it came into view. It then jolted to a halt before the cottage.

Madame Lemaire descended awkwardly, muttering under her breath as her *sabots* hit the ground with a dull thud. Her stout figure was swaddled in layers of skirts and shawls, their colors clashing like a forgotten patchwork quilt that settled around her and swished softly as she strode across the courtyard. Strands of gray hair had escaped her lopsided bun, framing a weathered face set in a permanent scowl. A large satchel hung from her shoulder, its contents rattling softly with each step.

---

[17] A *guérisseuse* (French) was a female folk healer who treated illness using herbs, salves, and traditional remedies. A *rebouteuse* (French) specialized in setting bones and treating sprains, dislocations, and muscular injuries through manual manipulation.

Madame Lemaire, Village Herbalist.

"Jeanne and Jean!" she barked, striding toward the cottage without pausing. "Where is he?"

Her sharp eyes swept the room the moment she crossed the threshold, taking in the scene with practiced ease. "Well, well! Nicolas Gaugien, hobbling like a lame mule! What were you thinking? You know better than to move barrels in the barn alone like a young man. Hmph!" She swished over to him. "A grown man with more pride than sense."

Nicolas, pale and grimacing in his chair, opened his mouth to respond, but Madame Lemaire silenced him with a glare as sharp as her tone. "Save your breath. I've no time for excuses. Let me see this leg of yours before you make it worse."

She dropped her satchel to the floor with a thud and knelt beside him, her skirts pooling around her. Glancing over her shoulder, she barked, "Colas, fetch me clean cloths and hot water. And hurry!"

Colas nodded quickly, crossing the stone kitchen floor to take the kettle from the fire. His mother gave him a bundle of cloths while Madame

Lemaire began unwrapping the bloodied bandages Jeanne and Grand-père had hastily applied earlier. Nicolas winced, gripping the chair's arms as her fingers prodded the swollen flesh. She muttered under her breath as she examined the knee, testing its range of motion and pressing along its edges.

Grand-père interjected, "Is it broken?"

"No, it's not broken. But it's slipped and the swelling tells me it will take some time to return. The cut will heal quickly enough, but the leg itself will take weeks. If you do as I say, you'll probably walk straight with the help of a cane again. If you don't, you will not." She dusted off her hands as she stood. "Your choice."

"Weeks?" Nicolas growled. "The vines…"

"Will wait," she interrupted sharply, pulling a jar of salve from her satchel. The smell of camphor and herbs filled the room as she lifted the lid. "Unless you'd rather cripple yourself permanently, in which case, by all means, stagger back out there."

Her words hung heavily in the air. Jeanne shot her husband a warning look as Madame Lemaire scooped a generous dollop of salve and began working it into the swollen skin.

"Five days of complete rest to start. Keep the leg raised, and don't put weight on it. After that, you'll start wrapping it tightly every morning and evening. The swelling will not go down overnight, but it will heal if you behave." She turned to Jeanne and handed her the salve. "Use this morning and night for the next five days. I'll collect it when I return, and by then, Doctor Mairet should be back. I am certain he will look in on him."

Nicolas's jaw tightened, but he said nothing, his frustration tempered by the pain and by the unmistakable finality in Madame Lemaire's tone. "If you take care of yourself with the same care you tend those vines, you'll be walking again before the end of summer."

Nicolas groaned and leaned back.

Colas returned with water in a wooden bowl and cloths, setting them down carefully beside her. She gently cleaned the blood from the cut across his knee. "There, the cut is not too bad. It will heal well." She rubbed a different salve around the cut and gave an approving nod before expertly wrapping the leg with clean linen from her satchel.

She glanced up at Nicolas with a glint of approval. "Your sons are men now, getting stronger by the day. They'll manage the work until you're fit again. That's what sons are for, isn't it?" Colas nodded, and Siméon stood taller. He looked at Madame, feeling momentarily proud that she recognized him as no longer a boy.

Nicolas's brow furrowed, but Jeanne stepped in before he could argue.

"Yes, we are blessed. We'll manage," she said firmly, though her hands trembled as she adjusted her apron.

Madame Lemaire smirked as she tied the final knot in the bandage. "Good." She jabbed a finger at Nicolas, "Sit still and let them help you, or I'll tie you to this chair myself."

"You'll also need to watch him," she said, addressing Colas. "Don't let him near the vines until I say so, or you'll be calling me back here to deal with the mess."

Her tone softened as she stood again and dusted off her skirts. "You're lucky it wasn't worse, Gaugien. Be thankful you have a family to care for you; not everyone does."

With that, she hoisted the satchel onto her shoulder and made for the door. "Five days, and I will come back. No work. No walking. If you're not smarter by then, Jeanne knows where to find me." She nodded to them both. "Good to see you, and Jeanne, I hope our patient will be cooperative."

And with a flurry, she was out the door, onto her cart, and trotting down the dusty path.

Jeanne squeezed Nicolas's shoulder. "You heard her. You're going to have to rest, no matter how impatient you feel!" Suddenly overwhelmed, she turned back to the hearth, stoking the flame to bring the big kettle hanging over it back to a boil.

Nicolas leaned back into the chair and stared at the ceiling.

The following days stretched long and heavy. With Nicolas confined, Siméon and Colas worked from dawn until the church bell tolled vespers, pruning vines, caring for the farm, and readying the stable for the cows' return each evening. The vines demanded their full attention. Grand-père's wisdom guided them in the mornings, though by afternoon the old man's strength waned, and Siméon and Colas grew accustomed to carrying on without him.

The weight of that responsibility revealed itself. Grand-père had warned them at breakfast that rain would come by midday, and the old man was rarely wrong. Racing to finish the lower slope before it arrived, Siméon misjudged the strain on a new hazel brace[18], cut green from the hedgerow, and woven into the trellis line. He pulled it too tight. With a dry crack, the brace splintered, whipping back across the back of his hand. Worse, the sudden release twisted the stake beside it, crushing the young, promising vine it was meant to support.

Colas was at his side in a moment. "Let me see," he said, his voice tight with concern. He inspected the hand, then the wounded vine, exhaling through his nose. "Papa had high hopes for this one," he murmured, acknowledging the loss.

A cold wave of failure washed over Siméon. He had been so focused on speed, on proving he could handle the work, that he had been careless.

He looked from his stinging hand to the damaged plant, a symbol of his recklessness. "I know," he muttered, shame heating his face.

But as Colas prepared to cobble together a repair, Siméon stopped him. "No. Wait." He studied the broken setup, his mind shifting from frustration to focus. He remembered an afternoon years ago, Père Charles at the millpond, asking why a stone thrown high traveled farther than one thrown flat. *What tells it to finally come down?* The answer had something to do with angles, with forces pulling against each other. He looked again at the splintered brace, the twisted stake, and suddenly saw it clearly.

---

[18] **Hazel** (*noisetiers* in French) grew abundantly in hedgerows and forests and provided vineyard families with inexpensive, flexible wood for stakes and supports. Viticulturists cut young branches while green, wove them into trellis lines, and replaced them seasonally as needed. This reliance on local materials continued until the phylloxera crisis of the 1860s devastated European vineyards and led to the widespread adoption of grafting onto resistant American rootstock, fundamentally transforming French viticulture.

"The post is set at the wrong angle. If we just re-tie it, it will snap again. We need to reset it entirely."

It took them the better part of an hour of grueling work as the sky darkened, growing heavy with rain. Siméon ignored the throb in his hand and directed the operation with a newfound calm, calculating the proper angle and depth. When the new post was set and the vine carefully re-secured, it was stronger than before.

Colas clapped him on his shoulder. "You set right what you broke. That's what matters."

Siméon nodded.

At home, Jeanne divided her time between caring for Nicolas, managing the household, and helping with the vines and farm. Her prayers grew longer, circling endlessly around her husband and sons, the vines, the animals, and Grand-père.

By the fifth day, Siméon and Colas returned home utterly spent, their clothes streaked with dirt and their shoulders heavy from long hours in the fields. They dropped into their chairs at the kitchen table without a word, the room filling only with the crackle of the hearth. Jeanne set steaming bowls of soup before them, her expression softening as she took in their weariness.

"You've done well."

Colas gave a faint smile and reached for his spoon. "Only because we've both worked like oxen," he muttered, though there was pride in his tone.

Siméon stirred his soup absently. "You've managed everything as if you've owned it all your life. Papa would be proud."

Colas gave a small shrug, though his glance lingered on his brother. "I only did what had to be done. And you, well, you've been paying attention all these years. It shows. Everything runs more easily with you here."

"If I'm honest... I've wondered how I was supposed to keep this place together on my own one day. Without you here. Without Papa, or Grand-père barking orders from every direction."

"Maybe it was never meant to be just me."

Siméon looked up, "You'd manage. You always do.

Colas laughed softly. "Maybe. But it's easier knowing you're here. You see things I miss: the small things.

Siméon replied drily, "Do not fret, big brother. I'm here now, aren't I?"

Jeanne glanced between them, her eyes glistening with quiet pride, before she turned back to the hearth.

Siméon said nothing more, but the words lingered. For now, his world was bound within the vineyard's borders.

Sitting by the fire, Nicolas stared at his swollen leg, the dull ache a constant reminder of the years of labor that had left him vulnerable. He watched Siméon return from the fields, shoulders bent, gaze distant. Nicolas had always known his son would leave. He had simply hoped the vines would prove stronger.

The next day, Doctor Marcel Mairet's cart appeared on the lane, and Madame Lemaire was seated beside him. Colas and Siméon were mending a fence near the road and straightened as the cart approached.

"Good day, young messieurs," Dr. Mairet called down from the seat. He was a thin, careful man with spectacles and a leather bag worn soft from years of use. "Is your father at home? I've come to examine his leg."

"He is, Doctor. Inside, by the fire."

They walked next to the cart as it stopped outside the cottage. Madame Lemaire descended from the cart with her usual bustle. "The swelling was considerable when I set it, Doctor, and the joint had slipped badly from its place. I applied a camphor salve and wrapped it tightly, as you know, and instructed complete rest for…"

"Thank you, Madame," Dr. Mairet said, his tone polite but final. "I shall see for myself."

They crossed the yard together, the doctor leading, Madame Lemaire a step behind, the brothers following. At the door, Jeanne appeared, wiping her hands on her apron. "Doctor Mairet, thank you for coming. Please, come in."

Inside, Nicolas sat in the high-backed chair, his wrapped leg resting on a stool. He made to rise, but the doctor waved him down. "Stay as you are, Monsieur Gaugien."

Madame Lemaire moved toward the patient, ready to point out her work, but Dr. Mairet turned to the room. "The sons may stay." His meaning was clear.

Jeanne touched Madame Lemaire's arm gently. "Come, I have some herbs to show you from the garden." The two women withdrew to the kitchen, Madame Lemaire's mouth pressed into a thin line, but offering no protest.

Dr. Mairet set his bag on the table, removed his coat, and rolled up his sleeves. He unwrapped the bandages slowly, pressed along the knee, tested its movement, and watched Nicolas's face.

"Tell me what happened."

Nicolas told him. The doctor listened without interruption, his fingers still probing the joint.

When he finished his examination, he rewrapped the leg with clean bandages from his own bag, his movements precise and unhurried.

"You are fortunate Madame Lemaire was able to attend you so quickly," he said. "The bone is sound. But the joint was badly strained. It will heal, though you'll have a permanent reminder." He looked at the boys, then at Nicolas directly. "You are fortunate to have two strapping sons. You will need to let lifting and carrying fall to other hands now."

Nicolas held the doctor's gaze. His sons remained silent.

"I understand," he said finally.

Dr. Mairet nodded and rose, rolling down his sleeves. "Another week of rest. Then, gentle movement only. Send for me if the swelling returns or the pain worsens."

He collected his bag and moved toward the kitchen doorway. "Madame Gaugien, Madame Lemaire, he must not overdo it. He needs more rest, and the wounds must be kept clean and covered."

At the door, Jeanne pressed a few coins into the doctor's hand. Dr. Mairet gave Madame Lemaire a small nod of acknowledgment. Something in her expression softened. Her work had been confirmed. That was enough.

Chapter Three:
Lettre de Recommandation

The following afternoon, Siméon suggested a hare would help his father's recovery. Jeanne nodded. It was the seventh day after Nicolas's accident and the first he had gingerly ventured from the house with a cane to check the vines. She understood Siméon needed time away from the farm. Still, her eyes lingered on him and she lowered her voice.

"Keep clear of *les bois du seigneur*. You know the *garde-chasse* patrols the boundary this time of year. On our land, a hare is a meal; in the seigneur's woods, it is theft. A pheasant in the wrong place means a fine for Papa," she leaned closer, adding in a whisper, "or worse."

Siméon gave her a half smile, one part reassurance and one part defiance. "Do not worry, Maman. I will bring back something, and no one will ever know where it came from." He winked at her with a roguish grin.

Jeanne's expression hardened briefly before softening again. "It is not only the seigneur's eyes that watch, Siméon. God sees all. It is best not to tempt either. Faith must live in both worlds." She paused. "Trust heaven for what we cannot guard, and tread carefully where men claim power."

The exchange hung between them.

Siméon kissed his mother's cheek and slipped out, musket slung over his shoulder.

Inside, Jeanne kept watch over Nicolas, his leg raised by the hearth after the difficult walk back from the cottage. He tried to hide his discomfort; she was not fooled. Then the steady clatter of hooves carried from the lane, announcing someone unexpected.

She smiled to herself as the familiar figure came into view. It was their parish priest in a wide-brimmed hat guiding his donkey cart along the dirt road toward the cottage. Père Charles was known for his pastoral rounds, and his appreciation for the Gaugien family's wine.

She sighed, smoothing her apron with deliberate care as the cart rolled to a stop, her practiced smile masking the weight of her worries. Though his visits were often cheerful, and she did have much to discuss regarding the Easter services, today's arrival was weightier. News of Nicolas's injury had traveled widely, no doubt from Madame Lemaire.

"Père Charles!" Jeanne called out, greeting him as he climbed from the cart. "What brought you our way so early?" she asked.

"The Lord's work, as always," he replied, tipping his hat respectfully. "Madame Lemaire's tongue runs faster than her spinning wheel." He grinned, his deep voice carrying a note of humor. "And, perhaps, the chance to share in the trials of your hearty red wine."

Jeanne chuckled despite her worries and led the priest inside. "Nicolas is resting," she said. "But I know my father-in-law will keep you company until Nicolas can see you."

"Then I shall offer my counsel and perhaps a small toast to Nicolas's recovery with Grand-père," Père Charles said with a warm smile.

Père Charles descended the steps into the cool wine cellar, his boots echoing softly on the stone. Grand-père Jean was there, inspecting a barrel with an appraising eye. He sipped from a small glass of red wine, then used his pocketknife to slice a thin strip of dried apple.

"Ah, Père Charles," Grand-père greeted him with a grin. "Are you here to sanctify the wine or indulge in its blessings?"

Père Charles chuckled, clasping his hands behind his back. "Perhaps both. But first, how is Nicolas? Jeanne tells me he has had a difficult few days."

Pére Charles, Parish Priest of Rosiéres

Grand-père nodded, swirling the wine thoughtfully. "My son works harder than his body allows. Stubborn as the day he was born. Sitting still is not his way. Letting the boys take over has been hard for him. Today he took his first walk in the vines. But the boys are capable and Nicolas will mend; he always does." He poured a second glass and passed it to the priest, then offered a slice of dried apple on the point of his knife. He raised his glass, clearing his throat.

"To recovery."

"To recovery," Père Charles echoed. He sipped, savoring the wine. "The vintage is delicious as ever."

Grand-père grinned. "It should be. This is the last cask my late wife, God rest her soul, helped press." Grand-père paused and silently made the sign of the cross. "It is very special to me. Every time I taste it, I am reminded of her touch, her care, and the love she brought to everything."

Père Charles nodded thoughtfully, his expression softening. "A beautiful tribute, Jean. The love you shared is woven into this cask, as much a part of them as the grapes themselves. She would be proud of the care you have taken to honor her memory."

They both took another sip, enjoying a moment of contemplative silence.

Père Charles broke the silence. "Shall we see if Nicolas is ready for a guest? I imagine he could use some company, and perhaps a story to lift his spirits."

Grand-père set the glass aside, leaning lightly on his cane. "I agree, and the fire is warmer by the hearth, my old bones will thank me."

In the sitting room next to the kitchen, Nicolas sat propped up in his chair near the fire, his injured leg extended. He glanced up as the priest entered with his father, offering a faint smile.

"Père," Nicolas said, gesturing to the chair beside him. "I imagine the whole village knows I am laid up like an old horse."

Père Charles chuckled as he settled in. "An old horse, perhaps, but not ready to be put out to pasture."

Jeanne appeared with three glasses of last year's vintage, placing them on the small table for the men to share before retreating to the kitchen. Nicolas raised his glass in a silent toast before taking a slow sip.

Père Charles savored the wine, nodding approvingly. "As fine as ever. Your vines never disappoint."

Jeanne smiled from the doorway. "Our vines are no finer than the Petit's or the Vauthrin's," she said with a smile. "But they are ours, and I think that makes the wine taste better," she added as she left the room.

Nicolas grunted softly, setting his glass down. He stared into the fire. "Père," he began, his tone low, "I need to ask you about Siméon. He talks of nothing but the war in America and fighting the British."

Père Charles's expression grew serious. "You know what war means for a common soldier. It is no place for a boy, though it can make a man."

"I know it," Nicolas said, his voice heavy. "But how do I argue with him? He says there is no future here but sweat and hunger."

"God does not waste what He shapes, Nicolas. I have watched that boy since he was seven years old."

He paused, the memory settling over him. In catechism, Siméon asked the questions other boys never thought to ask: why incense rises straight before it curls, why the bell rope feels lighter after the first pull. Maître Rets noticed it too, that the boy did not merely copy figures; he considered what they meant.

One afternoon by the millpond, Père Charles had watched him skip stones, counting under his breath, tracking each kiss of water. He approached quietly. "What happens, Siméon, if you throw it not just far, but high?"

The boy obeyed. This time he watched not the splashes but the moment the stone seemed to hang, weightless, before surrendering to its fall.

"It goes farther," he said, eyes bright.

"But why? And what tells it to finally come down?" Père Charles offered no answer. "These are the questions you must one day ask, and answer."

That night Siméon had not traced farm sums in the loft dust as usual. He drew the curve of the stone's path, marking where it rose, where it lingered, where it fell.

Père Charles folded his hands. "He has a mind for it, Nicolas. Not mere cleverness. Something rarer." His gaze sharpened. "A boy like that could find a place in the King's Artillery."

Nicolas looked up. "The artillery? That is for officers, for nobles."

"Not anymore. Not entirely," Père Charles said quietly. "Since the last war, they seek boys who can master the geometry of cannon fire. Precision and reason weigh more than title. It is dangerous, yes; but it would use his mind as well as his strength."

Père Charles leaned back, his gaze settling on the embers. "It is no small thing to be accepted. The examinations are demanding. But since the last war, a boy without noble birth may earn his place if he can reason, hold steady, and work with precision." He paused. "I remember well that Siméon could do all three."

Nicolas looked up, the firelight catching the bleakness in his eyes. "I am a farmer. I know soil and vines. I do not know anyone who could make such an introduction." His voice dropped. "Père, can you help us?"

Père Charles held his gaze as the fire settled between them. He took a slow breath.

"Perhaps. I studied under Archbishop de Durfort in Besançon, many years ago. He has long been sympathetic to promising youth of humble birth. If I were to write to him, invoking our old acquaintance, he might lend his name to a letter for Auxonne."

Nicolas could not speak. He had come hoping the priest would dissuade his son. The magnitude of what was being offered humbled him, and the worry he had carried for days gave way to something closer to relief.

"Thank you, Père." The words were all he had.

"I will see what can be done," Père Charles said, rising gently. "But remember, it is God who guides such things. If the boy is meant to go, the way will open. Now rest that leg."

When Siméon returned, the sun hung low and a plump young hare hung over his shoulder. Jeanne met him outside and took it with a wide smile. He told her about the pheasants and a young deer moving through the trees.

He did not mention that he had slowed at the forest's edge, where les bois du seigneur stretched dark and still beyond the hedgerows. For a moment he lingered, weighing risk against reward. He was a good shot and quick; no one would have known.

His eyes tracked a pheasant into the deep shadow. The desire to cross was less about the meat than the act itself: to tread where he was forbidden, to claim a sliver of that absolute liberty. Then, with a shake of his head, he turned homeward. He remembered the stocks. He had the hare.

As he stepped into the kitchen, the familiar warmth of bread and simmering herbs met him. Yet the silence of those shadowed woods stayed with him; the same silence that surrounded his father's chair, the same unspoken boundary now drawing him toward a more dangerous crossing. The forbidden and the possible were beginning to look alike.

Spring to Winter's Eve 1778

In the weeks leading up to Easter, the vineyard stirred from winter rest. Buds, then tender green leaves, unfurled beneath the strengthening sun, and the hills of Rosières-sur-Mance flushed with old, relentless life. Thawed earth and early blossoms scented the air. The first swallows wheeled overhead, sharp against the pale sky.

Siméon and Colas worked the slopes with pruning shears in hand, each cut deliberate. Their father had taught them to prune hard; to spare only one or two canes per vine and remove the rest so the year's strength would flow cleanly into new fruit. It was the method the Gaugien men knew well, rooted in foresight, patience, and restraint. Their cracked, calloused hands moved with practiced rhythm as they tied the chosen shoots with willow twine. Between the rows, they hoed the soil, breaking heavy clods to admit warmth and air. The sharp smell of manure rose in the morning light, mingling with faint smoke from the fires lit to guard against frost. Every movement carried inheritance. The vineyard was as much a prayer as a trade.

Their banter broke the silence.

"You missed a knot, little brother," Colas called, half mockery, half affection.

Siméon looked up, squinting against the sun. "That's because I'm not rushing like a fool. Keep cutting like that and your vines will weep before the season begins."

Colas grinned. "My rows are straighter than yours. Even Papa would agree."

"Straight, perhaps," Siméon replied, "but tied like a man with one good eye."

Their laughter drifted down the slope, blending with the chirr of *alouettes* (larks). They worked in easy rivalry, competitive without malice.

At the edge of the vineyard, Nicolas leaned on his walking stick and watched. Pride flickered behind the fatigue in his eyes. He remembered when the boys' voices came from the barn or the yard instead of the vines, when laughter filled the house while he mended tools or stacked barrels. That warmth returned as he watched them now, tempered by the knowledge that his sons were no longer boys. Siméon worked with a man's resolve, patient and enduring. Colas moved with grounded confidence. Together, they embodied the continuity Nicolas had spent his life building.

On Easter morning, April 19, 1778, the bell of Saint-Siméon rang across the valley. Its echoes rolled over misted fields and blossoming orchards toward the slow green bend of the Mance. Frogs croaked among the reeds, and the blackbirds and chaffinches were active in the hedgerow.

Inside the chapel, Père Charles's Holy Week sermons still lingered in the minds of the gathered parishioners. The Latin liturgy rose and fell like music, but it was the French homily, plain and direct, that took root. He spoke of sacrifice, of Christ's suffering mirrored in long winters, fruitful harvests, unending labor. He spoke of renewal, not as permission to wander, but as a call to return stronger.

As the family gathered for Easter dinner, talk turned to the vineyard. Colas and Claude discussed the work still to be done, while Nicolas and Grand-père offered thoughts from their places at each end of the table. The ease was palpable; Claude and his family belonged here, and everyone felt it.

Toward the meal's end, Père Charles cleared his throat, his gaze settling on Siméon. "Your Papa and I have spoken," he began, his tone measured. "About your ambitions for the artillery."

Siméon froze, the crust of bread suspended in his hand. "And? What...?"

"If you are truly committed and feel this is your path," the priest continued, choosing his words with care, "I am willing to make inquiries and suggest your name to those who might provide a *lettre de recommandation*."

He paused, letting the conditional nature of the offer sink in. "That alone will not be enough. You will still need to pass the examination and prove your skill in numbers and discipline."

Siméon's breath caught. The world seemed to narrow to the priest's face. *A lettre de recommandation.* This was no longer a boy's daydream. It was a fragile possibility: laid out by the two men he was most bound to obey. "You would do that for me?" he whispered.

"For your family," Père Charles corrected, his gaze unwavering. "But there are conditions. First, you must honor your duties here until the time comes. Your family needs you now more than ever."

Siméon nodded, a fierce, new determination solidifying in his eyes. "I will. I swear it."

"And second," the priest said, his voice firm, "you must understand what you are asking. The King's service is an eight-year enlistment. During that time, you will be discouraged from putting down roots. Your life will belong to the regiment." He leaned forward slightly, his eyes holding Siméon's. "War is no game, Siméon. It will test your body, your mind, and your faith. If you go, you must go as a young man knowing what he is sacrificing, not as a boy chasing adventure."

Siméon drew himself straighter, the weight of the moment settling not just over the table, but directly onto his shoulders. "I understand," he said, his voice low and solemn. He meant it.

The silence stretched, thick with the unspoken future. It was Nicolas who broke it. He raised his glass, his voice resolute, cutting through the tension. "To God's will," he said. "May we all be granted the strength and wisdom to follow His path."

Grand-père Jean nodded solemnly, his weathered hand gripping his own glass. "As I always say, it is a man's deeds, in service to God, that make him worthy of remembrance."

Siméon was silent. The path was real. The validation from Père Charles and the stunned consent in his father's eyes tightened his throat.

He looked at Colas, who offered a tense, unreadable smile. He looked at his father, who now stared into his glass as if reading a doom there. The hope remained, but it was now measured against time and duty.

That evening, the family gathered by the hearth. The scent of simmering stew filled the low-beamed room. Nicolas sat close to the fire, his leg propped up.

"You have been working harder than ever, boy," he said gruffly, though his voice held a rare note of pride. His eyes studied Siméon as if trying to see both the child he had raised and the young man now standing before him.

Siméon looked up from mending a tool handle. "The farm needs it, Papa," he said simply, though both men knew the truth that hung between them: the vineyard would feel his absence.

Across the room, Colas had been quiet, his elbows resting on his knees, eyes fixed on the fire. At last, he spoke. "If I had the choice, I would go too," he said, his tone half-light, half earnest. "See the world a bit before it buries me under a lifetime of grapes and cows."

Siméon laughed softly, though it caught in his throat. "You have more than enough to keep you busy here."

Colas looked at him, something unspoken tightening in his jaw. "Aye, and most of it is your doing lately. You have taken on more than half the chores I used to dread. If you go, I will be the one knee-deep in muck again, while you get to go off and play with guns."

The brothers shared a wry smile, but it did not reach their eyes. Colas's envy was a pale thing next to the dawning weight of inheritance. "You get to be the hero," Colas said, his voice dropping so only Siméon could hear. "And I get to be the son who stayed."

Jeanne caught Colas's look and shook her head gently. "Your brother's path is not an escape," she said softly. "It is a calling. And if it leads him away, then we will pray it leads him safely home again."

Nicolas grunted, eyes still on the fire. "Just make sure that fire does not burn you, boy," he muttered.

On the morning of May 25, the sun cast a pale golden glow over the vineyard, as if it too were prepared to begin the celebration of Rogation Days, locally understood as the blessing of the vines in France since AD

470[19]. The overnight rain clouds had dissipated, and the first warmth of the new day cast a sheen over the rows dotted with bright green new growth.

Père Charles stood at the head of the vines, cassock stirring in the breeze. In one hand he held a book of prayer, in the other a small vial of holy water. At his side, a server swung the thurible, its chain glinting as thin coils of frankincense smoke drifted over the field.

Blessing Of The Vines

Though many in Franche-Comté tended vines for both white and red, Nicolas Gaugien and his father before him believed their soil gave its truest heart to the dark grapes. From them came a wine the villagers called simply le rouge de Gaugien, or Gaugien Red, a labor of patience and faith that marked the family's craft for generations.

The small gathering included the Gaugien family, Claude and his wife Eloisa with their nephews Michel and Henri, and their neighbor Jean-Claude. All crossed themselves as the priest began in Latin, his voice solemn and measured:

---

[19] **Rogation Days**, from the Latin *rogare*, "to ask," originated around AD 470 when Bishop Mamertus of Vienne in Gaul instituted a triduum of prayer, fasting, and penitential processions during the three days preceding the Feast of the Ascension in response to earthquakes, floods, and other calamities. The practice spread throughout Gaul and was mandated by the Council of Orléans in 511. Sources: *Francis X. Weiser, S.J., Handbook of Christian Feasts and Customs: The Year of the Lord in Liturgy and Folklore (New York: Harcourt, Brace and Company, 1958), 41–42.*

"Benedic, Domine, vineam hanc, quam…"

He paused, then echoed in French so all might follow:

"Seigneur, bénis cette vigne…"

A soft murmur of responses rose. Jeanne clasped her rosary, lips moving in whispered petition. Nicolas bowed his head. Grand-père Jean had seen many blessings and many harvests; each one reminded him how much the land had given and how much it still asked.

Standing between Colas and his mother, Siméon replied when the responses came. He watched Père Charles move slowly down the rows, sprinkling holy water across the waking vines. One late frost, one storm, and all of it could still be lost. He thought of his father's accident, of the family's dependence on this crop, of Colas's responsibility, of his own restlessness. Each tied shoot was a bet against the weather. The vines seemed to speak of his own fate: tender, vulnerable, but reaching upward all the same.

The thurible swung wide, smoke drifting skyward, their eyes following it in silence.

When Père Charles returned, he rested a hand on Nicolas's shoulder. *"Que le Seigneur te donne force et guérison."* Nicolas's jaw tightened; he gave a firm nod, his hand finding Jeanne's. The priest moved on to Grand-père, to Colas, to Siméon, then to Claude and his kin, offering each a word of blessing for the season ahead.

The last of the incense curled into the clear morning sky. The solemn air eased. Already at the edges of the gathering, quieter talk stirred: late taxes, rumors of recruiters passing through neighboring towns, distant America.

They made their way toward the church, where the tables were laid with loaves of bread, bowls of fresh curds, and earthen cups of young wine. As neighbors arrived, the courtyard filled with laughter and chatter, boots muddying the flagstones. It was the season's first shared pause, and the village was not ready to let it end.

By midsummer, the Feast of Saint John the Baptist brought a rare evening free from toil. Bonfires blazed along the riverbank, their flames mirrored in the dark sweep of the Mance. Pipes and drums carried across the fields, and laughter mingled with the crackle of burning wood.

Colas stood with companions from the neighboring farms, a jug of young wine in hand, his easy grin catching the firelight. They spoke of the harvest, of horses, of girls, of whether the priest's sermon had run too long.

A few paces away, Siméon sat among his own circle. Their talk burned hotter: of France's fortunes in the war, of fleets and freedom, of what it might mean to fight for liberty.

When Colas passed by later, he clapped his younger brother on the shoulder. "Keep dreaming, little brother. France will need bread more than talk soon enough."

Siméon's smile was tight. "And will you be the one to bake it?"

Colas's grin faded. He leaned in, voice low beneath the noise. "Someone must. While you're off chasing glory, this land won't wait. Papa can't do it. So yes, I will. Just don't expect a hero's welcome when you come back to find nothing's changed." He gave Siméon's shoulder a hard, final squeeze and melted back into the crowd.

From the edge of the firelight, Nicolas and Jeanne watched their sons. Nicolas's jaw was set. Jeanne's hand moved steadily at her rosary, her prayers swallowed by the drumbeats, her eyes following Siméon as if trying to memorize the shape of him against the flames.

Jeanne moved ceaselessly between house and field. She checked the calves, gathered the fruits and nuts she had set out to dry, patched harnesses, tended the vegetable garden, and salted meat for the winter. When it was time to bake, she carried her dough to the seigneur's ovens, waiting her turn. The simplest tasks demanded hours, yet her hands were never still. Grand-père watched from the shade near the barn, his voice steady even as his body tired. In this world, family was labor, and labor was life itself.

Nicolas's recovery came slowly, slower than he liked. The limp remained, and with it a simmering frustration. One afternoon, watching

Siméon finish a row, his voice cut across the field. "Not like that. The knot goes under, or it will chafe the cane. Do you think you know better?"

The moment the words left him, sharp as a pruning hook, Nicolas turned away, rubbing his stiff leg. The true question hung unsaid in the summer air: *Will you even remember how it is done here?*

Siméon bristled beneath the criticism. He worked from sunup to sundown and found it harder each day to hold his tongue. The heat, the fatigue, the stubbornness of two men too alike; they all set the air between them crackling.

Jeanne's voice often cut between them, firm but even. "Enough," she would say, setting down her basket. "The land gives to us only when we work together."

Madame Lemaire visited often, bringing gossip and a touch of gentleness the farmhouse sorely needed.

At night, when the day's noise faded, Jeanne knelt by the bedside, her candle burning low. She prayed in silence, sometimes for strength, sometimes simply for peace.

Under Siméon and Colas's care, the vineyard flourished. The vines thickened, heavy with leaves and swelling grapes, and demanded constant weeding and pruning. They moved among them like vigilant craftsmen, Siméon working with deliberate, almost defiant care, as if each perfectly tied cane was an answer to his father's doubt. Each decision shaped the season's yield. Their days were filled with thoughts of the animals, soil, and vine health.

Nicolas scratched figures on a slate. "If the weather holds, we may see perhaps five *pièces*[20] this year," he murmured. "Enough for the

---

[20] **The** *pièce* (French) was the standard cask in which vignerons counted and sold their harvest across wine-producing regions of France. In the mid-eighteenth century, the priest of Volnay recorded his annual vintage in *pièces* of 228 liters, roughly equivalent to nearly five quarter casks. Capacity varied by locality under the Ancien Régime, which had no national standard for liquid measures, and barrel sizes continued to differ regionally even after the adoption of the metric system. Source: *Rod Phillips, "The Very Long and Very Short History of Barrel-Aged Wine," World of Fine Wine, January 5, 2026, https://www.worldoffinewine.com.*

authorities and the Church, trade for salt and cloth, and still have something for winter."

Jeanne nodded, also calculating silently. "And the tax man will come at *la Saint-Michel*," she said, "so perhaps one *pièce* for him, and another to see us through Lent."

Grand-père, sipping last year's vintage from an earthen cup, smiled faintly. "A good harvest raises a family's standing," he said. He looked at the slate, then at his son. "Spend them wisely, and the vines will remember. A good name lasts longer than coins."

Jeanne said nothing, but she knew both could be lost in a bad year. The vineyard was their life and their fortune.

Siméon's seventeenth birthday dawned bright and clear, his mother marked the occasion with a small loaf brushed with honey, set beside a crock of butter and the last of the previous summer's preserves. Grand-père reached for a jug saved for feast days. The cork came loose with a pop.

"Seventeen," Nicolas said, eyeing his younger son with a look that mixed pride and warning. "Strong enough to carry a man's work now. Which you already are."

Colas grinned across the table. "Aye, strong enough to carry the milk pails, at least. Maybe even keep up with me in the fields, if he does not stop to admire his reflection in the trough first."

Siméon laughed and threw a crust at him. "Strange talk from the one I beat chopping wood."

"I let you win," Colas shot back, his tone teasing but warm. "Did not want to shame you in front of the chickens."

"Enough, both of you," Jeanne said with a smile she did not quite hide. "Let your brother eat before you turn his head."

Grand-père raised his cup. "At seventeen, I thought myself invincible too," he said, chuckling softly. "The world was wide, and every road seemed mine to walk. Then life taught me otherwise."

Siméon smiled, but there was a faraway look in his eyes, fixed on some point beyond the kitchen wall. "I heard a man at the market talking about the American general, Washington," he said, his voice lower now. "He said the heat at Monmouth was so bad men were dropping where they stood, but Washington stayed on his horse all day and would not give the British an inch. They say he held them there by sheer will."

Siméon fell silent. Nicolas studied his son, not the boy's face but the set of his shoulders. After a long moment he gave a slow, considering nod. "I will say, I have heard he is a man of the soil," he rumbled. "A farmer. Like us."

A different weight settled over the room.

That afternoon, Jeanne slipped away to the chapel of Saint-Siméon. She lit a slender candle and bowed her head. "Grant him wisdom before courage, Lord," she whispered. "And if he must go, let him come back."

The celebration of Saint Matthew[21] passed, a last echo of summer. The sun worked the grapes now with focused, deep heat, and the vines bowed under the weight of their own gathering purpose.

Before the light failed, Siméon checked the iron pins on the ox cart. One had loosened in last week's journey back from town, and he had taken it to Bresson the smith at dawn. The blacksmith had tightened the bands and hammered the pin home, saying the cart would hold steady all the way to the *seigneur's* press.

Colas joined him with a weary huff, wiping his brow with a rag stiff from dust and sweat. "You've done well this year, little brother," he said, nodding to the lower rows where the vines near the oak grove thrived. "Papa says those are the strongest he's seen in years."

Siméon smiled, "It wasn't just me. You set the pruning right in spring. I only followed your lead."

Colas chuckled, giving him a rough nudge with his elbow. "Following my lead? I saw you up before dawn half the summer, fixing trellises before I even had my boots on. Don't think I didn't notice."

---

[21] **Saint Matthew's Day,** the feast of the Apostle and Evangelist Matthew, is observed in the Western Christian liturgical calendar on September 21.

They stood for a while in easy silence, the hum of crickets rising as dusk settled.

And then, it was time. The year's vendange began not with a decision, but with a collective intake of breath. That morning, laughter and song rose among the vines as neighbors worked side by side, baskets heaping with dark red clusters that left fingers and aprons stained deep violet. These grapes were the kind valued for their keeping quality, able to endure the journey and the wait before pressing. Every harvest held its risks; a sudden storm, a careless spill, or a delay at the seigneur's crowded press could spell ruin for months of toil.

The rows looked strong. It was shaping into a harvest to remember.

That evening the family raised their cups, laughter filling the room and echoing off the low beams. For a time, all other concerns fell away.

After the laughter faded and the house fell still, Jeanne lingered by the hearth. The embers glowed, soft and steady. She folded Siméon's freshly mended shirt, smoothed the sleeve, and pressed it briefly to her lips.

By October, the final grapes hung heavy on the vines, each day adding to the urgency. Wicker baskets filled with dark clusters as the family worked, their spirits lifted by the familiar songs of the vendange. Beneath the laughter lingered a quiet worry; every sunrise risked rot, rain, or a

sudden cold snap before their turn at the seigneur's press.

Fortune held. The weather remained kind, and the Gaugiens came through with only minimal losses.

Each quarter cask was filled and sealed carefully, then stored to age in the cellar. Siméon hefted them off the wagon one by one, the grooves of the cooper's handiwork rough against his palms, the sweet tang of freshly pressed juice rising from the wood. The cellar was cool and damp, the earthy smell of fermentation already settling into the stones.

"Careful, lad," Claude called from the doorway, half teasing, half in admiration. "You'll strain yourself."

Siméon Stacking Quarter Casks

Siméon smiled faintly, adjusting his grip on the barrel. "It's not so heavy," he replied, though the effort was plain in the tension of his arms.

Nicolas watched him work, as he remembered the scrawny boy trailing him in the fields years ago, blisters on his hands, stubborn fire in his eyes. Now, that boy had become a man, his strength matched by thoughtfulness.

Each lift and careful placement carried a precision Nicolas recognized; the focus of someone learning to shoulder more than the weight before him. The boy was readying himself for something far beyond this cellar, whether Nicolas was ready for it or not.

"I'm proud of you, son. You and your brother have held this family up when I could not."

"I only did what had to be done."

"You've done more than that," Nicolas said. "You're ready for what's ahead. Maybe more ready than I'd like."

Siméon said nothing, but the words settled deep.

With the wine safely aging, the family turned to the next necessity of the season. They slaughtered the pig they had fattened since spring. Nothing was wasted: hams and shoulders were rubbed with precious salt, then hung in the cellar to cure; blood became boudin, fat was rendered for cooking and candles, and the offal fed the family for days. Come spring, a new piglet would be purchased from a neighbor's litter, a small creature that would grow fat on scraps and forage until the following autumn brought its own reckoning.

From his chair by the wall, Grand-père shifted, his cane tapping once against the stone floor. His gaze, clouded yet still sharp beneath heavy lids, settled on Siméon.

"When I was your age, I thought the world ended at the edge of these hills. It was the stories of others, older boys who marched off and came home changed, that taught me otherwise."

He drew a long breath. "I had two close friends who followed their regiment across the border. They didn't die from bullets or glory, but to fever in a filthy camp, mud to the ankles, fouled water, sickness that swept through the tents faster than any enemy." He tapped his cane again, softer this time. "Remember that, lad. The battlefield is only one of the reapers."

The others fell silent.

Grand-père's voice grew quieter, though the conviction did not fade. "If your heart calls you beyond these fields, then go, boy. The world is larger than any one harvest. But do not mistake bigness for greatness. Carry the soil of this place with you, in your heart if not on your boots."

Siméon rose slightly, as though to speak, but his voice caught. "Merci, Grand-père."

The old man waved a hand gently. "Bah. Go if you must. Just come back with both your courage and your kindness intact."

As summer waned, the farm made its annual demands without pause. Vegetables were lifted, tools oiled, livestock sheltered, vines cut back and tied. Firewood rose in stacks against the barn wall. When Père Charles returned to bless the new wine and the hands that made it, his gaze found Siméon's across the rows. No words were needed.

Advent frost glazed the fields each morning. One evening Siméon paused at the vineyard's edge: behind him the farmhouse glowed warm through the fog; ahead, the dark hills and whatever lay beyond them.

At the market in Jussey, where he and Colas went to trade the last of the autumn apples, a new story was moving through the stalls.

"An American captain," the man said, his voice carrying over the clatter of carts. "Jones, they call him. Sailed right out of our port at Brest. Crossed the Channel and burnt a British ship in their own harbor, drank their ale in their pub and sailed back to Brest."

On the walk home, Colas glanced at his brother's silent, focused face. "You're thinking of that story," he said.

Siméon nodded, his breath misting in the cold air. "It changes everything, doesn't it? It means we're not just sending supplies or soldiers. We're in the fight."

That evening, by the hearth, Nicolas listened as Siméon recounted the tale. He said nothing, but his gaze lingered on his son's fervent face. Later, as the house settled into the deep silence of a winter night, Siméon stood as the farmhouse glowed behind him, but his eyes were fixed on the dark hills, imagining the flames in a British port.

Ranger

HISTORICAL NOTE: THE WHITEHAVEN RAID AND FRENCH INVOLVEMENT

In February 1778, France signed the Treaty of Alliance with the United States. Days later, the French ship of the line *Robuste* saluted Captain John Paul Jones's *Ranger* at Quiberon Bay, the first salute to the American flag from a foreign warship. On the night of April 22–23, sailing from Brest, Jones raided the English port of Whitehaven, spiking its coastal guns and setting fire to a merchant vessel. Two days later he captured HMS *Drake* off the Irish coast, the first British naval vessel taken by an American warship in European waters. Source: *Samuel Eliot Morison, John Paul Jones: A Sailor's Biography (Boston: Little, Brown, 1959).*

PART II
THE SOUND OF DRUMS

Chapter Four:
The Road to Auxonne

December 1778 to January 1779

Winter held the Gaugien house in a deep, quiet cold. Inside, warmth and preparation filled the rooms. Garlands of houx and buis draped the beams, fir boughs hung over the hearth. The scents of the coming celebration, roasted chestnuts, honey cakes, simmering sausages, mingled with the earthy cool rising from the cellar, where the 1777 vintage22 waited for its unveiling on the Feast of Saint Siméon.

One evening, Nicolas stood at the window, his gaze fixed on the sleeping vines.

"He is determined," Jeanne said without looking up from her mending. "Once Siméon sets his mind to something, there is no stopping him." A faint smile touched her lips. "Much like you."

---

[22] **Grapes were harvested** in September or October in late eighteenth-century eastern France, fermented for several weeks, and aged in oak barrels through the following year. Most families lacked the means to cellar wine beyond two winters; tapping a vintage typically occurred twelve to eighteen months after harvest, often timed to a local feast or saint's day. Source: *Daniel Roche, France in the Enlightenment (Cambridge: Harvard University Press, 2000).*

Nicolas turned. "Determined is one thing. War is not the vineyard. You cannot send a boy to face muskets the way you send him to plow. Out there, captains and generals will take their share of his sweat and blood, just as the seigneur takes our wine."

Her needle stilled. "And if we keep him here, would he forgive us?" She drew a quiet breath. "Grapes must be crushed to make wine; so must he be tested to learn what God intends of him."

Nicolas moved to the chair beside hers. "Beyond these walls is a world that does not care about him. How will he fare against men trained to kill?"

Jeanne set her mending aside and reached for his hand. "You have given him strength. I have given him faith. Together, that must be enough."

"And if he does not come back? What do we tell ourselves?"

"That we loved him enough to let him choose," she said. "That must be enough."

Nicolas stared at her, his features hard but beginning to crack. "You are right."

They sat in silence as the fire burned low. Outside, the first snow fell across the vines.

"God help him," Nicolas murmured. "And us."

Christmas Day brought the family together with neighbors, music, and shared bread. Laughter and storytelling filled the room, the warmth of the hearth pressing close.

Near the meal's end, Siméon set his fork down. "Père Charles, is there any word on the inquiries?"

The room fell still.

"There is," Père Charles said. "His Eminence, Archbishop de Durfort, has agreed to assist. He will provide a *lettre de recommandation*. Abbé Girard at Auxonne will receive you and present it to the officers of the King's artillery. With God's grace, your hands will be set to the guns."

Jeanne forced a smile. "Then he must wait until after Saint Siméon's Feast. It would not be right to go before *La Nuit des Rois*."

Grand-père nodded. "A proper farewell. That is how it should be done."

Colas stared at his brother, half disbelief, half pride. "So soon?" Then a grin tugged at his mouth. "Well, little brother, you will be making thunder of your own soon enough. And I suppose that is one way of getting out of cleaning the stable in the new year."

Claude cleared his throat. "The vineyard will be quieter without you, lad."

Père Charles glanced around the table. "His Eminence has suggested we join his representative in Auxonne after the holy days."

Nicolas nodded. "Thank you, Père Charles." His voice carried gratitude and resignation in equal measure.

Siméon was quietly exhilarated. His planned departure fell at the end of the very Twelve Days of Christmas he had celebrated all his life with his family. He took a steadying breath. "Thank you, Père."

Later, when the house had grown silent, Jeanne pressed her rosary into his hand. "This has carried me through many storms," she said softly. The dark beads were worn smooth, the crucifix a humble, timeworn carving. "Your Grand-mère gave this to me on my wedding day. Her prayers are in these beads, just as mine will be."

He closed his fingers around it. "I will carry it always, Maman. And I promise, I will return."

After Christmas, the cold deepened. Snow fell almost daily, and a low fog drifted up from the Mance, softening the hedgerows and settling over the dormant vines. Preparations for January 5th, the Feast of Saint Siméon and *La Nuit des Rois*, gathered pace as neighbors brought wood and food to share.

One day, Père Charles returned alone. He found Nicolas and Jeanne by the fire, the house quiet, their sons elsewhere. He sat with them and spoke plainly.

"There is more I wish to tell you about what I wrote to His Eminence, and what it may mean for your son."

"When I wrote to His Excellency concerning Siméon, I wrote not only as curé of this parish but as a former pupil. I commended your family to him: a household of faith, of honest labor, of steady character." He paused. "The Archbishop knows I would not attest to such things lightly."

Nicolas nodded slowly. "I would not have thought Monseigneur's attention could reach as far as Rosières."

"The Archbishop remembers those he has guided, and he trusts my word. Your son will be received with care and properly tested."

Jeanne crossed herself. "Thanks be to God. We will remember the Archbishop in our prayers, mon Père, and you as well."

On the Feast Day itself, the church filled early. The Mass was humble in its trappings, yet rich in devotion. For Siméon, every prayer and hymn carried a sharpened meaning. This might be the last.

By evening, laughter and warmth spilled from the barn. A fire roared in the courtyard. Children clustered near the tables, whispering about the *fève*, the hidden bean tucked into the Twelfth Night bread.

When Jeanne sliced the loaf, the crowd leaned in. The *fève* was found by little Marie Lenoir, who squealed when the bean clattered onto her plate. Crowned *reine du soir* with a garland of dried rosemary, she declared that Siméon must take the first taste of the new vintage.

At Nicolas's instruction, Siméon and Colas brought up the cask of the seventy-seven. But before Nicolas could tap it, Grand-père lifted a hand.

"Wait." He brought forward a small firkin. "A gift from the Château. Delivered this morning. The agent said the *seigneur* wished to share his benevolence."

A tense silence fell. They all knew: wine pressed from their own grapes, taken through the lord's press as a matter of right, and now returned as generosity.

"He calls it his *banalité*," Grand-père said quietly. "A fine word for a right that serves him alone."

Nicolas set his tap with a steady hand. Grand-père ignored the *seigneur's* gift and poured from the family's cask.

Feast of Saint Siméon le Stylites

Père Charles raised his goblet. "May this wine carry the faith and labor of all who have tended these vines, as we honor Saint Siméon le Stylites and the man who bears his name. May this Twelfth Night carry him forward with courage, and may this wine remind us that every good fruit comes from patient tending."

The room erupted in cheers. Claude lifted his mug, a flush already rising in his cheeks. "What the Americans are doing now, we will do here someday. The people will not be kept down forever."

The room hushed. Nicolas's expression hardened. "I will not hear careless talk against the King. Whatever men think of *seigneurs*, his Majesty is the pillar of France."

Claude glanced away, muttering. The cheer resumed, though an undercurrent of unease lingered.

Siméon slipped away.

In the cellar, the air was cool and still, the stone floor cold through the thick wood of his *sabots*. His hand brushed the oak casks, their scents wrapping around him: damp earth, oak, the faint sweetness of fermenting wine.

What if this becomes only a memory?

He rested his palm against a cask and bowed his head. After a long moment, he drew himself upright.

Footsteps creaked on the stairs. "I thought I would find you here," Colas said quietly. "You always came to the casks when you were thinking too hard."

Siméon gave a small, sheepish smile. "I just needed a moment."

Colas stepped closer. "You have the makings of it. If anyone is meant for the artillery, it is you." He squeezed Siméon's shoulder. "And if it does not work out, there will always be a place here. The vines do not forget their own."

He managed a nod.

Colas clapped him on the back. "Now come on. They will think you have run off already."

Together they walked back to the barn. When Siméon stepped into the light there was a new steadiness in his eyes.

That night, Jeanne knelt before a small wooden crucifix, a single candle flickering.

"Dear Lord," she whispered, "I place my son in Your hands."

A soft creak made her turn. Siméon stood in the doorway, barefoot. "I couldn't sleep."

"Come here, my son." She drew him into her arms. "My brave one," she murmured. Then she placed her hands on his shoulders and prayed aloud, her voice barely above a whisper. "Lord, keep watch over my son. Let Your hand be his shield, Your light his guide. When he walks through fear, walk with him."

She kissed his forehead. "Please get some sleep; dawn will come sooner than we wish." He kissed her forehead, then slipped back into the dark.

Epiphany dawned clear and bitterly cold. After Mass, there was no lingering.

Siméon stood in the courtyard, a small satchel over his shoulder. Inside were sturdy clothes, the rosary, and a *flasque* of Gaugien wine.

Jeanne stepped forward first, her hands trembling as she straightened his collar. "Go with God, Siméon," she whispered, her voice breaking. She pulled him into her arms.

Nicolas laid a steady hand on his son's shoulder. "Remember the land you come from. And the people waiting."

Colas's smile was faint but steady. "Whatever comes, you have a home waiting, and a brother who stands with you."

Siméon Departure on Epiphany 1779

Grand-père stepped forward last, leaning on his cane. He tapped a finger lightly against Siméon's chest. "As long as you carry it with you here, you will never be lost." He reached into his coat and pressed his worn pocketknife into Siméon's hand. "Steady hands and a clear mind will see you through."

Siméon turned the knife once in his palm, then met the old man's eyes. "*Merci*, I will keep it close."

Père Charles stood beside his parish cart, the mule shifting patiently. Siméon climbed up beside him.

As the cart lurched into motion, Siméon glanced back one last time. Jeanne stood in the doorway, arms wrapped tightly around herself. Grand-père was behind her. Nicolas and Colas lingered in the courtyard.

As they passed the smithy, Bresson stepped out, wiping his hands on a leather apron. He tipped his hat in a simple, wordless farewell.

A few hours later, in a wooded stretch far from any familiar landmark, the cart jolted hard as a wheel struck a hidden rut. Père Charles gripped the edge of the seat as the mule stumbled, its startled bray cutting through the cold air.

"Whoa," the priest called, pulling back on the reins.

Siméon jumped down and moved at once to the mule. Steam rose from its flanks as it pawed the frozen earth. He ran a hand along the harness, murmuring softly until it settled, then bent to check each leg in turn, fingers firm and practiced despite the chill.

Père Charles crouched by the wheel. "A spoke's cracked."

Siméon traced the break with his fingertips. "Not badly. If we bind it tight, it should hold until Gray."

"With what?"

"There should be a spare harness strap behind the seat."

Père Charles retrieved it and handed it over. Siméon crouched again, the leather stiff with cold as he wrapped it around the damaged spoke, knotting it with the ease of long habit. It held.

Père Charles tested the wheel with a firm push, then nodded. "Your father would be proud."

Siméon gave a faint smile and climbed back onto the cart. The wheel groaned with each turn, but it held.

Further on, when the road stretched empty ahead, Siméon reached for the *flasque*. He uncorked it, took a small sip, then offered it to the priest. "A parting gift from my father."

Père Charles accepted it with a nod, took a modest sip, and handed it back. "Thank you, Siméon."

They traveled on as the winter light thinned, the mule's hooves striking a slow, steady rhythm. With every mile, the world of the vineyard slipped a little farther behind.

They reached Gray as darkness gathered, the last light slipping behind rooftops and the river turning to ink. The Auberge de la Saône stood by the water, its windows promising warmth. The parish cart creaked to a halt in the courtyard, its strapped wheel groaning a final complaint. Siméon jumped down and crouched to inspect the damage. Cracks had spidered farther along the spoke.

"It will not hold to Auxonne," he said.

"A blessing we are here, then," Père Charles replied, climbing down stiffly.

Jacques Lemoine

The inn's door opened before they could knock. A sturdy man stood silhouetted against the candlelight. "I am Jacques Lemoine. You have arrived in time for *souper*." He glanced at the cart. "A rough ride."

"A cracked wheel," Père Charles said. "And the mule needs care."

Jacques smiled. "My brother is a wheelwright. I will send my boy." He called into the courtyard. "Gabriel."

A wiry boy of about twelve appeared from the stables. "Fetch your Uncle Louis. Then see to the gentlemen's mule."

"Come in," Jacques said, clapping him on the shoulder. "No more trouble tonight. Only a warm fire."

Inside, the common room was a haven. A fire crackled in the wide hearth. The rich aroma of stew mingled with spiced wine. Jacques led them to a table near the fire and brought steaming mugs of *vin chaud*.

Before long, Gabriel returned, breathless. "Uncle is coming."

Père Charles handed the boy a sou. "Thank you, Gabriel."

The boy's eyes lit up. He darted back toward the stables. Siméon smiled. He would have run all over for a coin at that age too.

For the first time since the wheel had cracked, they allowed themselves to relax.

Jacques placed logs on the fire. "Now, a meal and some wine."

They ate crusty bread, Jura cheese, and hearty stew before Jacques led them up a creaky staircase to a small cold room at the back of the inn.

"It is not much, but it will keep you warm," he said, pushing open the door. The wooden window rattled in the wind. Their breath misted in the air.

There was one long narrow bed. Both were too weary to care.

As the wind howled outside, Siméon stared up at the ceiling. Doubt came as images: a vine untended, his father at the edge of the vineyard, shoulders bowed, Colas alone beneath a barren sky. His grip tightened on his rosary until the crucifix pressed into his palm. He turned his face into the rough wool blanket.

"Holy Father, guide me," he whispered. "Help me find my way."

Eventually, sleep found him, troubled by dreams of vines and childhood sunlight, the very things that now felt like a farewell.

Morning came glazed with frost. Ice crystals feathered the corners of the windowpanes. Père Charles had already settled what was due. Siméon joined him in the common room for bread and steaming bowls of *gruau*. Outside, a pale fog clung to the Saône valley.

Père Charles took a sip of spiced wine. "Our cart will be ready shortly. Before we depart, I wish to stop at the Capuchin convent. There is a statue of the Blessed Virgin in its chapel, known for her miracles. We will offer prayers for our journey."

"Capuchins?" Siméon asked.

"Sons of Saint Francis," Père Charles said, his expression softening. "They live simply, serve the sick and hungry, and trust God for every need. Their brown robes remind them of the earth and their humility reminds them of heaven."

"And the chapel?"

"It houses a revered statue called Our Lady of Gray. Pilgrims have prayed before her for generations. Many speak of protection and healing."

"Do you believe she will protect us?"

"I do. Lighting a candle is a way to entrust our road to grace. It reminds us that none of us travels alone."

"Then I would like to honor her before we go."

Siméon's gaze drifted to the fog outside. A short walk later brought them to the Capuchin gate. A brown-robed friar greeted them, his sandals dusted white with frost.

"Peace be with you, travelers. Have you come for the Madonna?"

"Yes, Brother," Père Charles said. "We wish to offer prayers."

The friar smiled. "Then Our Lady will bless your road."

He led them through a narrow courtyard where the scent of rosemary and sage drifted from a sheltered herb garden. Another friar knelt near a wooden cart of candles, trimming wicks, whispering prayers.

The chapel doors creaked open, releasing a breath of beeswax and cold air. Inside, the soft glow of candles bathed the sanctuary. The air was chilled and still, yet warm with devotion.

Siméon paused at the threshold. The Madonna held the room in quiet command. Her modest form seemed imbued with the accumulated grace of more than a century and a half.

Père Charles leaned close. "Our Lady of Gray watches over travelers and the weary. For more than a century, pilgrims have come seeking comfort in illness, danger, and uncertainty."

Kneeling before the altar, he let his gaze rest on her serene face, seeking reassurance in her stillness.

Père Charles spoke softly. "Strength comes from prayer, not because it spares us from hardship, but because it steadies us to endure it."

A passing friar murmured gently to him. "She listens. She hears even the prayer you do not speak."

They knelt in the hush, surrounded by the soft murmur of others' prayers.

Père Charles lifted a taper and touched it to a flame. He gestured to Siméon.

Siméon praying to
Our Lady of Gray

Siméon's hands trembled as he brought the taper forward. A single flame rose to life.

"Faith is not the absence of fear," Père Charles said. "It is the courage to walk forward despite it."

Siméon made the sign of the cross and joined Père Charles at the back of the room.

Together they stepped back into the pale morning. Behind them, the friars tended the candles whose flames continued to glow, a living reminder of prayers left behind.

HISTORICAL NOTE: OUR LADY OF GRAY

The statue of Our Lady of Gray, standing just 14.5 centimeters tall, was carved in 1613 from black Montaigu oak by sculptor Jean Brange of Salins-les-Bains. The wood was considered sacred, cut from the tree in Belgium upon which an earlier miraculous statue of the Virgin had stood. A seventy-year-old widow commissioned the statuette after obtaining a piece of this venerated oak on pilgrimage; the Archbishop of Besançon blessed it for public veneration on April 4, 1613. It came to the Capuchin convent in Gray in 1616. After the Revolution expelled the Capuchins and destroyed their church, the Madonna was hidden at the Town Hall until the people of Gray demanded her restoration. She remains today in the Basilica of Notre-Dame de Gray, where for more than four centuries pilgrims have sought her protection and many miracles have been claimed. Source: *Christiane Claerr, "Statuette de pèlerinage: Vierge à l'Enfant dite Notre-Dame de Gray," Inventaire du patrimoine culturel de Bourgogne–Franche-Comté, 1991.*

The second day of travel felt shorter. They shared light conversation and long stretches of companionable silence. The fog lifted, and the sun shone weakly.

As they neared Auxonne, the sky dimmed. Fog gathered. They heard the city before they saw it.

Massive stone ramparts rose out of the haze, lanterns glimmering atop them. The smells hit him all at once: smoke, tallow, dung, fresh bread, the sharp tang of bodies and livestock.

Passing under the archway, the cold stone swallowed the last of the countryside's silence. Iron wheels clattered on slick stones. Boots struck in rhythm. Voices rose and fell in shouts, songs, and arguments. Lanternlight wavered over faces half hidden by hats and scarves.

Above it all, the clocher of Église Notre-Dame d'Auxonne pierced the haze, standing watch.

Officers strode through the crowd with crisp discipline. Siméon saw men who looked like those from home, the same coats and boots, yet their posture straighter. Nearby, a father and son embraced in farewell. An ordinary man bending toward an extraordinary call.

Siméon and Père Charles Enter Auxonne

"Welcome to Auxonne," Père Charles said. "This is where paths are forged."

The priest stopped the cart where recruits blocked the roadway. Siméon jumped down to guide the mule forward.

A young man sitting on a wooden crate caught his eye. His coat was threadbare and his boots caked with mud. His posture was upright and defiant despite the weariness in his eyes.

Siméon inclined his head.

"Here to enlist?" the young man asked. "Of course you are." He sized him up. "But you look like someone who still has a choice."

"I suppose I do," Siméon said. "And you?"

The young man let out a dry chuckle. "Already signed up. Not that I had much choice."

He leaned back. "When you have nothing left, the army starts to look like salvation. Or the next step to ruin."

He pulled up his sleeve, revealing a jagged scar along his forearm. "That is what I have left of our family fields. My father and I worked them until my mother and brother died from fever. We finished the harvest alone until I slipped with a sickle. Could not work for weeks. My father had to hire help, and the seigneur demanded more grain than we could spare. Taxes stripped us of everything. My father died cursing the soil he once loved."

"I am sorry," Siméon said.

The young man shrugged. "That is why I am here. Nowhere else to go. The King's bread is better than starving on land that is no longer yours."

"Perhaps this is a chance," Siméon said. "To fight for something greater."

The young man studied him, then extended a hand. "Henri."

"Siméon."

As the crowd thinned, Siméon returned to the cart. The banalité was not just a lord's right over presses and mills; it was a tax on hope itself. For his family, it had been a burden to be endured. For Henri, it had been a sentence carried out.

Before long, the cart stopped before the rectory beside the Church of Notre-Dame. A young priest appeared, lantern in hand. "Welcome. I am Père Mathieu. Abbé Girard has been expecting you."

Warmth and cooking scents enveloped them as they entered.

In the study, the Abbé rose and greeted them warmly. "Monsieur Gaugien, welcome to Auxonne. Dinner will be served shortly."

After they ate, the Abbé turned to their purpose. "His Eminence wrote that Siméon seeks to join the King's artillery."

"That is correct," Père Charles replied. "He is sincere and capable."

Abbé Girard studied Siméon and nodded. "I will prepare the *lettre de recommandation* and see that he is received for testing."

"You have our thanks," Père Charles said.

The Abbé's expression warmed. "And if you are willing, Père Charles, I would be glad to have your help at Mass this Sunday."

"I would be honored," Père Charles replied.

"Good," the Abbé said. "Then let us rest. There is much to attend to in the days ahead."

The next morning, Auxonne hummed with a martial rhythm. Drums rolled from the parade ground. Muskets clattered in steady time.

Siméon had risen long before dawn and walked the road alone, the Abbé's folded letter a stark rectangle against his chest. He touched it once, hearing the Abbé's quiet assurance: This will place you before the proper officers. His Eminence sends his blessing.

The recruitment station was damp and cold, heavy with the bitter tang of oil and spent powder. Not the familiar earth-and-wine scent of home. This was the smell of men gathered for war.

The yard was thick with recruits. Boys scarcely older than him shifted nervously. Older men, lined by winters and want, stood with grim stillness. The line moved with slow inevitability.

Siméon joined the end of it and held himself straight, though his palms were slick.

Beside him stood a young man with a patched coat and salt-cracked hands, the hands of nets and ropes as much as ploughs. His eyes held dry amusement, and when he spoke his voice carried the Breton coast.

"A fine gathering," he murmured, not looking at Siméon. "All eager to die for a King who would not know their names."

The line lurched forward. An officer barked names while a clerk marked them down, clipped and cold. Men were measured with a glance and dismissed with a flick of the quill. Near the front, a recruit was told to recite a sum. He faltered. The officer waved him aside.

The Breton clicked his tongue. "Arithmetic. Their favorite trick."

He stepped forward next, shoulders squared with lazy confidence.

"Name."

"Vincent Bruges."[23]

The officer handed him a slip of paper. "Read this."

Vincent glanced at it. "It concerns the price of flour in Lyon. Your handwriting is atrocious." He handed it back. "My father sold fish to scribes with better penmanship. They still cheated him on the count."

A few recruits snickered. The officer's eyes narrowed but he marked the ledger. Vincent stepped aside with a shrug, and Siméon caught the intelligence beneath the bravado.

Then it was Siméon's turn.

He offered the Abbé's letter. The officer took it between two fingers, glanced at the seal, and slipped it into the ledger without reading. A cold drop of doubt settled in Siméon's stomach.

"Name."

"Siméon Gaugien."

The officer pointed toward a group forming beneath the far archway. "With them."

Vincent appeared beside him again, hands tucked loosely in his coat. "You carry a seal. That helps. Let us hope your patron's name carries more weight than my wit."

"Not just connections," Siméon said. "A chance."

Vincent studied him, smirk softening. "We Bretons have a saying. Ar mor a zo frankiz. The sea is freedom. It gives and takes with the same hand. Your freedom might cost more than flour in Lyon."

---

[23] **Vincent Bruges,** born 1761 in Ambon, Brittany; enlisted in 1779 in the Régiment d'Artillerie d'Auxonne and was assigned to the Compagnie Bonnay de la Rouvrelle, where he served alongside Siméon Gaugien; served in the French Expédition Particulière under the command of Jean-Baptiste Donatien de Vimeur, comte de Rochambeau; fought in the Siege of Yorktown during the American War of Independence. Source: *Les combattants français de la guerre américaine, 1778 – 1783* (Washington: Imprimerie Nationale, 1905), 355.

The drills began. They shouldered muskets, marched in ragged lines, and struggled to find rhythm under barking orders. The musket felt familiar in Siméon's hands, but the formality of command set his pulse racing. Vincent moved with weary competence, his quiet quips a steadying anchor.

"Watch that captain. He counts paces like a priest counts sins, and spends just as much time punishing the last one." Siméon bit back a laugh. Later, as they struggled with the ramrods, Vincent muttered, "Easier to load a culverin on a rolling deck than to please this man on dry land."

Later, in a cramped tent thick with ink, sweat, and damp wool, an officer scrawled numbers on a slate and shoved it toward Siméon.

"Add these."

The sums were larger than any he had handled at home, but the logic was the same. He worked through them in silence and handed back the slate. The officer gave a single curt nod.

As Siméon stepped aside, Vincent brushed past with a low whisper. "Not bad."

He was being measured not for the strength of his back, but for the sharpness of his mind.

By day's end, shared exhaustion had done its work. When they were dismissed, Vincent fell into step beside him.

"You survived," he said.

"So did you."

Vincent pulled a dented *flasque* from his coat. The wine was harsh, but its warmth was a promise. He raised it in a mock toast. "Here is to fighting for a king who does not know our names, alongside a man who just learned yours."

"To the British!" Siméon replied.

Vincent took a swallow, passed the *flasque* back, and held Siméon's eyes. "To not drowning before we see it."

They parted with a nod, and the yard swallowed them again.

That evening, the rectory study glowed with candlelight. Père Charles read quietly while Abbé Girard poured three modest glasses of wine.

"Well then, mon garçon," the Abbé said, settling into his chair. "You made it through the first day of selection?"

Siméon eased into his own, his body aching yet his mind alight. "Yes, Père. There is a strange comfort in standing with men who have lost so much yet still choose to fight."

Père Charles closed his book. "Hardship binds faster than comfort. Remember that."

"Some of them carry anger," Siméon said. "Anger that does not fade."

"When a man is abandoned by his world," the Abbé replied gently, "he looks for meaning anywhere it might still live. But you, Siméon, you have something to return to. That makes your choice powerful."

Siméon looked into his cup. He had not come from despair, but conviction. He carried a home to fight for. They carried a home to avenge.

The Abbé lifted his glass. "To God's grace."

Père Charles bowed his head and raised his cup. Siméon followed, the soft chime of glass sealing the moment.

When he retired that night, he carried not only the ache of the drills but something steadier. Not certainty. Resolve.

HISTORICAL NOTE: ADMISSION TO THE RÉGIMENT D'ARTILLERIE D'AUXONNE

By the late 1770s, the French royal artillery was a technically elite corps, and admission to its regimental schools was highly selective. The 1776 regulations required candidates to present a lettre de recommandation from a respected patron, a noble, a high-ranking officer, or a prelate, and to demonstrate literacy and competence in arithmetic before artillery officers. Successful applicants entered as élèves canonniers (artillery trainees), taking the oath only after formal acceptance. Source: *Ernest Picard and Louis Jouan, L'artillerie française au XVIIIe siècle (Paris: Berger-Levrault, 1906).*

CHAPTER FIVE:
THE MAKING OF BROTHERS

January – February 1779

The gray light of morning seeped into the stone corridors of the rectory. Siméon rose early, though sleep had eluded him. Each motion, pulling on stockings, fastening his coat, felt deliberate, weighted.

Père Charles waited near the hearth, a cup of linden tea in hand. He looked up as Siméon entered, his expression calm but searching.

Silence pressed close around them, broken only by the hiss of firewood.

Père Charles gestured to the bench. "Sit with me, *mon fils.*"

"This oath you are about to take," he said quietly, "binds you not only to the King, but before God. It is a promise of service and conscience. If your heart hesitates, turn back now. Doubt is not a failing. The only dishonor is to swear what you cannot keep."[24]

---

[24] **Voluntary enlistments** in the French Royal Army during the later eighteenth century typically carried terms of approximately eight years. The Régiment d'Artillerie d'Auxonne, associated with one of France's principal artillery schools, was known for rigorous technical training and high standards of discipline. Soldiers serving in Europe were generally expected, though not always legally compelled, to delay marriage until completion of their term of service.

He set his cup down and folded his hands. "We could begin the return to Rosières today. No one would fault you. You have already done enough to make your family proud."

Siméon studied the fire. "Perhaps so. But I would think less of myself. Not for turning back, but for doing so before I had even begun."

Père Charles nodded, not in agreement, but in understanding. "Then I will walk with you to the gate."

Siméon and Père Charles stopped at the Église Notre-Dame d'Auxonne to offer prayers, then continued in silence through the early morning city.

The yard outside the enlistment depot was busier than the day before. Officers moved among the recruits in clipped tones, checking lists and issuing instructions. Smoke drifted from cook fires. Above the gate, the white flag of the Bourbons, adorned with golden fleurs-de-lis, stirred just enough to show its presence.

Siméon recognized some of the men from yesterday, Vincent among them, the sharp-faced boy from the coast with a permanent smirk.

Père Charles placed a hand on his shoulder. "Go, then. Remember what you carry: not just the rosary or the wine or the name of your family, but the strength of the people who raised you. And the prayers of a mother who will whisper your name each day."

Siméon turned to him, unable to speak. "Merci, Père. For everything."

"Walk with honor," Père Charles said softly. "And may your belief guide you when memory falters."

He shook his hand and kissed both cheeks.

Siméon stepped through the gate and took his place in the line. No one spoke.

When his turn came, he stood before two uniformed clerks.

"Name and parish," snapped the first, quill poised.

"Siméon Gaugien, of Rosières-sur-Mance."

The second clerk read the letter and declared, "Fit. Literate. Referred by ecclesiastical endorsement."

The first officer traced a finger down the record book, made his marks, wrote Siméon's name on an official document, and turned it across the table.

"Sign at the bottom."

Siméon signed.[25]

"Join the line for testing." The officer motioned to a second line and handed him the paper.

The *examinateur*, Louis Clément[26], tested Siméon's literacy, his skill with figures, and the steadiness of his bearing. Siméon answered clearly, worked the sums swiftly, and kept his composure.

Clément led him across the courtyard to Captain Bonnay and presented the evaluation with a faint nod, a silent signal between veteran and commander. The captain asked a few clipped questions about Siméon's schooling, then gave a short nod.

"Sufficient," he said, signing the register. He looked at Clément. "See that he learns the work properly. And have the chaplain administer the *serment* before he is quartered."

"Yes, sir," Clément said.

The recruits were directed to the small regimental chapel. Winter light fell through high windows in narrow columns across the stone floor. A regimental priest stood at the front, a large Bible on a wooden stand before him.

---

[25] **Siméon Gaugien's** signature, recreated from parish registers, Rosières-sur-Mance. Archives départementales de la Haute-Saône, France.

[26] **Louis Clément**, born 1746 in Poligny, Franche-Comté; enlisted in 1763 in the Régiment d'Artillerie d'Auxonne and was among the most seasoned members of the Compagnie Bonnay de la Rouvrelle; served alongside Siméon Gaugien in the French Expédition Particulière under the command of Jean-Baptiste Donatien de Vimeur, comte de Rochambeau, during the American War of Independence. Source: *Les combattants français de la guerre américaine, 1778 – 1783 (Washington: Imprimerie Nationale, 1905), 355.*

Vincent was already inside. When he spotted Siméon he grinned. *"Bien joué, vigneron."*

Soon it was Siméon's turn. He stepped toward the altar, his heart steady now rather than racing. The priest lifted the Bible. "Place your hand here."

Siméon set his palm on the worn leather cover. The priest's voice carried through the quiet chapel.

> *"Do you swear before Almighty God to be faithful and obedient to His Most Christian Majesty, King Louis XVI, and to serve in the Royal Army as a member of the Régiment d'Auxonne until your term is complete, His Majesty releases you from service, or death take you. So help you God?"*

"Je le jure (I swear it)."

The words hung in the still air. He kept his hand on the Bible a moment longer, the leather cool beneath his palm. In his pocket, his mother's rosary pressed against his thigh, a quiet witness.

The priest nodded. An officer stamped his papers and handed him a folded document. "Welcome to the artillery, cadet. Report to the quartermaster for your uniform, bedroll, and barracks assignment. Training begins at dawn. Next."

He walked from the chapel in silence, the document pressed between his palm and his mother's rosary. He was still the second son from Rosières; now one with a chosen path and an eight-year promise.

The quartermaster's office reeked of wool, wax, and oiled leather. Crates of uniforms stood against the walls; boots lined like sentries.

"Name?" barked a gruff sergeant without looking up.

"Siméon Gaugien."

The man scrawled his name in the ledger. His assistant measured Siméon's waist and looked him over. "Average build. Issue shirt, neckstock, waistcoat, breeches, boots, forage cap, and the habit: the regiment's blue coat."

Another assistant selected the items and handed Siméon a bundle: a white linen shirt, a black neckstock, a red wool waistcoat, white breeches, a blue coat in the traditional regimental cut faced with scarlet at the cuffs and lapels, and black leather boots stiff with polish. The wool smelled of storage and smoke, the brass buttons dulled by many fingers before him. A black felt tricorn hat with a white cockade, a forage cap, a white buff leather crossbelt, a brown leather belt, and a cartridge box stamped with the royal arms completed the set.[27]

Siméon Gaugien, French Artilleryman

In a narrow chamber, the men struggled into their new uniforms. The air was thick with coarse fabric, sweat, and bursts of laughter as they tried to make sense of the layers.

---

[27] **French artillerymen** were distinguished by blue coats with red facings, cuffs, and lapels. The Ordonnance du Roi of February 1779 standardized royal artillery dress under Louis XVI, introducing blue small clothes across artillery regiments. The extent to which individual regiments had fully implemented this regulation by the time of Siméon Gaugien's enlistment in 1779 remains uncertain in the available sources. The uniform depicted reflects the dress of the Régiment d'Artillerie d'Auxonne as reconstructed from surviving documentation; any errors of historical detail are the author's own. Source: *René Chartrand, The French Army in the War of American Independence, Men-at-Arms Series 244 (London: Osprey Publishing, 1991).*

Vincent elbowed Siméon as he passed. "Try not to tear it, vineyard boy. Linen to the eye, but sackcloth to the skin." He chuckled as he failed to fasten a crooked row of buttons.

"Careful," Siméon said. "They'll have you stitching those back on yourself."

"Bah. My stitches would shame a drunken seamstress."

There were boots that refused to bend, crossbelts that kept sliding, and jackets that seemed designed to trap an arm at just the wrong angle. Yet the room filled with camaraderie, young men helping each other tug sleeves into place, exchanging quips to mask their nerves.

"One would think the King's coffers could stretch to a coat that fits," someone grumbled.

"Oh, they do fit. Just not humans."

At last they stumbled into the courtyard, tugging at collars as if that might make them appear more soldierly. The midday sun glinted off brass buttons.

Vincent gave Siméon a quick once-over and offered a half-salute. "Respectable enough for a vineyard boy."

"Not so bad for a sea urchin yourself," Siméon replied.

Vincent nudged him toward the water trough. "Go on. See if you still recognize the farm boy."

Siméon leaned in. The water gave him back a stranger in blue and red, brass flashing when he moved. He looked for the vineyard boy and found him, pushed down but not gone.

"Not bad," Vincent said, peering over his shoulder. "Though I've seen handsomer scarecrows."

Siméon didn't look up. "Don't be so hard on yourself."

The men laughed, and the stiffness of the new cloth eased with it.

Tonight he would sleep in barracks, not in the quiet of the Abbé's quarters or beneath the beams of his family's cottage. Tomorrow his new life would begin.

As the day unfolded, the new recruits were led through the inner gates of the barracks compound. They were issued bedrolls and straw pads, found their assigned quarters, and set their civilian belongings aside in neat bundles. Siméon tucked the freshly signed parchment into his satchel with care. It bore his name and his assignment to the Régiment d'Auxonne, artillery corps. The same regiment where capable men were taught not only to fight, but to calculate, to measure, to think. Engineers of destruction. Keepers of thunder.

The stone walls of Auxonne, once forbidding, now seemed to draw him inward with purpose. There was no music, no fanfare, only the steady shuffle of boots on packed earth and the low instructions of junior officers guiding the bewildered line. Yet for Siméon, passing beneath those arches felt like entering a mighty church.

That night he slept more deeply than he had in weeks.

At dawn the recruits stood shoulder to shoulder in the freezing cold, their uniforms untested, their boots still new and stiff. The courtyard smelled of damp earth and woodsmoke.

A grizzled sergeant strode toward them, a ledger tucked under one arm. "Vous, recrues. Fall in. Drills at the field in ten minutes. Move."

They marched toward the practice ground, where three cannons stood in a row, dark shapes against the rising sun. A ripple of awe passed through the recruits. These machines, these monsters of metal and fire, would one day be entrusted to their hands.

The day that followed was spent far from the cannons, for before any man approached artillery, he had first to master the discipline of the regiment itself. They learned to stand, to march, to answer a command before the breath behind it had cooled. The new rhythm of their days began before dawn and did not ease until darkness, a cadence that pressed the habits of soldiering into bone and muscle long before powder or flame would touch their fingers.

HISTORICAL NOTE: THE RÉGIMENT D'AUXONNE - ARTILLERIE

The Régiment d'Auxonne, created in 1755 under King Louis XV, was an elite artillery regiment of the French Army. Stationed in the fortified town of Auxonne, it became one of France's foremost training centers for gunners and engineers, where mathematics, mechanics, and battlefield discipline were fused. Its colors displayed a white cross on yellow and green quarters, each bearing the artillery's flaming grenade: the emblem of controlled fire and technical mastery. From 1780 onward, the regiment formed part of the artillery contingent of Rochambeau's expeditionary corps, fighting alongside American forces in the War of Independence. Sources: *Louis Susane, Histoire de l'Artillerie Française, Tome I (Paris: J. Dumaine, 1874), 206–210; Service historique de la Défense (Vincennes). Sous-série Yb, Régiment d'Auxonne.*

The cadets' days quickly settled into a familiar routine. They were woken by drumbeat at half past four, the réveil cutting through sleep like a blade. Bleary-eyed, they washed at the pump, straightened their bedding, and assembled for muster by five. Names were called, orders barked, a salute offered to the King. Then silence, broken only by the shuffle of boots on frozen ground during inspection.

From six to eight came marching drills: endless turns, pivots, the stock-strike of muskets in unison. Even future artillerymen began with the infantry basics: formations, manual of arms, hauling gun carriages across the parade ground.

The morning meal was brief: bread, hard cheese, and watered wine. Then came the heart of Auxonne's reputation. From half past eight until noon, they bent over slates and compasses, learning the mathematics of war: arithmetic, geometry, and the ballistics explored by Robins and Euler. They drew parabolic arcs, calculated powder charges and trajectories. Instructors spoke of the Gribeauval system and of precision as the language of victory. The air smelled of chalk, oil, and cold iron.

Here, in the quiet scrape of chalk and the certainty of numbers, Siméon felt the vineyard boy receding. In his place rose the artilleryman, a soldier whose weapon was not only force but thought.

HISTORICAL NOTE: THE GRIBEAUVAL SYSTEM AND RATE OF FIRE

The Gribeauval system, adopted by France beginning in 1765 and fully implemented by 1776, standardized field artillery into three principal calibers: the 4-pounder, 8-pounder, and 12-pounder. The reforms emphasized lighter gun tubes, improved carriages, calibrated sights, and interchangeable parts. A minimum of six men could serve any piece. Under favorable conditions, a trained 8-pounder crew could fire approximately two rounds per minute; a 12-pounder crew approximately one. In practice, sustained rates dropped due to barrel heating, fouling, and fatigue. At Yorktown, the Auxonne artillery carried Gribeauval guns. Sources: *Robert A. Selig, March to Victory: Washington, Rochambeau, and the Yorktown Campaign of 1781, U.S. Army Center of Military History; David G. Chandler, The Campaigns of Napoléon.*

Dinner came at midday: ragout or salted meat carried in steaming tubs, and afterward a short respite. Some men wrote letters home; others polished their brass buttons or mended torn cuffs. Siméon sent word home when he could, brief letters to his father assuring the family he was well and describing what little he was permitted to share.[28]

By afternoon, the drills began anew. The recruits hauled field pieces across the packed earth, practiced harnessing horses, and rehearsed the delicate choreography of loading and firing with inert charges. Occasionally, distant echoes of live rounds carried from the Saône range, a promise of what was to come.

As dusk fell, the men took their *souper*: bread, soup, a ladle of beans if fortune allowed, then evening formation. Roll calls again, small punishments for dust on a musket or tardiness in the ranks. Sometimes by

---

[28] **Unmarried sons** in eighteenth-century French households customarily corresponded with the *chef de famille* (French, "head of household"), typically the father, who would share news with the wider family and convey their collective replies. This pattern of communication remained common during periods of extended military service.

candlelight, lessons continued: geometry problems traced in chalk, quiet reading of the artillery service manuals.

After drills, the recruits spilled into the barracks yard for the games that passed for leisure in a soldier's life: the clack of a *paume* ball against the barrack wall, the rumble of wooden quilles pins scattering, the solid *thock* of an iron *boules* ball finding its mark. These contests required focus and a steady hand, draining restless energy into friendly rivalry. Occupied men were obedient men.

Games of pure chance were a different matter. Dice and cards were officially forbidden and flourished accordingly: behind the stables, in hushed tents after curfew. They led too swiftly to heated words, bitter debts, and stolen rations.

Lights-out came at the ninth hour. Even Sundays offered little rest beyond Mass and a brief reprieve from drills.

Through it all, Siméon felt something take root within him. Not pride, not yet, but a deeper awareness, as though the steady beat of the drums had carved a new rhythm into him.

Purpose, he realized, was not a single choice but a daily repetition: the scrape of the rammer, the angle of the quadrant, the quiet vow made each morning in the cold light of dawn. He had not turned back. In that steadfastness he began to recognize the man he was becoming.

The next morning, the call to muster came with the now-familiar drumbeat. Siméon groaned softly as he stretched, muscles aching from unfamiliar labor, but a quiet determination pulled him upright.

Vincent was already tugging on his boots, muttering curses. "Up, vineyard boy. If we're late, I'm blaming your noble dreams."

"You were snoring like a hound in the straw," Siméon replied. "And if I dreamed, it was about better wine than the slop we had last night."

Louis Bayrettes[29] had already dressed and stood by the door, his dark eyes alert even through his sleep-mussed hair. "Move faster, *mes braves*. Today we are a day closer to touching guns."

"Do not listen to him; he says that every day," said another recruit, stretching his arms above his head.

Siméon laughed, but the sound was enough to shake off the last of the cobwebs. They washed quickly with cold water, dressed in semidarkness, and filed out into the early mist. As the recruits lined up for roll call, the three cannons loomed at the far end of the training field, glinting with dew in the first light: heavy, patient, and deadly.

Vincent let out a low whistle. "If those things could talk, I am certain they would be asking which one of us they will eat first."

"Not me," Louis declared, stepping forward with a grin broad enough to warm the chill air. He was a handsome slender man who carried himself with the easy confidence of someone who already knew the rules and how to bend them. "Cannons and I have an agreement. I do not question their temper; they do not question my size. Or at least that is true for my part."

Siméon felt the tension in his shoulders loosen. "Since you have this agreement, perhaps you can introduce us later. Preferably when they are not firing at us."

Vincent elbowed him lightly. "Careful. Encourage him and we will never get any peace."

"Peace?" Louis said, falling into step with them. "You two joined the wrong army for that."

For a moment, the three of them were young men at dawn.

They fell into formation with the others. And there, already waiting near the guns, stood a solid man with a jaw like an anvil: older, late thirties at least, but holding himself like a man half his age. His coat bore the faded marks of long service.

---

[29] **Louis Bayrettes**, born 1762 in Verrières, Champagne; enlisted in February 1779 at approximately seventeen years of age in the Régiment d'Artillerie d'Auxonne and was assigned to the Compagnie Bonnay de la Rouvrelle; served alongside Siméon Gaugien in the French Expédition Particulière under the command of Jean-Baptiste Donatien de Vimeur, comte de Rochambeau, during the American War of Independence. Source: *Les combattants français de la guerre américaine, 1778 – 1783 (Washington: Imprimerie Nationale, 1905), 355.*

One of the seasoned soldiers stepped forward: Louis Clément, the examiner who had tested many of them at enlistment. He gestured toward a man moving among the recruits with the heavy, deliberate grace of an old dragoon.

"Eyes forward," Clément said. "This is Sergeant François Le Boeuf[30]. He will be leading your field instruction."

Jean Baptiste Dutrule[31], a veteran who already knew the rosters and rhythms of Auxonne, leaned toward Siméon, his whisper dry rather than conspiratorial. They call him Sans Soucy. Apparently, he does not have a care in the world."

Siméon exhaled slowly. "I believe that as much as I believe cannons grow flowers."

Sans Soucy's voice cut through the murmur before it could settle. Low and intensely serious, like gravel shifting beneath the weight of a gun carriage.

"I do not care where you come from. I do not care if you are the sons of barons or the sons of whores. In this yard, you are *canonniers*. And you will be trained to be worthy of the title."

His eyes swept across them, slow and grinding.

"But first," he said, "you will learn to be soldiers.

A few recruits laughed nervously. Siméon did not. There was something behind the sergeant's gaze, not bluster, not ritual. Weight. Experience. Loss.

---

[30] **François Le Boeuf, known as Sans Soucy**, born 1745 in Villers-les-Pots, Comté de Bourgogne; enlisted December 5, 1773, in the Régiment d'Artillerie d'Auxonne and was assigned to the Compagnie Bonnay de la Rouvrelle; served alongside Siméon Gaugien in the French Expédition Particulière under the command of Jean-Baptiste Donatien de Vimeur, comte de Rochambeau, during the American War of Independence. Source: *Les combattants français de la guerre américaine, 1778 – 1783 (Washington: Imprimerie Nationale, 1905), 355.*

[31] **Jean-Baptiste Dutrule**; born 1744 in Etuz, parish of Cusey, Comté de Bourgogne; enlisted May 12, 1760, in the Régiment d'Artillerie d'Auxonne and reenlisted September 1, 1777, for an additional eight-year term; was assigned to the Compagnie Bonnay de la Rouvrelle; served alongside Siméon Gaugien in the French Expédition Particulière under the command of Jean-Baptiste Donatien de Vimeur, comte de Rochambeau, during the American War of Independence. Source: *Les combattants français de la guerre américaine, 1778–1783 (Washington: Imprimerie Nationale, 1905), 355.*

Sans Soucy moved down the line, correcting a slouch with a shove, snapping a chin upward with two fingers, yanking a loose strap tight without breaking stride. He stopped in front of Siméon.

"Fresh. What did you do before this?"

"My family's vineyard and farm."

Sans Soucy grunted. "Good. You know how to work." Already turning away: "Now we will teach you how to fight."

Vincent murmured from the corner of his mouth. "He might be more terrifying than my mother."

Louis snorted. "That is quite a memory of your mother."

Sans Soucy's voice came back over his shoulder. "If you have breath to joke, you have breath to drill."

Silence fell instantly. And without ceremony, their formal initiation had begun.

He did not need to raise his voice twice. The first command carried the weight of the battlefield behind it. No bluster, only precision and a grim patience born of too many campaigns and too few survivors.

The days passed in a blur of routine: shouted commands, dragging equipment, learning the name of every part of the gun. They practiced forming a gun team, rotating through every position until any man could fill any post. They did not yet fire. Their training was about ritual, rhythm, discipline. A misstep around a cannon could mean death.

As they became more familiar with the pieces, Siméon found himself grateful to share a squad with Louis and Vincent. The rest of their crew filled in around them: Claude François Moraux[32] from Salins, broad-shouldered and strong as an ox, known as Divertissant for the easy humor that kept spirits up. Jean-Baptiste Dutrule was older than the rest, a former cooper returned to the army to learn the guns, who loaded his pipe in a

---

[32] **Claude-François Moraux, known as "Divertissant"** ("the Entertainer"); born 1757 in Salins, Franche-Comté; enlisted June 1, 1774, in the Régiment d'Artillerie d'Auxonne; was assigned to the Compagnie Bonnay de la Rouvrelle and served alongside Siméon Gaugien in the French Expédition Particulière under the command of Jean-Baptiste Donatien de Vimeur, comte de Rochambeau, during the American War of Independence; discharged July 7, 1783. Source: *Les combattants français de la guerre américaine, 1778 – 1783 (Washington: Imprimerie Nationale, 1905), 355.*

single practiced motion as if the ritual steadied him. Michel Caillet[33] solid as oak, moving with the measured care of a man who understood weight and balance. And Pierre Stenietz[34], a tall, slender artisan whose precision seemed almost mechanical.

Together with Siméon they made seven. The eighth position remained empty, and they found themselves wondering who would fill it.

The work left their bodies ragged: splinters in raw hands, blisters on heels, bruises across shoulders from hauling the limbers. Yet slowly their movements aligned; the rhythm of sponging, ramming, priming, and aiming became second nature.

During a short pause one day, Siméon found himself beside Sans Soucy, watching him pack and ram the powder with swift, economical movements.

"You watch everything," the sergeant said without turning.

"Yes, Sergeant. I want to understand it all."

"Good. Understanding keeps you alive. Thinking too long will kill you." He glanced over. "But still: keep watching. You have the right eyes for it."

Sans Soucy moved on.

When the sun dipped low and drills ended, the recruits trudged back toward the barracks, uniforms stiff with sweat and dirt. Yet Siméon felt a quiet satisfaction in his exhaustion. Later, he, Vincent, and Louis gathered outside the barracks wall, where the stone still radiated the day's warmth. Vincent shared a sliver of mountain cheese, and Louis passed around candied nuts won in a quick game of cards.

---

[33] **Michel Caillet,** (referred to as the Oak in this book); born 1755 in Jussey, Franche-Comté; entered military service October 23, 1774, in the Régiment d'Artillerie d'Auxonne and reenlisted September 12, 1779, for an additional eight-year term; was assigned to the Compagnie Bonnay de la Rouvrelle and served alongside Siméon Gaugien in the French Expédition Particulière under the command of Jean-Baptiste Donatien de Vimeur, comte de Rochambeau, during the American War of Independence. Source: *Les combattants français de la guerre américaine, 1778 – 1783 (Washington: Imprimerie Nationale, 1905), 355.*

[34] **Pierre Stenietz,** (referred to as the Reed in this book); born 1756 in Saint-Jean-de-Rohrbach, Lorraine; enlisted in April 1776 in the Régiment d'Artillerie d'Auxonne; was assigned to the Compagnie Bonnay de la Rouvrelle and served alongside Siméon Gaugien in the French Expédition Particulière under the command of Jean-Baptiste Donatien de Vimeur, comte de Rochambeau, during the American War of Independence. Source: *Les combattants français de la guerre américaine, 1778 – 1783 (Washington: Imprimerie Nationale, 1905), 355.*

Siméon drew the *flasque* from his satchel, took a single sip, and handed it to Vincent.

"A taste of Rosières," he said.

Vincent drank and raised his brow. "The wine from home. I am surprised you have any left. Miracles do happen."

Louis drank and passed it back with a nod.

"Why artillery, Siméon?" Louis said, settling in. "Why not infantry? Or the dragoons with their fine plumes and fancy horses?"

Siméon watched the dark sky. "Because the artillery builds something. Even if it is destruction. There is a craft to it. A measure. Like tending vines. You do each step right, and the outcome matters."

Vincent gave a half smile. "Or maybe you just like the bang."

Making of Brothers

"Maybe a bit of both," Siméon admitted.

From the shadows, a familiar gruff voice cut through. "You three will never become qualified *canonnier-soldats* sitting around gossiping like washerwomen."

Sans Soucy stood there, arms crossed, but there was no real menace in his tone.

"Sergeant," Louis said quickly, scrambling to his feet.

"At ease, *Champenois*." Sans Soucy looked at Siméon. "You speak well, farm boy. Better than most."

"I listen well too," Siméon replied.

"Good. Then listen to this, all of you: you will see men break before the cannon does. Do not be one of them."

He turned to leave but paused. "Keep your *flasque* hidden. Share it only with men worth trusting. You have chosen two decent ones here. That is not nothing."

He walked off into the dark.

The three of them sat in silence, listening to the night settle: the distant murmur of other recruits, the sigh of wind dragging across the parade ground.

"Sans Soucy," Vincent whispered at last. "'Without worries,' they say. That man has more ghosts than bones."

Louis huffed a quiet laugh, softer than usual, almost reverent. "You do not know the half of it. On my first day, green as spring grass and twice as stupid, I nearly got myself tossed out."

Vincent raised a brow. "You? Too charming for that, surely."

"Oh, I was charming. And quick to say the wrong thing and throw a punch." He leaned back on his elbows. "Sans Soucy dragged me out of the fire. Did not scold me, did not shout. Just looked at me like he already knew every mistake I would make before I made them. Then showed me how not to make them."

Siméon's gaze followed the direction the sergeant had vanished. "He watches everything. As if he has already calculated where danger will come from."

"Because he has," Louis said. "I asked him once how he knew so much. He said, 'You live long enough, you learn what kills a man and what does not.'"

Vincent shivered, though the night was not cold. "And here I thought I was the dramatic one."

Louis grinned. "You are. But Sans Soucy? He is the real thing."

"I am glad he is our sergeant," Siméon said quietly.

"Glad?" Vincent snorted. "I am grateful. Safer having him within shouting distance."

Louis nodded. "Stick close to him and you will come out the other side alive. The sergeant does not waste the men he believes in."

Vincent's crooked smile formed. "Well then. Let us give him a reason to believe in us."

"Now that," Louis said, "is the smartest thing you have said all day."

All three of them laughed, quietly, but together.

Siméon leaned back against the wall and looked toward the darkened yard where the cannon slept. He had chosen his path and was living it now. Leaving his family had been hard, his grand-père most of all. His hand found his breast pocket where the old man's knife rested. Perhaps, in this rough place of fire and iron, he would find something worth becoming.

By the end of his first month, the word "pay" ran like a current through the barracks. Ten sous a day for an artilleryman, better than the infantry's eight. Fifteen livres in a month: enough, Siméon thought, to send something home.

The recruits queued before the paymaster's table, a stout man in a powdered wig with a box of coins and an endless list of deductions.

"Name?"

"Siméon Gaugien."

"First installment, clothing fund: deducted. Bedding and mess tin: deducted. Levy for the prévôté: deducted. Barber-surgeon fee: deducted."

A few small coins clinked onto the table. "Three livres, two sous. Next."

Siméon stared at the pitiful sum. Beside him, Vincent had already pocketed his own. "First taste of the King's arithmetic, vineyard boy. The coat on your back is not yours until you have paid for it ten times over. The *prévôté* fee is forever. Welcome to the army."

Others grumbled, some laughing bitterly. One Burgundian admitted he had already wagered more than his pay, deep in debt from borrowed coin.

Siméon pocketed the coins. Here, a month's service vanished into deductions and, for others, into dice and drink. His service, for now, was for learning, a bed, and food. That would have to be enough.

That night, Siméon followed his comrades into town. The tavern roared. Pipe smoke clung to the beams, catching the dim glow of tallow dips. Dice clattered on scarred tables. Cards slapped down in games of lansquenet and la prime. The air was thick with sour wine, sweat, and woodsmoke.

Women moved through the crush with practiced ease, tankards balanced on hips, laughter thin but knowing. Some leaned close over dice throws. Others settled onto waiting knees. They knew the rhythm of a soldier's pay.

Songs rose in ragged bursts. Tankards sloshed. Coins changed hands faster than any ledger could keep pace.

Siméon stood at the edge of it, letting the noise break over him.

Michel Caillet occupied half a bench near the door, tankard in hand. Pierre sat beside him, narrow as a reed, nursing a single cup. The two made an unlikely pair, the oak and the reed; somewhere in the shared crucible of training they had settled into an unspoken arrangement. When a drunken infantryman strayed too close, Michel shifted once and the man drifted elsewhere.

Jean-Baptiste drank steadily, then disappeared toward the river wall with the veterans.

Divertissant climbed onto a table and launched into a ballad from Salins. The tavern split between heartbreak and obscenity until the rafters shook. Vincent answered with something bawdier. Louis shouted corrections from the counter, grinning at a girl with chestnut curls.

Siméon drank a mug of vin coupé, then another. Three unlucky throws of dice later, a good part of his pay was gone. He pressed the remaining coins deep into his pocket.

A blonde girl with hopeful eyes made a slow circuit around him. When she realized he would not spend, she turned elsewhere. He did not begrudge her.

Vincent sauntered over, wiping ale from his chin. "You look like a man studying insects. Dangerous ones."

"They certainly feed on something," Siméon replied.

Louis dropped into the seat beside them, mug raised. "Glory! And poor decisions."

"Mostly the second," Siméon muttered.

Their laughter came easier now.

Later, when the air grew heavy, Siméon slipped outside. The night was cold and clean. Stars hung over the rooftops.

"Oy, Philosopher!" Vincent called, catching up. "Retreating from human experience?"

"Pacing myself," Siméon said.

Louis stumbled out behind them, straightening with exaggerated dignity. "Comrades walk home together," he announced, slinging an arm around each of them. "Especially when one cannot see straight."

They walked back through the dark, boots striking the cobbles in uneven rhythm.

That night, lying in the straw-smelling barracks, Siméon turned the few remaining coins in his palm before tucking them away. There would be little for home. Not yet.

He closed his fist over the rosary in his pocket.

He had sworn. He would endure.

Chapter Six:
Le Trio Infernal and The Thornflower

February – April 1779

Siméon rose at the first drumbeat echoing through the courtyard. He brushed down his uniform and prepared it for inspection. His arms ached from the previous day's drills.

He stretched, pulled on his coat, and met Vincent's mock scowl.

"You look disgustingly awake," Vincent grumbled, fumbling with his boots. "Dream you were back home in your vineyard?"

"No," Siméon replied, smiling. "Dreamt our gun crew ran the best times in the yard."

Louis sat up in his bunk with a loud yawn. "Dreaming of drills? Saints, farm boy. You need to get better dreams."

A thin morning mist clung to the parade road as the three of them trudged toward the training ground, muskets slung over their shoulders, the cold still biting through their coats. Behind them the barracks were only beginning to stir. The clang of a pot, a shouted curse, and a slammed door echoed in the pale light.

Louis kicked a pebble ahead of them. "If we spend the rest of our lives marching between barracks and the yard, I will forget what it feels like to go anywhere else."

Vincent arched an eyebrow. "Anywhere else? Like what, the tavern? That place is basically an extension of the barracks."

Louis elbowed him. "I am being serious."

Siméon adjusted his musket strap, eyes on the path. "I keep thinking there must be more than drills. A posting, a campaign." He hesitated. "Do you think they will send us beyond these walls? Maybe even beyond France?"

Vincent gave a low whistle. "Listen to you, dreaming of glory already."

"That is not what I meant," Siméon muttered, though a shy smile tugged at him. "I only wonder when they will tell us something."

France was at war with Britain; the fighting now stretched from the Caribbean to the Indian Ocean. In taverns and barracks, men wondered which regiments might be sent overseas.

A barked voice cut through the mist.

"You three!"

Sans Soucy strode up behind them.

"Always with your heads together," he growled. "I do not know if you are plotting a mutiny or the meaning of life but stop looking so pleased with yourselves."

Louis snapped upright. Vincent failed to hide a grin. Siméon nearly tripped over his own boots.

"Yes, Sergeant," they chorused.

Siméon hesitated, then spoke up. "Sergeant, would we be assigned an eighth man?"

Sans Soucy glanced at him, eyes sharp.

"A full gun crew is eight, Sergeant."

Sans Soucy grunted. "Soon enough. Any day now."

He resumed his march, then called back over his shoulder, "Try not to kill him his first week."

Once he was out of earshot, Vincent murmured, "That is practically encouragement."

Louis snorted. Siméon tried not to smile and failed. Shoulder to shoulder, they continued toward the training ground. The horizon felt a little wider.

But it was not Sergeant Le Boeuf who waited for them that morning.

As the recruits fell into their companies, a new figure approached from across the yard. He walked tall and straight-backed, his uniform impeccably pressed despite the Burgundian grime. A cocked hat sat at a deliberate tilt, and his dark eyes swept the field with practiced ease. He moved with the quiet confidence of a man long accustomed to command.

Every man knew France was at war. Every man wondered whether orders would come. Now, seeing this officer cross the yard with purpose, the question stirred again: *Would they soon be sent to fight the British?*

"Attention!" a junior officer barked.

Siméon recognized him from the day of his enrollment. His voice carried easily, steady but not harsh.

"I am Captain Jean-Baptiste Bonnay de la Rouvrelle," he introduced himself. "Welcome to the bombardier company, gentlemen. You may call me Captain Bonnay. I trust Sergeant Le Boeuf has not scared the courage out of you yet."

Laughter rippled through the line.

Bonnay's presence contrasted sharply with the bark of the sergeants. Where Sans Soucy drilled with blunt force, Bonnay carried a charm edged with steel. He was no martinet, yet his authority was undeniable. At thirty-six, he commanded with the quiet certainty of a man accustomed to leading, not from birth alone. The men sensed the difference. This was no court ornament.

His gaze caught on Siméon, Louis, and Vincent, who it appeared had deliberately stood next to each other in formation.

"Ah," Bonnay said, almost to himself. *"Le Trio Infernal."*

A few of the recruits snickered.

Vincent raised an eyebrow. "Infernal already, sir? We haven't even broken anything."

Captain Bonnay smiled. "Not yet. But I know your kind. Quick friends, heads full of mischief, and just enough wit to survive. A dangerous combination." He paused, then nodded. "I like it."

With that he turned and walked down the line to speak with other recruits.

Louis said nothing but was beaming. He half turned to Siméon and Vincent and whispered urgently, "That is it! We are *Le Trio Infernal!*"

From that moment, the name stuck. *Le Trio Infernal.*

That morning, their training intensified. Though no live firing was yet allowed, Bonnay introduced them to the rhythms and rituals of artillery.

For the first time, Siméon saw it not as a list of tasks, but as a living machine. Each man was a moving part: the *servant à l'éponge* (sponger) to swab out smoldering embers, the loader to ram home the charge, the powder man to measure and pass cartridges, the firer to set the match.

"Artillery," Bonnay said as he strolled among them, "is the scientific arm of the army. We bring precision, gentlemen, not brute strength. Your lives, and the lives of your comrades, depend upon rhythm as exact as a clock."

They drilled in endless sequence: sponge, load, ram, prime, aim. Ramrods weighted with iron grew heavier by the hour. Shoulders burned, arms shook, palms blistered, and still the sergeants shouted for more. The great Gribeauval pieces demanded discipline and unity. Even without powder, the guns carried enough weight to remind each man he served not alone, but as a cog in something larger.

HISTORICAL NOTE: CAPTAIN JEAN-BAPTISTE DE BONNAY DE LA ROUVRELLE

Captain Jean-Baptiste de Bonnay de La Rouvrelle (1743 – 1809) came from a noble Argonne family and held the feudal title Seigneur de Biesme, a domain in the Austrian Netherlands. Like many nobles from the border provinces, he belonged to a tradition in which landholding and military service crossed political frontiers, supported by training in mathematics, engineering, and patronage networks that opened paths across dynastic boundaries. By age thirty-six he commanded a company in the Régiment d'Auxonne's 2nd Battalion. From 1780 to 1783 he served in the War of American Independence as part of Rochambeau's expeditionary forces, then continued with the regiment until departing Auxonne in 1787. Returning to Biesme, he expanded the family glassworks, specializing in window glass and beginning exports to the United States. By 1789 the enterprise employed more than two hundred workers; the French Revolution brought that growth to an abrupt halt. Source: *Marie-Christine Jannin, "Verreries d'Argonne, quoi de neuf?" Bulletin de l'AFAV (2020).*

A few days later, a new figure appeared in the yard, escorted by a familiar face, Louis Clément, the seasoned artilleryman who had examined many of them at enlistment. The boy was thin as a reed and blinking against the sunlight. His uniform looked too large, and his pale hands clutched his papers tightly as he scanned the unfamiliar faces.

Sans Soucy straightened as they approached. "Ah, there you are. Reinforcement from Lorraine, no, Offenbach, was it not?"

The boy nodded and stepped forward, handing Sans Soucy his papers with trembling hands. "Sergeant, Jacques-Cristianne Closset,[35] reporting for bombardier assignment." His voice was soft, tinged with a melodic German accent.

---

[35] **Jacques-Cristianne Closset, known as "Fleur d'Épine"** ("Thornflower"); born 1762 in Offenbach am Main, Landgraviate of Hesse-Darmstadt, a state of the Holy Roman Empire; enlisted December 20, 1778, in the Régiment d'Artillerie d'Auxonne; was assigned to the Compagnie Bonnay de la Rouvrelle and served alongside Siméon Gaugien in the French Expédition Particulière under the command of Jean-Baptiste Donatien de Vimeur, comte de Rochambeau, during the American War of Independence. Source: *Les combattants français de la guerre américaine, 1778 – 1783 (Washington: Imprimerie Nationale, 1905), 355.*

Fleur d'Épine (Thornflower)

Clément gave the boy a brief nod of encouragement, then stepped back to join the other artillerymen who had gathered to observe the new arrival.

Sans Soucy glanced at the papers, then looked up with a slight grin. "Gentlemen, meet Jacques-Cristianne."

Vincent elbowed Louis lightly. "*Un petit oiseau,*" he murmured. A little bird.

Sans Soucy's grin widened, overhearing him. "Yes, yes. Do not let that fool you. Even his papers call him *Fleur d'Épine* (Thornflower.)" He folded the papers and handed them back to Closset with a look that was equal parts amusement and assessment.

The boy flushed with embarrassment, though a quick flicker of pride showed in his eyes. Siméon estimated that he was a couple of years younger than himself.

"You will pair with Gaugien's team," Sans Soucy added, gesturing toward the eight men who had gathered to observe. "Your gun crew. Keep him alive, you three," he said, singling out Siméon, Louis, and Vincent with a pointed look, "or I will put your pay toward funeral candles."

Dutrule, the eldest, gave a brief nod from where he stood at the edge of the group, pipe unlit in his hand. Divertissant offered an easy grin. Caillet and Stenietz acknowledged the boy with the quiet reserve of older soldiers who had seen many new recruits arrive and knew better than to make promises about survival.

Then Siméon stepped forward, Louis and Vincent flanking him. He reached out his hand. "I am Siméon. These two are Louis and Vincent. The rest you will know soon enough. They call you Fleur d'Épine?"

The boy nodded and shook Siméon's hand, his grip firmer than expected. "I am pleased to meet you," he said earnestly. "I will do my best not to be a burden."

Siméon grinned at the clipped precision of his accent, already wondering what his story was. A subject of the Holy Roman Emperor, serving the French King. There was a tale in that, if he ever chose to tell it.

"You already speak better French than Vincent," Louis quipped, reaching out to shake hands.

"Better manners too," Vincent added with an ironic grin. "Stick with us, and we will toughen you up."

Later, as they lined up for more drills, Fleur d'Épine stood a bit too rigidly at Siméon's side. Vincent gave him a nudge. "Relax," Siméon said, "you will be fine." The teen dropped his shoulders a little.

"Do not worry, petite fleur," Vincent said. "We only haze the ones we like."

For the first time, Fleur d'Épine smiled. Mischief flickered behind his reserve. "I will get you in your sleep."

Vincent let out a surprised laugh. "Then you will fit right in."

Folded into the rhythm of training, into shared rations and sore muscles and whispered stories after lights out. Fleur was the youngest among them, born in late '62, just sixteen, but quick to learn and eager to prove himself.

When the drills left him breathless and sweating, he never complained. Not once. Even though there was a lot they could complain about.

Fleur's first night, as they sat cleaning their gear by lantern light, Louis asked what they were all thinking. "So, Fleur, Offenbach. That is a long way from Auxonne. What brings a German boy to the French King's guns?"

Fleur did not look up from the buckle he was polishing. "My father is a tanner. Four sons. The shop goes to the eldest. The second joined the church. The third apprenticed to a cousin." He shrugged, a small motion. "I am the fourth."

"And the French artillery pays better than German leather," Vincent said.

"The French artillery," Fleur replied quietly, "goes places."

Louis asked, "And *Fleur d'Épine*?"

Fleur gave a faint shrug. "My mother's garden. Thornflowers grew along the fence. White ones. Pretty enough. Drew blood if you were not careful."

Vincent grinned. "Good to know!"

Fleur's mouth twitched.

No one pressed further. That was enough.

In March, on another inspection, Captain Bonnay watched them as they practiced the motions of loading under pressure.

"Gaugien," he said suddenly, pointing to the team. "Let us see what you have learned. Full sequence, thirty beats."

He gestured toward the canon de 4 Gribeauval, the light field piece favored for training.

They scrambled into position, working as one. Bonnay's voice carried over the yard, firm and even, the rhythm every man matched by step and voice.

"Un! Épongez!

Deux! Chargez!

Trois! En place!"

The rhythm took hold. Fleur d'Épine set the primer with precision. Louis drove the charge home. Vincent called each command to keep the tempo. Siméon stood at the rear, guiding their pace with calm authority, his voice steady where others hurried.

They hit every mark, thirty-two by Bonnay's count.

At its edge, a lone figure had stopped to watch. Bonnay noticed him at once and straightened, the ease leaving his posture. It was Colonel François-Marie d'Aboville[36], commander of the French artillery. He had come without announcement, his coat plain, his manner spare. Among the men, his presence carried immediate weight.

He watched in silence as the men reset their positions.

"Again," d'Aboville said quietly, without looking at Bonnay. "Accuracy before speed."

Bonnay inclined his head. "You heard the colonel," he said. "Again."

The familiar sharpness returned to his voice. "*Mon Dieu*. Did someone grease their brains with their cannon this morning?" He looked them over, a smile tugging at his lips. "My *Trio Infernal* seems to have acquired a fourth devil. Let us see if your hellish efficiency improves."

They grinned, breathless and proud. Even Sans Soucy, standing nearby with his arms crossed, gave a slow approving nod.

"Again," Bonnay ordered. "Faster this time, and if you beat thirty beats, Fleur d'Épine earns the last apple from my saddlebag."

"Challenge accepted, *mon capitaine*," Siméon replied, smiling.

They drove themselves harder. *Épongez. Chargez. En place.* Ram, sponge, load, prime. The rhythm tightened, each movement precise and sure.

This time they finished in twenty-eight counts.

---

[36] **François-Marie d'Aboville** (1730 – 1817) was the senior commander of French artillery serving under Jean-Baptiste Donatien de Vimeur, comte de Rochambeau, during the American War of Independence. A career artillery officer, he commanded the French artillery deployed to North America, organized largely around elements of the Metz and Auxonne artillery regiments, including the 2nd Battalion of the 6th Regiment of Foot Artillery. At the Siege of Yorktown in 1781, the disciplined and methodical deployment of French guns under his direction played a decisive role in the Allied victory. His conduct during the campaign earned acknowledgment from General George Washington and promotion to brigadier of infantry on December 5, 1781. Source: *"Aboville, François Marie, Comte d'," Encyclopedia of the American Revolution: Library of Military History, Encyclopedia.com.*

That night, in the barracks, Fleur d'Épine polished the apple to a shine before quartering it and passing the slices around, insisting Siméon take the largest piece. They sat on the floor playing dice for matchsticks, the day's tension giving way to laughter.

Vincent took his piece of apple and leaned back against the bunk, one hand behind his head. "We may just survive all this after all."

Louis nodded, voice low. "As long as we are a team."

Siméon smiled. The barracks still smelled of sweat and gunpowder, but he hardly noticed anymore.

Outside, the yard had fallen quiet. The guns stood cold and still in the dark.

Tonight they were young men with sore muscles and the sweet taste of apple in their mouths.

The days turned into weeks. Recruits became soldiers, then *canonniers*. Their days fell into a pattern: mornings of musket drills and marching, afternoons of artillery handling and maintaining the heavy guns. Operating together as a trained cannon crew became second nature, each man trained for every role, and Fleur d'Épine cemented his place within their core group.

French artillery was no ordinary branch of service. Precision mattered. Knowledge mattered. Every man trained for every post, because when the firing began, hesitation was fatal.

What broke the monotony was the slow but steady tightening of bonds among them. Siméon, Vincent, Louis, and Fleur grew into something more than comrades, their banter and laughter bridging the drudgery of endless drills.

Evenings slipped into their familiar pattern: rough barracks, a shared fire, cards shuffled or dice rolled more from habit than thrill, and quiet wagers that no longer surprised anyone. Sans Soucy often drifted into their circle by the fire, where conversation swung between Rousseau, Voltaire, Montesquieu, and camp gossip. Some nights they argued about reason, justice, and whether men could truly govern themselves. In the smoky glow of the campfires, they were young men with ideas as much as they were *canonniers* in training.

One night, Captain Bonnay joined them near the fire, his voice calm and measured. "You boys speak of philosophers as if they were comrades," he said with a faint smile. "Perhaps that is not far from the truth. Officers who value learning bring books with them. Even Voltaire travels in our baggage, though such reading is best kept among those who understand its purpose."

He studied the flames for a moment before continuing. "My family's trade is glassmaking. A title is a small thing without skill, so my father insisted I learn every step of the craft. Measuring heat, calculating pressure, judging the color of molten sand. It teaches patience. It teaches that perfection comes only from exactness."

His gaze moved deliberately around the circle. "That is why I chose the artillery. It rewards precision of mind as much as strength of body."

The fire cracked, sparks lifting into the dark.

"You will not speak of these things beyond yourselves," he added quietly. "Your King prefers soldiers who fight for order, not ideas."

No one replied. The fire burned lower. The words stayed.

Their talk did not stop at philosophy. Around those same fires, the young men traded stories that had drifted through Auxonne from distant America: tales of General Washington's battles along the Hudson, of desperate winter marches, and of the young Marquis de Lafayette, whose courage had become a point of national pride. Every Frenchman knew his name, and every Frenchman told the story differently. He was nineteen when he crossed the Atlantic at his own expense, defying the King's explicit orders and purchasing his own ship to carry him to war. He fought bravely at Brandywine and returned to face royal censure for his disobedience. Eight days confined to the Hôtel de Noailles, they said, yet even that rebuke became part of his legend. He emerged not chastened but celebrated, welcomed in the salons of Paris and spoken of in the taverns of Dijon as proof that French courage and generosity were reshaping the world. Now he lobbied tirelessly at Versailles for greater aid to the American cause. To men like Siméon, his story made the distant war feel personal, and entirely French in spirit.

Marquis De Lafayette

HISTORICAL NOTE: MARIE-JOSEPH PAUL YVES ROCH GILBERT DU MOTIER, MARQUIS DE LAFAYETTE

Gilbert du Motier, Marquis de Lafayette (1757 – 1834), defied King Louis XVI's explicit orders by purchasing a ship he named La Victoire and sailing for America in 1777 to serve in the Continental Army. George Washington quickly recognized his sincerity, particularly since Lafayette volunteered without pay. Wounded at Brandywine in September 1777, he earned the respect of Continental officers through personal bravery. Returning to France in February 1779, he faced royal censure: Louis XVI confined him to the Hôtel de Noailles for eight days, a symbolic rebuke that only burnished his reputation. Lafayette emerged as a persuasive advocate for the American cause, lobbying Versailles for greater military commitment. His advocacy contributed directly to the approval of the Expédition Particulière in March 1780, the force of over 5,000 soldiers under Rochambeau dispatched to reinforce Washington, and helped secure Admiral de Grasse's fleet for North American waters in 1781. Returning to America, he commanded forces in Virginia, his strategic patience helping set the stage for Yorktown. Sources: *Harlow Giles Unger, Lafayette (New York: Wiley, 2002); Louis Gottschalk, Lafayette and the Close of the American Revolution (Chicago: University of Chicago Press, 1942).*

One night Fleur spoke up, his accent thick but his eyes bright with conviction. He told them of a Prussian officer serving with the Americans, Baron von Steuben, who had taken a ragged army and given it discipline. Fleur said he had heard that the Baron was fierce in drill, sharp in his commands, and trusted by General Washington himself, a rare honor for any foreigner. The idea that a German could help shape a new army across the ocean filled him with a quiet pride.

He said the Americans now drilled by the Baron's regulations, marching and firing in a single rhythm, their movements crisp even in winter camps. Some French officers in Auxonne had spoken of the Prussian with respect, saying his work at Valley Forge had helped turn Washington's men into soldiers who could stand in a European line.

Fleur's voice softened as he looked toward the fire. "He is one of ours," he said. "German-born, but he fights for freedom."

HISTORICAL NOTE: BARON FRIEDRICH WILHELM VON STEUBEN

Friedrich Wilhelm von Steuben (1730 – 1794) was a Prussian-born officer who served as Inspector General of the Continental Army during the War of American Independence. Arriving at Valley Forge in 1778, he introduced rigorous drill, standardized training, and a unified manual of arms that transformed the Continental Army into a disciplined fighting force. His Regulations for the Order and Discipline of the Troops of the United States remained the army's foundational drill manual for decades. Serving directly under General George Washington, von Steuben earned a reputation as a master of military science that was widely recognized among European officers, including those in the French artillery. Sources: *Friedrich Wilhelm von Steuben, Regulations for the Order and Discipline of the Troops of the United States (Philadelphia, 1779); Paul Lockhart. The Drillmaster of Valley Forge: The Baron de Steuben and the Making of the American Army. New York: HarperCollins, 2008.*

In their daily drills, the cannon crew became more than a collection of roles. Siméon was training mainly as gunner and chief of piece and found himself not only calculating ranges and setting elevations but binding together the rhythm of the crew. Beside him Vincent worked tirelessly as loader, his relentless strength and reliability matching Siméon's precision. Louis darted as powder runner, his quick feet and quicker tongue finding humor where others found only urgency, while Fleur d'Épine handled the sponge and worm with meticulous care, his sharp wit never far from his precise hands. Divertissant Moraux rammed charges home, Jean-Baptiste Dutrule guarded the vent with the calm assurance of an older veteran, Michel Caillet, oak-solid, handled the trail for aim, his strength shifting the massive gun with precision, while Pierre Stenietz, tall and slight as a reed, worked the magazines with a glassworker's focus, pressing each cartridge into Louis's waiting hands.

As they moved from dry drills to live rounds, as the roar of powder and the cannon's recoil shook the ground beneath their boots, their laughter quieted and their firelit debates grew more somber.

One evening, after a flawless drill, Bonnay walked the line in silence. He stopped before Siméon's crew, studied each face, and gave a single nod. Then he turned and walked on.

"Feu!"

The command cracked across the muddy training ground. The cannon answered with thunder. Smoke surged upward in a thick, acrid plume, chased by the reek of powder and scorched cloth. The recoil shuddered through the carriage and into the bones of the crew, who gritted their teeth and worked through the rhythm drilled into them for months.

The first live round struck Siméon like a blow to the chest. He stepped back to make room for Louis to load the next shot, his shoulder throbbing from bracing the wheel, his cheeks streaked with soot. The ache sharpened his focus. The smell of sulfur, oil, tar, and iron clung to the air.

Out on the parade ground, the team began to work as one, gaining confidence with each live round under the steady gaze of Sergeant Le Boeuf.

"You're too polite with the fire," Sans Soucy growled one morning, watching Siméon hesitate before touching match to fuse. "The enemy will not wait for courtesy. Burn it like you mean it."

Siméon grinned despite himself. *"Oui, mon sergent."*

"It's not your fault, you're from Franche-Comté," Sans Soucy said, sniffing as if he'd caught wind of milk gone sour. "A good wine comes from there maybe once in a decade."

"And never a drinkable drop from Bourgogne?" Siméon shot back, too fast to think.

Sans Soucy laughed, a deep bark of mirth. "That's the spirit, Comtois. Now let's see if you can aim half as well as you talk."

The days passed in smoke and sweat, boots sliding in mud, cheeks chafed by wind and grit. Fleur d'Épine surprised them constantly. Slender and pale, he was wiry rather than weak, and his wit was as sharp as the thorny name he carried. He shocked them one evening with a clever idea for sabotage: blocking the vent hole of an enemy gun with hardening soap paste disguised as wax, rendering it useless at a critical moment.

Vincent gasped. "Where did you learn that?"

"I imagine things," Fleur said, tapping his temple. "That, and my uncle was a sapper in the Seven Years' War. He told stories that would make you think."

Smaller and slight, Fleur became a younger brother to the group: protected, teased, fiercely defended.

When a brutish conscript from another unit mocked his accent and knocked him down, Louis launched himself from ten paces away. He threw precise punches without hesitation and had to be dragged off before he broke the man's jaw.

"He's with us," Louis spat, wiping blood from his knuckles. "Say another word and I'll knock your teeth into Strasbourg."

Nobody gave Fleur a hard time again.

That night, they shared wine in the barracks, bundled in blankets as Fleur recited bawdy poetry in German-accented French until they were breathless with laughter.

Sans Soucy, though gruff with others, became their mentor. He taught more than *école de pièce*; he taught how to find dry wood in wet forests, how to pack a knapsack without chafing, how to lead without barking.

"Orders are easy," he said once as they cleaned the breech. "But trust: earned by listening. By bleeding with them. If you want to lead, know when to shout, and when to say nothing."

Siméon absorbed every word.

Sans Soucy taught him how to read the wind when aiming, how to keep calm when a charge misfired, how to dig a firing pit in damp, stubborn earth. And though he claimed to despise sentiment, he was often seen slipping crusts of bread to Fleur when rations were thin.

Most evenings, Siméon and Sans Soucy argued the merits of

Franche-Comté Rosières-sur-Mance versus Bourgogne Côte de Nuits. Neither ever conceded. Both smiled through the debate.

The letter arrived on a damp, grey afternoon in early April, its seal bearing the familiar mark of the Rosières syndic. Siméon was called from the powder magazine, his hands still grey with grit.

Letter From Home

He read it twice before the words took hold.

Passed in his sleep on Tuesday last… laid to rest Thursday morning beside your dear grandmother. The curé spoke well of him. Your mother placed his rosary in his hands. The ground was soft from the spring rains, and we finished before noon.

Thursday. The word stood apart. He counted back the days. His grandfather had been in the ground nearly two weeks.

Vincent found him behind the stables, sitting on an overturned crate, the letter limp in his hands.

"My grandfather," Siméon said, his voice distant to his own ears.

"They buried him two weeks ago."

Vincent cursed softly and sat beside him. Fleur appeared moments later, squeezing Siméon's arm. Louis followed, pulling him into an embrace. "I'm sorry, my friend."

Sans Soucy arrived within the hour. He'd already spoken to Captain Bonnay.

"Pack your things," he said. "Five days' compassionate leave. A cart is arranged. We leave before dusk."

"We?" Siméon looked up.

"I'll see you there and back." Sans Soucy's voice was matter-of-fact, but not unkind. "It's not right to travel with grief alone. And someone has to make sure the Franche-Comté boy doesn't wander off and join a monastery."

Siméon's throat tightened. "Thank you."

"Get your belongings," Sans Soucy said.

The packing took no time. A few clothes, his rosary, the small knife his grandfather had given him.

The others gathered at the cart to see him off. Vincent embraced him hard enough to drive the breath from his lungs. Louis clasped his arm, solemn and steady. Fleur d'Épine pressed a small, worn volume of Voltaire into his hands. "For when the thoughts get too heavy," Fleur said softly. "It helped me when I first came here."

"You'll return," Fleur added. "Stronger, I think."

Vincent stepped back and saluted. "Give the old man our respects."

By dusk, the cart was rolling north. After miles of silence, Sans Soucy passed him a wineskin.

"Bourgogne," he said. "Your grandfather would have hated it."

Siméon managed a half-smile. "He said it tasted like cold soup and regret."

"That's called character."

That night they slept beneath the cart, cloaks pulled tight against the spring chill. By the next evening, the hills of home rose ahead.

The black crepe ribbon on the door was the blow he had braced for and could not soften.

Sans Soucy reined the mule to a halt and said nothing.

The silence here was not the brittle hush of a barracks yard. It was softer, layered with doves in the eaves, the distant clatter of a pail, the grinding of the miller's wheel, a world enduring absence.

The door opened. Nicolas stood in the frame, leaning on his cane, his face drawn but steady.

"Papa, this is Sergeant Le Boeuf," Siméon said quietly. "He brought me home."

Nicolas extended his hand. Sans Soucy took it firmly.

"You are welcome here, Sergeant. We are in your debt."

"Your son is a fine soldier, Monsieur Gaugien. I am sorry for your loss."

Inside, the warmth of the hearth wrapped around him, but so did the grief. The scent of warm bread and cider hung in the air, sweet and familiar, yet beneath it lingered the ghost of pipe tobacco, clinging to the empty chair by the fire.

His father poured wine. Colas hovered near the door.

"You've grown," his father said finally. "And shrunk, somehow. Thinner in the face."

"You look older," Siméon replied, then caught himself.

His father only nodded. "We are. Loss adds years faster than rain ages stone."

Siméon understood he might not be speaking only of Grand-père.

The next morning, his mother walked with him toward the vineyard. The vines were bright with new growth, the sky the pale, soft gray of a dove's breast.

"The whole village came," she said quietly, not looking at him. "Père Charles spoke of his long service to the land. It was a good farewell." She paused, her gaze fixed on the distant hills, recounting the last few days with Grand-père. "He asked for you at the end. He was confused. Said he heard drums."

Siméon stopped walking. The life he had chosen, echoing in his grandfather's final hours.

He went alone to the churchyard.

The earth of the new grave had begun to settle, darker than the older, moss-grown mounds around it. No wreath remained, only a simple wooden cross: JEAN GAUGIEN. The date of burial was the Thursday Siméon had spent ramming powder charges, unaware.

He stood there a long time. All he had was settling soil and a name.

"He believed in the path you chose."

Siméon turned. Père Charles stood a few paces away, his hands folded into his sleeves.

"I should have been here," Siméon said, the words scraping his throat.

"You were where your duty placed you. He knew that. Sometimes honoring a life means standing where they cannot, not where they fell."

The priest rested a hand on Siméon's shoulder. "He was proud, Siméon. He said the vineyard soil was in your bones, but the army would put iron in your spine."

Siméon placed a hand on the damp wood of the cross. He offered a prayer. The vineyard and the iron: that was the inheritance.

On the walk back, he passed the smithy. His childhood friends fell silent as he approached. They admired his uniform, his polished boots, but their talk of frost and seed prices was stilted, polite.

He lingered by the church wall, watching them return to their conversations.

But the promise to the cross, and the echo of the drums, anchored him.

He returned to the warm hearth of home and a sergeant from another world.

That evening, the talk turned to the farm: plowing, fencing, spring planting. Nicolas worried aloud about taxes and seigneurial dues, the same worries Siméon remembered from childhood. He listened in silence, feeling the weight of the empty chair and the empty place in the fields his hands no longer filled.

When the others had gone and the fire burned low, he lingered at the table with his father. Neither spoke for a long while.

Siméon reached into his coat and drew out a small purse. "For the house."

His father looked at it, then at him. "You've done enough just by coming home."

"It isn't much. But Grand-père would have wanted me to do my part."

Nicolas nodded once, his rough fingers resting on the worn leather. "He would have," he said quietly. "And I thank you, my son."

The fire popped.

Later, Siméon found Sans Soucy alone by the hearth, nursing the last of the wine. When the sergeant asked about Grand-père, the words came easily.

"He was a hard man," Siméon said. "But fair. The kind who never explained his feelings. You just knew by how he showed you things."

Sans Soucy nodded slowly. "Men like that don't go quietly, even when they die in their sleep."

The fire crackled. Siméon turned his cup in his hands.

"You've known loss too," he said. It wasn't quite a question.

For a long moment, Sans Soucy didn't answer. When he spoke, his voice was quieter than Siméon had ever heard it.

"I was twenty-eight, on leave. My younger brother, Alain, died while I was gone. Alain was about your age. He watched things. The way you do."

He took a slow drink.

"My wife, Charlotte, had given birth while I was away. A girl. Lucie." He stared into the fire as though he could see them there. "She was as beautiful as her mother."

Siméon said nothing. He understood that silence was what this story required.

"The pox came through the village. Charlotte fell ill, then Lucie. She was so small… there was never any chance." Sans Soucy's jaw tightened. "I buried them both within a month of coming home. First my daughter. Then my wife."

The fire hissed. A log settled.

"I nearly drank myself into the grave. One dawn the priest found me in the church stables, half-dead. He gave me water and bread and said, 'Wine is warmer than memory. But as long as you're breathing, God isn't finished with you.'"

Sans Soucy let out a slow breath.

"He said Charlotte would want me to stand. Lucie would want her papa to fight on."

He was quiet a moment. Then, almost to himself: "After that, you learn to recognize it. The way the eyes go dull. The way the breath changes. You never forget."

Siméon did not ask what "it" was. He knew. The pox. The thing that had taken them. The thing Sans Soucy now watched for in every camp, every hospital tent, every boy who coughed too long in the night.

Siméon thought of Grand-père, of the drums, of the promise at the grave.

"That's what matters," he said quietly. "The carrying forward."

Sans Soucy looked at him, a long, measuring look. Then he raised his cup.

"Well, Siméon, as your grandfather would say: it's the struggle of the vine on rocky soil that makes the richest wine."

Siméon raised his own cup.

"I'll drink to that."

The morning of departure came too soon.

Siméon filled his *flasque* from his father's cask. His mother pressed dried fruit and bread into his hands, then held him for a long moment, her face against his shoulder.

Colas clasped his hand, then pulled him into a rough embrace. "Give them hell, little brother."

His father walked him to the cart where Sans Soucy waited, reins in hand.

Nicolas stood with his arms crossed, his face unreadable. Then he spoke.

"I had my doubts about this path. About whether it was right for you."

Siméon opened his mouth, but nothing came.

"I was wrong," his father said, voice gruff but steady. "You're becoming the man your grandfather believed you could be."

He extended his hand. Siméon took it, and his father pulled him into an embrace, brief and fierce.

"Come back to us," Nicolas said quietly. "When you can."

"I will."

Siméon climbed onto the cart. Sans Soucy clicked his tongue, and the wheels began to roll.

He looked back once. His father stood in the lane, one hand raised. His mother watched from the doorway, her shawl pulled tight. Colas leaned against the doorframe, arms folded, a faint smile on his face.

The house grew smaller. Beyond it, the vineyard stretched out, young vines clinging to their trellises beneath the pale spring sky. From the chimney, a thin line of smoke rose straight and quiet.

He turned forward.

The road to Auxonne unspooled ahead, and beside him, Sans Soucy sat in comfortable silence. Somewhere ahead, Vincent and Louis and Fleur d'Épine waited.

Siméon settled into the seat, the *flasque* pressing against his ribs, the weight of his grandfather's knife in his pocket.

He was ready.

Part III
Onward to Yorktown

Chapter Seven:
The Channel Coast

April – September 1779

When Siméon returned to the artillery camp at Auxonne with Sans Soucy, it felt like the first full breath after holding one too long.

The familiar smell of smoke and leather wrapped around him. The churned mud of the drill yard, the echo of boots on stone, the barked commands carrying across the parade ground.

Captain Bonnay was the first officer he saw. The captain crossed the yard with his measured stride, eyes sharp but kind. He stopped before Siméon and studied him a moment.

"You did what duty required," Bonnay said quietly. "Your grandfather would be proud of how you carried yourself."

Siméon bowed his head. "Thank you, *mon capitaine.*"

Bonnay placed a hand briefly on his shoulder. "The company is glad to have you back."

With that, the captain moved on.

Vincent smacked Siméon's back hard enough to jostle his pack. "Back from the land of vines and cows!"

Fleur d'Épine stepped forward and placed a folded sheet of paper into Siméon's hand with a solemn flourish. "A poem," he said. "For grief and return." His sincere expression shifted into mischief. "It also contains my mother's recipe for wild onion soup." The mischief faded to something softer. "She would make this whenever I came in from the cold, or when I needed warming, inside or out. It always worked."

Siméon tucked the poem and recipe into the pages of the book Fleur had given him and set it aside in his kit beside the knife from Grand-père and the rosary from his mother.

Over the following days, Siméon slipped back into the rhythm of morning drills, afternoon maintenance, evenings spent with *Le Trio Infernal* and its Thornflower.

The rumor of deployment reached Auxonne like a fever.

Siméon felt it crackle through the barracks yard, a current beneath the usual drills. He was still scrubbing grease from his kit when Sans Soucy appeared, his voice stripped of its dry humor.

"Battalion assembly. Now."

The yard filled quickly. Companies formed by regiment, guns drawn up behind them, officers in place. Captain Bonnay stood with his men, hands clasped behind his back, his expression unreadable.

When Colonel François-Marie d'Aboville stepped forward, the last murmurs died away.

He did not raise his voice. He did not need to.

"You have trained for movement as much as for fire," he said, his words measured, precise. "The time has come to prove both. Orders have been received. The artillery of Auxonne will march north to the coast."

No flourish followed. No promise. Just fact.

"What awaits us there will depend on the King's will," d'Aboville continued. "You will conduct yourselves accordingly. Discipline will matter.

Timing will matter. Every piece, every horse, every man."

He paused once, letting the weight settle.

"Make yourselves ready."

That was all.

Bonnay saluted and turned back to his company. The yard buzzed the moment the formation broke. The north coast could mean anything: defense against a British raid, reinforcement of a naval port, or something larger still.

Fleur d'Épine, who had a gift for finding things out, disappeared many evenings and returned with fragments of rumor. Spain had entered the war. A great fleet was gathering. Some said the target was England itself.

"England," Louis repeated, his voice caught between disbelief and hunger. "They would not. Would they?"

No one slept well. By the end of the second week, the whole camp hummed with a single word: invasion.

On the morning of departure, packs were cinched tight. Cannons were hitched to their teams, the horses stamping and blowing in the cool air. Captain Bonnay rode to the head of the column and turned his horse to face them. For a long moment he simply looked at them, his eyes passing over each man as if counting them, weighing them.

Then he spoke.

"You know why we march." His voice was calm, but it carried across the silent yard like a struck bell. "Now you will know where. To the Channel coast. To join the greatest fleet France has assembled in a generation."

He paused. Somewhere a horse stamped.

"We are going to invade England."

The words hung in the morning air.

Bonnay let the silence hold a moment longer.

"Spain has joined us. The combined fleet will command the Channel. The army will cross, and when we do, our guns will break whatever resistance we find." His jaw tightened. "This is what you have trained for. This is why the Régiment d'Auxonne exists. You will not waste this chance."

He turned his horse and raised one hand.

"Column forward."

The drums began. The wheels groaned into motion. And Siméon, his Grand-père's knife in his pocket, marched north toward a war he could finally see.

England. They were going to invade England.

The landscape shifted day by day: vineyards gave way to wheat fields, then to pastures dotted with pale cattle, then to forests that broke the horizon into dark green waves. Church spires marked villages Siméon had never heard of. Rivers he could not name flowed under bridges his boots crossed without pause.

Fleur d'Épine produced a crumpled broadsheet from a peddler two villages back and read it aloud by firelight, stumbling over the longer words: Spain had joined the war, and the combined fleet would number several score ships of the line.[37] The British, it claimed, were in a panic. Michel and Pierre cheered and passed a bottle. Divertissant climbed onto a supply crate and began a mock plea in King George's voice until Jean-Baptiste hauled him down before an officer saw.

Siméon's shoulders ached from the ropes when they had to help the horses haul the guns up a slope. His skin darkened under the sun until his mother would not have recognized him. But beneath the exhaustion, something burned. Every step north was a step toward England, toward the enemy.

The column pressed on. And somewhere ahead, invisible but calling, the sea waited.

They smelled it before they saw it.

The wind shifted on the morning of the fourth week, carrying something Siméon had never encountered: a sharpness beneath the air, briny

---

[37] **Ships of the line** were eighteenth-century warships large and heavily armed enough to participate in the line of battle, the prevailing naval tactic in which opposing fleets formed parallel lines to exchange broadsides.

and ancient, that cut through the dust and sweat of the march. Vincent lifted his head like a hound catching a scent.

"The sea," he said quietly. "We are close."

The column crested a long ridge in the early afternoon.

He stopped walking.

He had read of the sea. He had heard Vincent speak of it. But no words had prepared him for this: the sheer impossibility of so much water, heaving and glittering under the summer sky, swallowing the horizon whole.

"God in heaven," Louis breathed beside him.

Fleur d'Épine said nothing. His mouth hung open, his usual wit struck silent.

Vincent watched them with a strange expression, half pride and half sorrow. This was his country. The salt air was his childhood. He had grown up in a fishing village on the coast where boys learned to read the tides before they learned to read letters. The smell of brine and tar was as familiar to him as the smell of gunpowder had become.

"Come on," Sans Soucy called from ahead. "You will have plenty of time to gawk. Move."

They descended toward the coast.

And then they saw the fleet.

It filled the harbor like a forest of masts. Ships of the line rode at anchor, their hulls dark against the water, their rigging a tangle of rope and canvas that reached toward the sky. Smaller vessels darted between them: barges, launches, boats Siméon could not name. Flags snapped in the wind, the white of France everywhere he looked. Beyond the breakwater, more sails dotted the horizon, an armada gathering from every port on the Atlantic coast.

Siméon counted ships until he lost track. Twenty. Thirty. Forty. More. All French.

"This is it," Louis said, his voice hushed. "This is really happening."

Tents stretched in uneven rows across the dunes and fields, thousands of them, more soldiers than Siméon had ever seen gathered in one place. Cook fires sent thin smoke into the sky. The sound of hammers rang from the shipyards.

And amid it all, long lines of soldiers filing toward the harbor. Men with packs on their backs and muskets on their shoulders, boarding launches that would carry them to the great ships at anchor.

"They are embarking," Fleur said. "They are already boarding."

Vincent nodded slowly, his eyes on the ships. "They want to be ready. When the Spanish arrive, they will sail at once."

This was it. The ships were waiting. The men were boarding. England lay just beyond that gray horizon.

The column halted at the edge of the artillery park, a vast field of guns and caissons and wagons arranged in ordered rows. Sergeants shouted. Officers conferred. Siméon and his crew stood with their cannon, waiting for the order that would send them to the ships.

Captain Bonnay rode up and dismounted. He spoke briefly with the company's sergeants, then turned to Louis Clément, who had already appeared at his side with the company's papers.

"Find Colonel d'Aboville's headquarters," Bonnay said. "Present our compliments and report our arrival. Learn what orders await us."

Clément saluted and disappeared into the chaos of the camp.

The crew waited. Around them, infantry continued to file toward the harbor. Launches pushed off from the shore, heavy with men. The ships seemed to pull at their anchors, eager to be gone.

Clément returned within the hour, his face unreadable.

"Colonel d'Aboville sends his acknowledgement," he reported to Bonnay. "Orders from Admiral d'Orvilliers: all artillery is to remain ashore. The guns will not be loaded until sailing orders are confirmed. We are to establish the battery park and await further instructions."

Bonnay nodded slowly. "And the sailing orders?"

"Dependent on the Spanish fleet, mon capitaine. The Admiral expects them daily."

Bonnay dismissed him and walked the line, his face composed but his jaw tight. He stopped before each gun crew, spoke a few words, and moved on. "You will remain here," he said. "The guns stay ashore until sailing is confirmed. Your duty is to maintain the battery and await further orders."

Louis stepped forward. "Mon capitaine, the ships are boarding. When do we embark?"

Bonnay smiled. "*Le Trio Infernal* wants to board early? And will you leave the Thornflower behind?" His expression changed. "When the order comes. Not before."

"But the Spanish," Vincent said. "They could arrive any day. The winds are favorable. If we're not aboard when they come..."

"Then you will board when you are told to board." Bonnay's voice was not unkind, but it was final. "Heavy artillery does not load on speculation. The guns are too valuable, the process too slow. We wait for confirmation that the fleet will sail. Until then, you guard what you have carried here."

He moved on to the next crew, leaving them standing in the salt wind.

And the artillery of Auxonne stood in a muddy field, watching.

"Bonnay explained it," Louis repeated. "And the men climbing into those boats? They did not march further than we did. They are not braver than we are. But they will set foot on English soil."

No one had an answer for that.

Sans Soucy appeared behind them, silent as always. "You heard the captain. Set up the tents. Dig the latrines. Check your powder stores. We could be here for days or weeks. Make yourselves useful."

"And if the Spanish arrive tomorrow?" Louis asked. "If the fleet sails while we are still unpacking?"

Sans Soucy met his eyes. "Then we will board when we are told to board. Until then, we wait."

Vincent turned to look at the sea.

"The wind is good," Vincent said quietly, almost to himself. "If the Spanish were here, we could sail today."

"But they are not here," Sans Soucy said. "So we dig latrines."

He walked away.

That night, Siméon lay in his tent and listened to the unfamiliar sounds of the coast: the cry of gulls, the distant crash of waves, the creak of ships at anchor. Through the canvas, he could see the glow of lanterns on the water, hundreds of them.

Somewhere out there, men were settling into hammocks below decks, ready to sail at dawn if the word came. They would be the first wave. They would land on English soil and make history.

And Siméon was here, in a tent, guarding cannons that might never fire.

Every morning, the same routine: check the guns, oil the mechanisms, inspect the powder for damp. Every morning, no orders. Drill with the crew until the movements were automatic. Eat whatever the quartermasters provided. Watch the harbor.

Thirty thousand men and four hundred ships, all waiting for word that the Channel was clear.

Then one morning the ships of the line began to move. Vincent noticed first. One by one they slipped from the harbor, sailing out behind Admiral d'Orvilliers' flagship. The transports did not follow.

Louis spoke loudly enough for all to hear. "I told you. They would sail without us. And there they go." He was only giving voice to what every man was thinking. There had been no notice.

The warships were gone more than a week before it was confirmed. D'Orvilliers had taken the fleet south to meet the Spanish. Now every day the camp waited for news of the rendezvous. Every day, nothing came.

"Where are the Spanish?" Louis asked one evening, staring at the empty horizon. No one had an answer, but someone asked it every night.

Vincent shook his head.

"They will come," Sans Soucy said. "Spain signed the treaty. They have as much to gain as we do."

"Then where are they?"

No one answered.

The Spanish fleet scattered by a storm, the Spanish admiral a coward, Madrid betraying Versailles. Each story spread through the camp, believed for an hour, forgotten by nightfall, replaced by something worse. And through it all, the transports sat empty, the army drilled on the beaches, and the artillery of Auxonne stood guard over guns that gathered dew in the morning and rust by afternoon.

Fleur returned one evening with darker news.

"They left Brest under-provisioned," he said, his voice low. "Deliberately. To slip past the British patrols. They were supposed to meet the Spanish within days. Now they have been waiting off the coast at a place called La Coruña for a month."

Vincent's face went pale. "A month at sea with short supplies? In summer, in those waters?" He shook his head slowly. "The water will turn. Men will sicken."

Then word came by dispatch riders and sailors returning to port. Men were dying on the fleet. Not in battle; there had been no battle. They were dying of fever, of flux, of foul water and close air. The bodies were sewn into canvas, weighted with shot, and given to the sea. There were no crosses, no graves, only the gray water closing over what remained.

"It happens," Sans Soucy said when Louis asked about it. "Men get sick. Men die. It is not the war that kills most soldiers. It is the waiting."

He said it like a fact, not a warning. But Siméon noticed that he began insisting they boil their water before drinking it, and that he moved their latrine further from the tents than regulations required.

"They are dying out there," Vincent said one night. His voice was hollow. "A sailor came in yesterday from a supply run to the fleet. He said they have already buried many men at sea, and the Spanish have not yet arrived."

Louis shifted uncomfortably. "Maybe it will be different when we cross."

"Maybe." Vincent did not sound convinced.

The fleet could not return without abandoning the rendezvous. The army could not cross without the fleet. So they all waited: the sailors off Spain, the soldiers on the beaches, the gunners in their camps.

It was late July when a dispatch rider galloped into camp at midday, his horse lathered and heaving. Within the hour, the word had spread to every tent, every fire, every man who had spent six weeks waiting and wondering.

The Spanish had arrived.

The camp erupted. Men poured from their tents, cheering and embracing with relief. Sixty-six ships of the line were now sailing north toward the Channel.

"They are coming," Louis shouted, grabbing Siméon by the shoulders. "The fleet is coming!"

Fleur d'Épine was already running toward the artillery park, shouting over his shoulder. "Come on! We will be loading within the week!"

No orders were needed.

This was it. The fleet was sailing. Within days, perhaps a week, they would be crossing to England.

Siméon was tightening a rope on the gun carriage when Captain Bonnay rode up.

"Stand down," Bonnay said. His voice was calm but firm.

Louis looked up. "*Mon capitaine?*"

"Stand down. Secure the guns. Return to your tents."

"But the fleet has sailed," Siméon said. "We should be loading the transports."

Bonnay's face was composed, but something flickered behind his eyes. "The fleet must first engage the British and secure the Channel. Until that is confirmed, we remain in place. No guns load onto transports until we have word that the crossing is clear."

"How long?" Louis asked.

"Days. Perhaps a week or two. The armada must find the British fleet and defeat it, or drive it into port." Bonnay's jaw tightened. "Until then, we wait."

He moved on before anyone could respond.

The crew exchanged glances. Around them, the chaos of preparation continued, but the initial surge of energy was already beginning to cool. The transports still sat empty in the harbor. The army still drilled on the beaches. Nothing had actually changed except the news.

Vincent had not moved from his position by the gun. His eyes were fixed on the northern horizon, as if he could see the armada sailing toward the Channel.

"What is it?" Siméon asked.

Vincent did not answer immediately.

"It took them a week to sail after the Spanish arrived," he finally said. "A week to sort out signal codes and formations. A week the fleet did not have.

Half of them were sick." He turned to look at Siméon, and his eyes held something that might have been despair. "If they had sailed in June, when the wind was fair and the crews were healthy…"

He did not finish the sentence.

He did not need to.

The fleet had sailed, but the army remained on shore. Each day brought nothing.

Then, in mid-August, Fleur came running back toward the tent, breathless. He had been gone since morning, and his face was flushed with more than exertion.

"The armada has entered the Channel," he said. "The combined fleet was sighted off Plymouth. England herself is within reach."

"They did it," Louis said, his face alight. "They are there. We will be crossing any day now."

The camp buzzed with renewed energy. Men checked their equipment for the hundredth time. Officers conferred over maps. The transports were readied, their holds prepared for guns and horses and men.

Captain Bonnay assembled the company. His expression was composed, but something flickered in his eyes.

"The armada has drawn first blood," he said. "HMS Ardent[38], a British ship of the line, was captured by a French squadron. Her captain mistook our ships for friendly sails until it was too late."

A cheer went up from the men. Bonnay let it run its course.

"We await orders to embark. Until then, maintain readiness."

He dismissed them. As the men dispersed, Vincent stood apart, his arms crossed.

"One ship," he said quietly. "One ship, and we still have not landed a single man."

The winds turned. An easterly gale drove the armada back into the Atlantic. Then fog rolled in, and the British fleet, which had been lurking near the Scilly Isles, slipped past them entirely. The armada gave chase but could not catch them. By the end of August, the British had reached the safety of Portsmouth, and the combined fleet was scattered across the western approaches, its crews decimated by disease.

Siméon first understood the scale of it when the ships began returning to port.

He was on the beach with Vincent, helping to unload supplies for a vessel that had put in for fresh water, when another boat passed them heading for shore. It rode low in the water, heavy with men. At first Siméon thought they were reinforcements. Then he saw how they lay.

They were not sitting. They were sprawled against one another, too weak to hold themselves upright. A few raised their heads as the boat

---

[38] *HMS Ardent*, a sixty-four-gun ship of the line, was captured on August 17, 1779. Captain Phillip Boteler sailed from Plymouth unaware that the Franco-Spanish armada was already in the Channel. When Ardent encountered a squadron and signaled for identification, the French, reportedly in possession of the Royal Navy's signal codebook, gave the correct response. The ship approached and was taken under fire before her crew understood the deception; Boteler struck his colors after brief resistance. Ardent was recaptured by the British at the Battle of the Saintes in 1782. Source: *Rif Winfield, British Warships in the Age of Sail, 1714 – 1792 (Barnsley, UK: Seaforth Publishing, 2007).*

ground onto the sand. Most did not move at all.

"Sick detail," Vincent said quietly. "They are bringing them off the ships."

Two men from the hospital tents came down to meet them. They lifted the first man under the arms and dragged him up the beach. He made no sound.

His head hung loose, his feet trailing furrows in the sand.

"How many today?" Siméon asked.

Vincent shook his head. "I do not know. But that is the third boat I have seen this morning."

It was not yet noon.

The hospital tents filled, then overflowed. Men lay on blankets in the open air, too sick to move, too numerous to shelter. The surgeons worked without rest, but there was little they could do. No medicine could cure what the ships had bred. The sailors spoke of men too weak to climb to the deck, of bodies sewn into canvas and given to the sea without ceremony.

"More than a hundred burials at sea yesterday," Fleur said one evening. "And that was just what they could count."

Louis stared at the fire. He had grown quieter since the news of the Ardent. "How many total?"

"No one knows."

"Thousands," Vincent said. He was sitting apart, his back against a supply crate, his eyes on the harbor where the battered ships rode at anchor. "I talked to a bosun's mate from the Bretagne this afternoon. He said they have lost half their crew since June. Half. And there are sixty-six warships out there, all of them the same or worse."

No one spoke.

"This is wrong," Louis said. "We should be crossing. We should be invading. The fleet reached the Channel. They were right there."

"This is not the war," he said. "This is just the dying."

The artillery crews had been spared the worst of it. They remained on shore, breathing clean air, drinking from wells that had not yet spoiled. The guns stayed in the artillery park, oiled and ready, waiting for orders that never came.

Fleur d'Épine, who could befriend a stone if given half an hour, had found a sailor from the *Bretagne* recovering in the hospital tents. The man had been carried off his ship with the flux when she put in for fresh water, and was slowly mending. Fleur visited him most evenings, bringing tobacco when he could find it, and returned with accounts that made the others fall silent.

"He says the gun deck was a charnel house," Fleur reported one night, his voice stripped of its usual lightness. "Men too sick to move lying in their own filth. The healthy ones, what few remain, too exhausted to clean it. They just step over the bodies."

"Bodies?" Louis asked.

"The ones waiting to be sewn up. They could not bury them fast enough. Sometimes a man died in his hammock and no one noticed for hours."

"The water barrels went foul weeks ago," Fleur continued. "Green slime on the surface. They drank it anyway because there was nothing else. And the air below decks…" He shook his head. "He said you could taste it. Like breathing through a corpse's mouth."

Vincent stared at the ships riding at anchor in the harbor, their lanterns flickering in the dark. "How long can they last?"

"Not long." Fleur's voice was quiet. "He said some ships barely have enough men to raise anchor. Even if the orders came tomorrow, half the fleet could not sail."

They could all see it was true.

The sickness came for them three days later.

Fleur was the first to fall. He had spent evenings in the hospital tents, sitting with his sailor friend, breathing the same air as the dying. He woke one morning pale and shaking, and by noon he could not keep water down.

"Serves me right," he managed, trying to smile. "Should have stuck to making friends with healthy people."

They kept him in the tent, away from the hospital he had come to know too well. For two days he suffered, but his case was mild. By the third day he was sitting up, weak but lucid, complaining about the taste of boiled water.

Vincent was sick only a day, but Louis was not so lucky.

He woke in the night with cramps that bent him double. By morning he could not stand. By noon he was burning with fever, his skin dry and hot, his eyes glassy and unfocused.

"Get him to the hospital tent," Sans Soucy ordered. But when they tried to lift him, Louis cried out in pain so sharp that they set him down again.

"No," he gasped. "Not the hospital. Men go in there and do not come out."

"You need help," Siméon said. "The surgeons…"

"The surgeons cannot do anything." Louis grabbed Siméon's arm, his grip weak but desperate. "Keep me here. Keep me with the crew. I will get better. I just need rest. I just need…" He broke off, seized by another cramp, and curled into himself.

They looked at Sans Soucy. The sergeant's face was unreadable, but after a long moment he nodded.

"Keep him in the tent. Boiled water only. Clean rags. If he gets worse, he goes to the surgeons whether he wants to or not."

For three days, Louis burned. He drifted in and out of consciousness, sometimes lucid enough to recognize their faces, sometimes lost in fever dreams that made him cry out against his blankets. Siméon took turns with Vincent and Fleur sitting beside him, pressing wet cloths to his forehead, forcing water between his cracked lips.

On the fourth day, the fever broke.

Louis opened his eyes, clear for the first time in days, and looked around the tent as if seeing it for the first time. He was pale and thin, his cheeks sunken, but he was alive.

"Still here," he said. His voice was a croak.

"Still here," Siméon confirmed.

"Scared myself." Louis tried to smile, but it came out as more of a grimace. "What did I miss?"

"Nothing good. The fleet is scattered. Men are still dying."

"So the usual." Louis closed his eyes. "Wake me when the war starts."

He slept for two more days, a real sleep this time, without fever or dreams. When he finally woke again, he was weak but healing.

Siméon fell ill last, a mild case that left him weak and shaking for a week but never threatened his life. He lay in his tent and listened to the sounds of the camp: the coughing and the groaning and the occasional cry of grief.

The fleet had reached England. They had seen her shores. They had taken a prize. And still the invasion had not come. The British had slipped away, the crews had sickened, and now the armada was limping back to port.

All that waiting. All that death. And nothing to show for it but empty transports and unmarked graves at sea.

The mood in the camp grew darker with each passing day.

Siméon had recovered enough to resume his duties, but the camp he returned to was not the one he remembered. The energy of May, the anticipation of June, the desperate hope of July, the brief elation of August when they had come so close: what remained was exhaustion. Men moved through their tasks like sleepwalkers, going through the motions because the motions were all they had left.

The hospital boats came more frequently now, each one riding low with men too sick to sit upright. The sailors who rowed them no longer looked at the shore. They simply delivered their burden, pushed off, and returned to the ships for more.

"How many?" Louis asked one evening. He had regained some of his strength, but not his spirit. The illness had hollowed him out in ways that went beyond the physical.

Fleur had the numbers. He always had the numbers now, gathered from sailors and soldiers and anyone who would talk. Gathering the facts was his way of bearing witness.

"They are saying eight thousand. Since June."

No one spoke. Eight thousand men. An army's worth of dead, and not one of them killed by the enemy.

"This fleet cannot sail again," Vincent said. His voice was flat, reciting facts he no longer had the energy to feel. "Half the ships do not have enough crew to man the guns. Some could barely make port."

"What does it mean?" Fleur asked quietly. "For the invasion?"

Vincent did not look at him. "It has been over for weeks. The commanders just have not admitted it yet."

By late August, the camp felt hollowed out. Men who had once dreamed of glory now dreamed only of survival. The songs that had carried them north were forgotten. In their place: silence, or worse, the thin sound of dying drifting from tents and ships alike.

Siméon found himself spending more time on the headland, staring out at the gray water. It had become a kind of ritual, a way to escape the stench and despair of the camp. Sometimes Vincent joined him. Sometimes he went alone.

One evening, near the end of August, he climbed the path to the headland and found Captain Bonnay already there.

The captain stood at the edge of the cliff, his hands clasped behind his back, looking out at the battered ships in the harbor. He did not turn when Siméon approached. He did not speak.

Siméon stopped. He had never seen Bonnay like this, alone and still, the weight of the summer visible in the slope of his shoulders. The captain who always had answers, who always knew the next step, stood watching a fleet that had sailed so far and come so close, only to limp home in defeat. For a long moment he was just a man.

Bonnay turned. Their eyes met.

He did not speak. Neither did Siméon. There was nothing to say that both did not already know.

After a moment, Bonnay nodded once, slowly, and walked past him down the path toward the camp.

"Get some sleep," he said. "Tomorrow will be another long day."

He was gone before Siméon could respond.

The order came on the third of September.

Louis Clément returned from Colonel d'Aboville's tent in the early morning, moving quickly through the camp toward Captain Bonnay's quarters. Everyone who saw him pass could tell the message was urgent.

There was no fanfare. No assembly. No speech. Within the hour, Sans Soucy found them by the cannon, where they had been pretending to check the lashings again.

"Pack your kit," he said. "We march at dawn."

Louis looked up. "We are boarding?"

"We are leaving." Sans Soucy's voice was flat. "The invasion is cancelled. We return to Auxonne."

For a moment no one spoke. The words hung in the salt air, impossible and yet inevitable.

"Cancelled," Fleur repeated. "Just like that."

"Just like that."

"But the fleet…" Siméon started.

"The fleet is returning to Brest. The Spanish are going home. The army is dispersing to winter quarters." Sans Soucy looked at each of them in turn. "It is over. There will be no invasion. Not this year. Perhaps not ever."

He turned and walked away before any of them could ask the questions they all had.

The camp dissolved into controlled chaos. Tents came down. Wagons were loaded. The guns were hitched to their teams with a weariness that had nothing to do with the weight of the iron. The living moved through the motions of departure.

Siméon helped lash the cannon and tried to feel something. But there was only a dull hollowness where the anticipation had been. They had marched four hundred miles. They had waited four months. They had watched thousands of men die in the shadow of the greatest fleet France had ever assembled. And now they were retreating from the coast, having never fired a shot, never seen the enemy, never set foot on a single ship.

The artillery had stayed on shore. They had guarded the guns, maintained the equipment, waited for orders that never came. And because of that, they survived.

Three days later, as the company formed up for the first leg of the march south, Captain Bonnay rode the line.

He stopped before Siméon's crew and looked at them a long moment.

"You did everything that was asked of you," he said. "Remember that. This failure belongs to winds, tides, and disease."

He rode on without waiting for a response.

The drums began. The column lurched into motion.

Most of the dead never came ashore. Those who died on land were buried quickly near the ports, often without names.

Siméon did not look back.

Chapter Eight:
Pour le Roi

October 1779 – April 1780

The villages that had cheered them watched from behind closed shutters. They marched as men already defeated, haunted by the stench of the camp they had left behind, by the memory of boats riding low with dying men, by the knowledge that everything they had endured had been for nothing.

No one sang. No one joked. Even Louis, who had always found something to laugh about, walked in silence, his face drawn and pale. The illness had left him thinner than before, and he tired easily, falling behind the column.

"I will be fine," he said whenever they asked. "Just need to get my legs back."

Vincent kept apart, his gaze distant, bearing the quiet weight of having known. From the first weeks on the coast, he had seen what the others could not, and the knowledge had brought him no comfort. Now he walked with the look of a man who had been proved right and wished he had been wrong.

Fleur d'Épine tried once to lift their spirits with a poem, something about soldiers returning home with honor. But his voice faltered halfway through, and he put the paper away without finishing.

"Some things cannot be made into verses," he said quietly. "Not yet."

The rain continued. The roads turned to mud. The column stretched and contracted as men struggled to keep pace. At night they made camp in fields that had already been stripped by the harvest, eating cold rations because the wood was too wet to burn. No one complained.

They were only days from Auxonne when the news reached them.

Siméon was crouched beside a sputtering fire, turning his boots toward the weak heat when the courier arrived. He did not see the man ride in, but he heard the commotion from the officers' tents, the sudden sharpness of voices that cut through the steady patter of rain.

Within the hour, the story was everywhere.

"Savannah," Vincent said. He had come back from the sergeants' fire with his face set like stone. "The assault in America failed. The siege abandoned. The British hold the city."

Siméon looked up. "When?"

"October. While we were marching home."

The words landed like a blow. October 9th. They had been somewhere in Champagne, slogging through the rain, cursing the mud, thinking of nothing but the next mile and the meal at the end of it. And on that same day, across the ocean, French soldiers had been dying in a swamp they would never see.

That night, the camp was quieter than usual. Men sat around their fires and stared into the flames, thinking of what awaited them, if anything awaited them at all. The invasion of England had been a fantasy. The war in America was real, and it was going badly.

"Hundreds dead," Louis muttered. His voice was hoarse from the cough that would not leave him. "And for what? A city they could not hold."

Vincent shook his head slowly. "They say d'Estaing[39] ordered the assault against the advice of his own officers. Rushed it. No proper siege, no time to prepare."

"No artillery," Fleur d'Épine said quietly. He looked up at the others. "I heard one of the lieutenants say it. They had naval guns. Ship cannons dragged ashore. Not siege guns. Not like ours."

The words hung in the cold air. Siméon turned them over in his mind, but before he could speak, a voice cut through the darkness.

"On your feet."

Captain Bonnay stood at the edge of the firelight, his breath clouding in the frozen air. He was not a man given to speeches, and the men rose at once, wary and silent. He let them stand a moment, his eyes passing over each face.

"You have heard about Savannah," he said. It was not a question. "Good. You should hear it. Every man here should know what happened, because what happened there is why Auxonne must be ready to go wherever the King needs to send us."

He stepped closer to the fire, and the light carved deep shadows beneath his eyes.

"Nearly six hundred French soldiers killed or wounded on that field. They fought with courage. Admiral d'Estaing bled alongside them, wounded twice and still leading from the front. No one who was there that day lacked for bravery." He paused. "What they lacked was time. What they lacked was a proper siege. And what they lacked," his voice hardened, "was artillery fit for the task."

Bonnay's gaze swept across the young gunners.

"They had naval guns. Cannons built to fire from the decks of ships. They did not bring their artillery to bear long enough to breach walls or

---

[39] **Admiral Charles-Henri-Théodat, comte d'Estaing** (1729 – 1794), commanded French naval forces during the Siege of Savannah, September – October 1779. Wounded twice while personally leading the assault, he was praised for bravery yet criticized for attacking before completing adequate siege preparations. Deteriorating weather threatened his fleet, and standing orders required his return to France, contributing to the decision to launch a premature assault. The failed operation, which resulted in approximately 600 French casualties, influenced subsequent Allied planning, particularly the emphasis on proper artillery preparation at the Siege of Yorktown. Source: *David G. Smith, The Siege of Savannah: A Pivotal Battle in the American Revolution (Columbia: University of South Carolina Press, 2005).*

reduce fortifications. They did not have trained crews who could place a shell through a redoubt window at four hundred yards." He let that settle. "They did not have the Régiment d'Auxonne."

"Savannah proved what this war requires," Bonnay continued. "The men who plan at Versailles are watching. They will see what naval guns could not do, and they will know what must come next. Proper siege artillery. Trained crews. Men who understand how to break a fortification, not merely bombard it." He paused. "When the next expedition sails, and it will sail, it will not fail for want of guns. It will not fail for want of us. Victory will be decided by artillery. By you."

He stopped. For a moment, the only sound was the crackle of burning wood.

"The men who died at Savannah did not die so that we could waver. They died proving what this war demands." His voice dropped, quieter now but no less firm. "So when you reach Auxonne, you will not brood over what failed on the coast. You will train harder than you ever have. Because when the orders come, and they will come, you will be ready."

Bonnay turned and walked back into the darkness without another word.

No one spoke for a long time. The fire hissed and popped.

Finally, Sans Soucy's voice broke the silence, low and steady. "You heard the captain. Get some sleep. We have work to do."

His eyes met Siméon's for a moment in the firelight. Then he turned and disappeared into the dark.

The march resumed at dawn.

The men walked with their heads up, their steps steadier despite the autumn rain. They had failed to invade England. Their countrymen had died at Savannah. But the war was not over.

Siméon marched south with his grandfather's knife in his pocket, his mother's rosary around his neck and Bonnay's words in his ears. The road to Auxonne lay ahead. Beyond it, maybe America.

HISTORICAL NOTE: THE FRANCO-SPANISH ALLIANCE OF 1779

The Treaty of Aranjuez, signed April 12, 1779, brought Spain into the war against Britain and committed both nations to a joint invasion of England. The combined Armada assembled sixty-six ships of the line and four hundred transports, the largest invasion fleet to threaten England since 1588. But the Spanish fleet's delayed departure from Cádiz pushed the rendezvous back two critical months, and disease ravaged French crews waiting at sea. The combined fleet entered the Channel in late July, came within sight of England, and captured one British warship. Contrary winds, fog, and the escape of the British fleet doomed the enterprise. By September, dysentery and typhus had killed an estimated eight thousand men. Admiral d'Orvilliers, who had lost his only son to the sickness, resigned his command. Source: *Sam Willis, The Struggle for Sea Power (W.W. Norton, 2016).*

Back at Auxonne, word came through the barracks, passed from officer to sergeant to the men themselves: the English king had addressed his Parliament. His words, translated and repeated until they became common knowledge, carried a tone the men recognized.

"The designs and attempts of our enemies to invade this kingdom have, by the blessing of Providence, been hitherto frustrated and disappointed."[40]

Frustrated. Disappointed. The English gave Providence credit for what the weather and dysentery had accomplished. No mention of the men left in unmarked graves along the coast. No acknowledgement of the fleet that had sailed. Only relief dressed as piety.

It was Captain Bonnay who gave them the gift, not of coin or privilege, but of leave.

The company assembled in the yard on a late December morning, the cold biting through their coats. Bonnay stood before them, his breath

---

[40] **George III**, "Speech from the Throne," November 25, 1779, Source: *Journals of the House of Commons, vol. 37 (1779), 530.*

clouding in the still air. He did not waste words.

"You have endured a hard year," he said. "The coast took something from all of us. Men we trained with. Men we buried." He let that settle. "The army asks much of you, and it will ask more. But before it does, you deserve time to remember why you serve."

He paused, his gaze moving across the ranks.

"Any man with family within traveling distance has leave until the Feast of the Holy Innocents.[41] If you have family, surprise them. Refresh your soul after what we have all experienced." His voice softened, just slightly. "Not a day later."

A murmur moved through the ranks. Men glanced at one another, disbelief giving way to something like hope.

"Dismissed."

The yard broke into motion. Men clustered together, calculating distances, making plans. Some had family a day's walk away. Others had no one to visit and would remain in barracks. Fleur d'Épine was already shaking his head.

"Offenbach is too far," he said quietly. "Even if I left now, I would arrive with no time to return."

Louis clapped him on the shoulder. "Then you will drink with me. My family is in Lorraine."

Vincent added, "I have you all beat. I would have to walk back to the Channel Coast."

They would stay.

Siméon felt the pull immediately. Rosières-sur-Mance. His father. Colas. Two days by donkey cart, but he had no cart, no donkey. On foot in winter, it would take three days each way. Six days of travel for two days at home. The mathematics were cruel.

Sans Soucy found him an hour later, cleaning tack in the stable.

"Gaugien."

Siméon looked up.

---

[41] **The Feast of the Holy Innocents** is observed on December 28 in the Western Christian liturgical calendar.

"There is a bay mare in the third stall. She is steady and knows the roads." Sans Soucy's voice was flat, as if discussing routine matters. "She will get you to Rosières and back in time."

"Sergeant, I cannot…"

"You can. I have spoken with Captain Bonnay." Sans Soucy turned to go, then paused at the stable door. "I have been to your father's house. I know how far it is. See your family."

He was gone before Siméon could thank him.

The ride north took two days. The mare was sure-footed. Siméon pushed her as fast as the conditions allowed, stopping only to water her and rest. By late afternoon on Christmas Eve, the familiar hills of Franche-Comté rose around him, the vineyards stripped and dormant under a thin crust of snow.

He smelled the woodsmoke before he saw the house.

Colas was in the yard, splitting kindling, his breath rising in white puffs with each swing of the axe. He looked up at the sound of hooves and froze, the axe hanging loose in his grip.

"Siméon?"

"Joyeux Noël, brother."

Colas let the axe fall and crossed the yard in three strides. They embraced hard, Colas pounding his back with a force that drove the breath from his lungs.

"You are here," Colas said, pulling back to look at him. "How are you here?"

"A kind captain who cares for his men. And a sergeant who remembers many things."

Their father appeared in the doorway, drawn by the voices. For a moment he simply stood there, one hand braced against the frame, his face working through surprise into something that might have been joy. Close behind him, their mother came to the door, wiping her hands on her apron, and when she saw Siméon she pressed a hand to her mouth, as if to steady herself. Then she crossed the yard and pulled him into her arms, holding him there a moment longer than custom allowed.

That night they walked together to midnight mass, the four of them side by side on the frozen path to the village church. The bells rang out across the valley as they had every Christmas of Siméon's life. Inside, the candles flickered and the familiar Latin washed over him, unchanged since childhood. He stood between his parents, with Colas at his shoulder. This first Christmas without Grand-père was harder on all of them than they had expected.

The réveillon afterward was simple. Jeanne had prepared what she could: a chicken roasted with herbs from the garden, bread kept warm from the neighbor's oven, wine from their own vines. They ate slowly, talking of small things at first, the state of the vineyard, the winter's harshness, news from the village. Their father listened more than he spoke, while Jeanne watched her sons with the quiet attention of a woman counting blessings she had not dared to expect.

Later, when the fire had burned low and the wine was nearly gone, Colas leaned back in his chair and studied Siméon across the table.

"You look different," he said. "Older."

"It has been a hard year."

Colas nodded slowly. "We heard about the coast. The sickness. Men said thousands died without ever seeing battle."

"It is true."

"And you survived."

"I survived."

Their father rose and placed another log on the fire. The flames caught and climbed, casting long shadows across the room. He did not turn around when he spoke.

"And now? What comes next?"

"I do not know," Siméon said. "There is talk of America. But nothing is certain."

Colas raised his cup. "Then we will drink to the brother who came home for Christmas."

They drank.

Christmas Day passed in the quiet rhythms of the house. Siméon helped Colas with the morning chores, their breath fogging as they fed the animals. The cold was sharp and familiar.

He left at dawn the next morning. Colas walked with him to where the mare was tied, neither of them speaking. The sky was pale and clear, a winter morning that promised hard cold.

"Come back," Colas said.

"I will."

They embraced once more. Siméon mounted and turned the mare south toward Auxonne. At the crest of the first hill, he looked back. Colas was still standing in the yard, one hand raised.

Siméon raised his own hand in return. He rode on.

The men of the *Régiment d'Artillerie d'Auxonne* had returned from the Coast hollowed by sickness and disappointment, but Captain Bonnay's words on that rain-lashed road still hung in the air. Savannah. Failure. Being the answer. A challenge none of them yet knew how to meet.

They drilled. They cleaned their guns. They welcomed new recruits and trained them hard. Wagons were kept serviceable. Equipment lists were checked and rechecked. Nothing was said aloud, but everyone understood they were training to move.

Among the new faces was Alexis Le Bru,[42] a quiet boy from Granges-le-Bourg in the Comté, born the same year as Siméon and raised less than fifty miles from Auxonne. He had enlisted in December, drawn by the same rumors of America that now filled every barracks conversation.

January tightened its grip. Sergeant Le Boeuf drove them harder.

---

[42] **Alexis Le Bru**, born 1761 in Granges-le-Bourg, Franche-Comté; enlisted in December 1779 in the Régiment d'Artillerie d'Auxonne and was assigned to the Compagnie Bonnay de la Rouvrelle; served alongside Siméon Gaugien in the French Expédition Particulière under the command of Jean-Baptiste Donatien de Vimeur, comte de Rochambeau, during the American War of Independence. Source: *Les combattants français de la guerre américaine, 1778 – 1783 (Washington: Imprimerie Nationale, 1905), 355.*

"We are not polishing cannonballs for ceremony," he told them, his breath clouding in the air. "We are preparing for war. A real one."

The squad moved as one machine: Siméon at the sight; Vincent, quieter now, at the loader's position; Louis, his humor turned dark, running powder; Fleur with his sponge and worm; Jean-Baptiste at the vent; Divertissant at the ramrod; Michel at the trail; Pierre from the magazines. They worked in a silence that understood what waited for them across the ocean.

By February, snow lay deep across the parade ground, packed hard by boots and wheels. The Saône froze solid in places, something even Louis Clément said he had never seen in all his years at Auxonne.

By early March, war became real again. Orders were posted.

Deployment. Brest. The march begins in three days.

The yard assembled that afternoon, companies drawn up in the snow. Captain Bonnay stood with his men, silent. Colonel François-Marie d'Aboville stepped forward, frost dusting his coat, his expression unchanged by the cold.

"You will depart for Brest as ordered," he said, his voice carrying easily. "The comte de Rochambeau has been appointed to command the expedition to America. He stood before the King at Versailles and made one request: that Auxonne accompany him. The infantry was already chosen. The ships already assigned. But Rochambeau insisted the expedition could not succeed without trained siege artillery. Without you."

He let his gaze pass once over the ranks.

"The King agreed."

The words settled heavily in the frozen air.

"You have been trained for movement, endurance, and discipline," d'Aboville continued. "Those standards do not change with weather, delay, or uncertainty. They will not change on the road. See to your equipment. See to your teams. Be ready."

He drew himself to full height.

"Pour le Roi. Pour la France."

The formation answered as one. Only then did the colonel turn and leave the yard.

"Bonnay was right," Jean-Baptiste said, grinning. "And the King agreed. Pack up, boys. We're going to America."

They left Auxonne before dawn.

The road west cuts across all of France. Dijon. Angers. The Loire. Rennes. Siméon's life became a map drawn by the army's needs. The guns moved at the pace of oxen and horses, even slower when the thaw turned roads to mire. Every sixth or seventh day brought a little rest, unless swollen rivers or broken wheels stole it first.

When winter loosened its grip, the road turned against them. The thaw came fast, swallowing boots, sinking wheels to their hubs. Men leaned into ropes that cut their hands raw. Horses shuddered, flanks slick with mud. By nightfall, breeches stiffened with salt and grime.

The Loire tested them most. Snowmelt swelled the river, icy and fast. Men waded waist-deep beside the beasts, teeth chattering, water dragging at their clothes. Captain Bonnay rode the bank through each crossing, his voice steady above the roar. Without it, the line might have broken.

At night, they slept where they could; frozen ground at first, then sodden turf as the thaw caught them, lulled by the low murmur of shared endurance. Each morning they scraped dried muck from their coats and stood inspection as steam rose from damp wool. Vincent joked that if mud earned medals, they would all be generals by now. Their laughter, rough and weary, was the last thing that still sounded clean.

By the time they reached Rennes in mid-April, their blue coats were dulled to gray, shoulders sore, spirits stretched thin, but unbroken.

It was early afternoon, and the market square was alive with noise and the smell of fresh bread. While officers arranged provisions and billets, the men were told they would remain in Rennes for two days before continuing to Brest.

Siméon asked permission to go into town. He still had a few sous from his last pay and wanted something fresh to share.

Head down, distracted, he turned a corner near the market and collided hard with someone.

Siméon meets Laure

"*Merde!*" he exclaimed, staggering back.

A basket of herbs and flowers spilled across the stones, blush-pink peonies, wild buttercups, lavender, white spring blossoms scattered like snow. The young woman who had been carrying it bent to gather them, startled but laughing.

"Forgive me," Siméon said, dropping to his knees beside her.

Their eyes met.

She had dark curls and eyes that studied him with open curiosity. Her cheeks were flushed, not with anger but with amusement.

"Well," she said lightly, "if you meant to empty my basket, you might have warned me."

He laughed. "Allow me to apologize properly. I will replace them all."

"They don't need replacing," she said, smiling. "But you may walk with me."

"Siméon Gaugien," he said. "King's artillery."

"Laurence Hudel,"[43] she replied. "But everyone calls me Laure."

"It suits you," he said, before he could stop himself.

She smiled. "I was named after my godmother, Laurence Jacquinot de Rosières."

"Rosières?" Siméon repeated, suddenly still. "Rosières-sur-Mance?"

Laure looked at him in surprise. "Yes. My parents married there. I was born there. Why?"

"That's where I'm from," he said, his heart lifting. "My family has lived there for generations."

She studied him anew, then nodded slowly. "Perhaps our families knew each other."

They gathered the last of the scattered flowers and walked through the side streets near the market, the city moving around them. Their conversation was unhurried, familiar in a way that surprised them both.

"My parents died when I was young," Laure said quietly as they walked. "I was five years old when my father passed, it was then I came to Rennes to live with my cousin. Julien Hudel. He has been good to me."

She paused, studying him more closely. "You are from Rosières? That seems impossible."

"Why impossible?" Siméon asked.

"It is so far away. I have never met anyone from there. I remember almost nothing of the village itself."

For a moment, Siméon was silent. The name Hudel did not surprise him. Of course he knew it. Noël Hudel was a few years older than he was, closer in age to his brother Colas.

"I don't know him well," Siméon said at last, "but my brother does. They grew up closer together. Noël is known at church. We were all saddened when your mother passed. He did what he could for her. Everyone knew that."

---

[43] **Laurence Hudel**, (referred to as Laure in this book); born April 12, 1761, in Rosières-sur-Mance, Haute-Saône, France, daughter of Noël Hudel (1718 – 1766) and Élisabeth Richard (1719 – 1775); married Siméon Gaugien on January 29, 1788, in Rosières-sur-Mance; emigrated June 5, 1832, to Jefferson County, New York, settling in the French community of Rosiere in the town of Cape Vincent; died there August 2, 1847. Sources: *Registres paroissiaux et d'état civil, Rosières-sur-Mance, Archives départementales de la Haute-Saône; and civil records, Jefferson County, New York.*

Laure lowered her eyes, then nodded. "Thank you for telling me," she said quietly. "I received word that she had passed, but little more."

He smiled then, the moment easing between them. "It's not impossible," he said. "Just a very long road that has brought us to the same corner."

After a pause, Laure continued, her voice thoughtful. "The cousin who took me in, Julien Hudel, runs a small linen trade. He has been very kind to me. The woman who sells beside us in the market knows the old remedies, which flowers ease a headache, which roots settle a stomach. She took me under her wing. I've begun learning which plants are edible, and which ones can truly help people."

"That's a good thing," Siméon said with genuine warmth. "We have a gifted herbalist in Rosières, Madame Lemaire. She helped my father when he injured his knee badly. She knows every plant and remedy." He smiled. "She is fierce about following her instructions, but she truly knows her craft."

Laure's eyes brightened. "Perhaps she knew my parents, or my godmother."

"I wouldn't be surprised," Siméon said. "It's a small village. Everyone's lives are woven together."

By the time they parted, they had agreed to meet again.

When Siméon returned to the men, Louis noticed immediately.

"Well," he said, grinning, "where's the bread?"

Vincent circled him slowly. "Something's happened."

Fleur joined in, nodding gravely. "Very serious. I should come next time. Make sure you find the bakery."

"Please don't," Siméon said, helplessly smiling.

The next afternoon, Siméon asked Sans Soucy if he might go into town again. The sergeant studied him, then shrugged.

"Be back before dark."

Siméon presented himself at Julien Hudel's door within the hour. Julien received him with folded arms and the wary look of a man who had seen too many soldiers pass through Rennes.

"Your family?"

"Vineyard workers in Franche-Comté, *Monsieur*."

Julien studied him. "Faith and family are important to you?"

"Yes, *Monsieur*. They are."

"And yet you are a soldier. Soldiers leave. Many do not return." Julien's voice was flat, without accusation. "What are your intentions toward my charge?"

Julien was silent for a long moment. Then he unfolded his arms.

"She has had enough loss in her life. Do not add to it."

"I will not, monsieur."

When Laure walked him to the door afterward, she was quiet for a moment. Then she smiled. "He didn't warn me against you."

"From my guardian. It is practically a blessing."

On the afternoon before departure, Siméon found her again near the market as stalls were closing. They walked together along the quieter lanes, the air warm with late spring.

Laure paused at a stall being packed away and chose a small white blossom. She wrapped it in her handkerchief and slipped it into the lining of his jacket.

"For the road," she said.

He covered her hand for a moment. When they reached her door, neither spoke.

At last, Siméon bowed and kissed her hand, as custom allowed. Laure inclined her head and stepped back into the doorway.

He did not look back.

At dawn, the regiment left Rennes. Every step west carried Laure's face with him, steady as the road beneath his boots.

Fields flushed green beneath a softer sky, lambs calling from distant meadows. Villages were dressed for Easter, ribbons on doors, bells ringing as the column passed. Children waved. Women paused in doorways. The soldiers returned the gestures briefly before the road narrowed and the weight of their guns pulled them onward.

They reached Carhaix on the evening of April twenty-second, the old garrison town set deep in the Breton interior where roads converged before the final push to the coast. Stone barracks lined one edge of the town, the Casernes de Carhaix, long accustomed to housing troops moving east or west as the King required.

"Carhaix," Louis said, glancing at the worn buildings.

Vincent shook his head. "Carhaix-Plouguer," he corrected quietly. "That's what people here call it. Always have."

The halt was short but welcome. Stores were refreshed, harness mended, hooves tended.

On Easter morning, April 23rd, the entire regiment assembled and marched not for the road, but for Mass. They filled the Église de Saint-Trémeur, a great Gothic structure of stone and shadow, built centuries before, its height and arches so vast that to men fresh from the road it might have passed for a cathedral. Yet its purpose was local and familiar, a parish church serving farmers, tradesmen, and soldiers alike.

Blue coats pressed among wool and linen. Candles flickered beneath ribbed vaults darkened by generations of smoke. The Mass was spoken in Latin, the responses murmured as one. Resurrection. Endurance. Promise after suffering.

Siméon stood with his head bowed, thinking of the long road already behind him and the longer one still ahead. Around him, all good Catholic boys, every man of Auxonne, crossed himself with practiced ease.

They left Carhaix the next morning.

Brest was a city turned fortress. Soldiers and sailors pressed shoulder to shoulder. Wagons creaked beneath powder casks. Cannonballs lay stacked along the quays, dull iron glinting in the pale light. The harbor itself churned with motion: ships crowded the anchorage, barges ferried supplies, and the air was thick with shouted orders in Breton, French, and naval slang.

As they arrived, whispers ran through the camps. First division. Second division. Who would sail. Who would wait.

"How can there not be enough ships?" Louis asked one night, his voice rough after overhearing an officer's conversation.

"You getting sick?" Siméon asked, ignoring the question.

Louis shook his head. "Everyone's coughing."

"Who goes and who stays?" Vincent muttered. "If it's by seniority, we're lost. If it's by usefulness…" His gaze drifted to the cannon lined like iron sentinels.

Louis snorted. "Infantry can march without guns. But without us? An army without artillery is no army at all."

Siméon said little. If they were left behind, Laure was closer. But what would that mean? To miss the fight. To wait in obscurity while others sailed into history.

Word moved through the battery like fire. The Order of Battle was fixed. Rochambeau himself had chosen. Four infantry regiments would sail first: Soissonnais, Saintonge, Bourbonnais, Royal Deux-Ponts. Lauzun's Legion would follow without their horses.

And Auxonne.

The siege guns would go. The mortars. The seasoned gunners.

Some men cheered. Others only nodded. The veterans of the Channel coast remained quiet. They had heard promises before.

Louis smiled at last, genuine relief breaking through the pallor that had settled into his cheeks. "We're going," he said. "Finally."

Siméon clasped his shoulder and felt how thin it had become beneath the coat. The thought flickered, then faded. Everyone had lost weight in the Brest mud. It meant nothing.

Or so he told himself.

Vincent caught Siméon's eye and gave a small nod.

Not celebration. Recognition.

Chapter Nine:
The Crossing

May – August 1780

The intended date of departure proved impossible to pin down, since nothing at Brest ever moved as neatly as a number written in a ledger. Confusion grew as the embarkation unfolded in uneven stages. Some warships and a handful of transports had already worked their way into the roadstead, the wide anchorage just offshore where the fleet waited, but most of the army still crowded the quays: carts, animals, crates, and weary officers trying to impose order on the impossible.

For Siméon and the gunners of the Auxonne regiment, the long wait was over. Their cannon rolled toward the water's edge behind an oxen team, the wheels clattering over wet stone. Captain Bonnay strode beside the team with his tablet tucked under one arm, calling out orders above the din.

The air shook with noise. Sails snapped in the wind. Crates thudded into place. Gulls wheeled overhead.

Rumors churned through the ranks. Some men said Admiral de Ternay[44] and the lead ships had already tried to sail and had been forced back by contrary winds. One morning word ran down the quay that the transport *Comtesse de Noailles* had struck the seventy-four-gun *Conquérant*. Men rushed in time to see the injured vessel creeping toward harbor, her bowsprit splintered and her carved figurehead broken away. Baron von Closen, one of Rochambeau's aides, would later joke that only the Countess's face had been lost. Her commander offered the shipwrights fifteen *louis*, a gold reward worth more than a year of a craftsman's wages, if they could restore her by the next day. It seemed impossible. Yet by nightfall the battered, headless ship had been hauled back into line.

Amid the turmoil, Bonnay marched at the head of the column, as they made their way to their ship, the *flûte Le Pluvier*. He stopped often to check a manifest or confer with a harried naval officer about the sequence of loading. All around them, barrels of powder, shot, food, wine, tools, and frightened animals swung into the air on straining ropes while sailors shouted orders that vanished in the wind.

Louis grinned. "Let us hope we stay afloat. Have you seen how much they loaded onto this ship?"

Siméon groaned. "Always the realist. Enjoy the moment."

Vincent laughed. "We will be fine. I have seen ships ride lower in the water than this." With sudden mischief he grabbed Fleur's hat and sprinted for the ladder. "Come on, *tortues* (turtles)!"

They boarded and descended below, found their hammocks, and tucked away what little they carried. Two men shared each hammock, taking turns while the other stretched across bare planks. The air already held the weight of tar, damp wool, penned livestock, and the unmistakable smell of the ship's dogs.

---

[44] **Charles-Henri d'Arsac de Ternay** held the rank of Chef d'escadre, equivalent to Rear Admiral in English naval terminology, though history most often refers to him simply as Admiral de Ternay, a convention followed here. A veteran naval officer with decades of service, he commanded the squadron that transported Rochambeau's expeditionary force across the Atlantic to Newport in 1780. The seventy-day voyage through storms, disease, and the constant threat of British interception demanded exceptional seamanship; de Ternay's steady command delivered the army safely, a feat that made everything that followed possible. Once at Newport, he maintained vigilant watch over his fleet while coordinating closely with Rochambeau on the defense of the French position. Sources: *Maurice Linjer de La Barbée, Le chevalier de Ternay: Vie de Charles Henry Louis d'Arsac de Ternay, chef d'escadre des armées navales, 1723 – 1780*, 2 vols. (Grenoble: Éditions des 4 Seigneurs, 1972); *Lee Kennett, The French Forces in America, 1780 – 1783* (Westport, CT: Greenwood Press, 1977).

Fleur d'Épine could not stand still, his excitement tumbling out of his mouth in rapid observations. "Did you see the sails? They could swallow the sky. And how many sailors are on the masts? I think we will be leaving soon. Is there more to load? Let's get back on deck and watch!"

They were all excited and a little afraid; they had seen the ocean from Channel beaches the year before, but none, except Vincent, had ever set foot on a ship bound for open water. The memory of that summer, and the thousands who had died, hung unspoken between them.

The decision to sail had not been made lightly. Rochambeau knew that only part of the force could be carried with the ships available. Men, artillery, and supplies intended for a second division would wait behind in France, not for want of readiness, but for lack of transport. Yet the season, the winds, and the threat of the British fleet left little room for delay. To remain concentrated at Brest risked losing the moment altogether. If anything had been learned it was that waiting could have severe consequences. He chose to move with what transport he had. The second division, everyone believed, would sail soon after.

At last, on May 2, 1780, the final crates were stowed and the gangplanks hauled aboard *Le Pluvier*. Ropes tightened, masts groaned, and the wind filled her sails. As the anchors rose, the heavy-laden *flûte* turned west to join the main body of the fleet. Signal flags climbed the mizzen of the flagship, the *Duc de Bourgogne*.

Ahead lay the great ships of the line, with the transports stretching out behind them. Using a narrow passage off the coast, the expedition slipped toward open water, though where it was bound the men could only guess. The *Duc de Bourgogne* led the formation, with the *Neptune* and the *Conquérant* close astern. Siméon, Vincent, Louis, and Fleur d'Épine watched from the rail as the cliffs of Brittany faded into a pale haze.

"Here we go, boys! Off to victory!" Fleur shouted into the wind.

Louis smiled faintly. "We have to get there first."

The convoy was striking to behold. Seven ships of the line formed its armored core, adding the *Provence, Jason, Zélé, and Ardent,* supported by frigates, smaller escort vessels, and a long train of transports carrying the army. Admiral de Ternay directed the formation at sea, while General

Rochambeau moved among the transports, as France once more committed men, ships, and hope to the American cause.[45]

The Crossing

De Ternay and Rochambeau sailed with the knowledge that Spain's war effort, now in its second year, was forcing Britain to defend on multiple fronts. The siege of Gibraltar consumed British ships and soldiers. Admiral Córdova's fleet threatened the Atlantic sea lanes. Gálvez pressed the Gulf Coast. Every British vessel guarding the Rock or chasing Spanish convoys was one fewer hunting the French crossing. The alliance that had failed so catastrophically in the Channel in 1779 was now, at a distance, doing what it had always promised: stretching British resources until they frayed.

The soldiers on the transports knew none of this. They knew only the rhythm of the waves, the creak of the hull, and the uncertainty of

[45]**The Fleet** composition of Rochambeau's expeditionary army and the enumeration of Admiral Charles-Henri-Louis d'Arsac, chevalier de Ternay's fleet at the time of departure from Brest in May 1780, including the ships of the line Duc de Bourgogne, Neptune, Conquérant, Provence, Jason, Zélé, and Ardent, the British vessel captured in the Channel in August 1779 and then sailing under French colors, together with supporting warships and transports. Source: *Marins et soldats français en Amérique, vol. I, Armée de Rochambeau, 1780 (Paris, 1903)*.

what awaited them across the sea. For the young men of Auxonne, the horizon looked like the edge of the world.

The next morning, as the convoy cleared the Raz de Sein, the treacherous strait marking Brittany's last reach into the Atlantic, a cutter from the rear-guard caught up with the flagship. Word spread quickly through the transports: two young officers, the Berthier brothers, had chased down the fleet, appearing aboard the *Duc de Bourgogne* in canvas jackets and sailor's breeches. They carried letters of authorization from the prince de Montbarey himself, begging for any berth at all. They would serve as common matelots if it meant reaching America.

But there was no room. Not on the flagship, not on any vessel in the convoy. The Admiral de Ternay sent them back aboard *La Bellone*, which turned for France that evening carrying dispatches.[46]

Below deck, twenty-two men squeezed into a chamber barely fifteen feet long, twelve wide, and low enough to force most to stoop. Soldiers muttered. Dogs barked. Every breath carried the close, humid press of men packed too tightly together.

Fleur tried to grin. "A tarry little tub. And this is only the first day aboard."

Of them all, only Vincent moved easily among the ropes and rigging, explaining the ship's movements to his friends, laughing when they gripped the rail at every roll.

Then the wind shifted. The fair breeze that carried them out of Brest Roads lasted less than a week. By May 9th, as they fought their way past Cape Ortegal on the treacherous Spanish coast, the wind turned violent. By four o'clock, it had become a real tempest.

The Bay of Biscay rose in a chaos of water and wind. Ships pitched and groaned, timbers crying out under the strain. The storm was not a passing squall but a days-long siege.

---

[46] **Louis-Alexandre Berthier and Charles-Louis-Jean Berthier** reached the fleet on May 3, 1780. Rochambeau wrote that same day to the comte de Montbarey: "They joined us in canvas jackets and breeches, offering to sail with us as sailors. The chevalier de Ternay could not assign them a place on his ship or on any of his fleet. The poor young men are interesting and desperate, but the chevalier de Ternay truly does not know where to put them." Undeterred, Louis-Alexandre Berthier made his own way to America via the West Indies, arriving at Newport on September 30, 1780. In January 1781 he was assigned to Rochambeau's staff, where he produced more than one hundred detailed campaign maps. He later became Napoléon Bonaparte's chief of staff and a Marshal of the Empire. Source: *Noailles, Marins et soldats français en Amérique (Paris, 1903)*.

On *Le Pluvier*, the young artillerymen, who had never imagined such fury, clung to whatever was fixed, their earlier excitement replaced by a cold, enduring fear. The sailors moved with a sharpened urgency that told them everything they needed to know. It seemed like almost everyone on the ship was seasick. Even the cooks were not serving meals.

The true scale of the danger became clear when word spread through the convulsing ship: the *Provence*, a mighty ship of the line, had lost her foretop mast. The damage was so severe her captain prepared to leave the squadron, a desperate move in an enemy-patrolled ocean. Only the frantic work of carpenters managed a temporary repair in the punishing gale and kept the *Provence* with the fleet.

The storms gave way to a constant, steady breath from the north and northeast, the famed trade winds. The convoy surged forward, the ships at last able to stretch their sails. On their best days, they covered forty-six leagues, the ocean hissing along the hulls.

Yet, for all their speed, progress was a game of hurry-up-and-wait. The warships, capable of greater speed, were constantly reefing their sails and "laying by" for the laggards of the convoy, the tubby transports and store-ships that wallowed in their wake. The daily report of leagues made was always followed by the sight of the fleet scattered across the horizon, slowly rallying around the flagship.

The creak of timbers and the slow, ceaseless roll of the deck became background noise, no longer remarked upon, only endured. In the hold, frustration thickened the air. Health became a quiet, constant concern. Louis coughed often into his sleeve, dismissing it as the foul air, though the sound lingered longer than it should have.

The one topic that never lost its energy was their destination. The fleet was driving relentlessly south, not west, and with each drop in latitude, the rumors grew more specific. The hope for a direct run to New England was fading, replaced by theories of Caribbean landfalls.

"Twenty-nine degrees? We are as far south as the Canaries!" Fleur d'Épine announced, having befriended a sailor who understood the navigator's charts. "They are taking us to the Indies, I tell you. Jamaica, or Saint-Domingue.

"Why would we go there?" Louis asked curiously. "Do they hate the British too?"

"To join the Spanish," Vincent suggested, leaning against the rail. "Or to sack a British sugar island. There's more gold in sugar than in all of Washington's army."

Siméon listened, letting their theories spin themselves out. He already knew better. Earlier that morning, he had caught a snatch of conversation between Captain Bonnay and another officer; calm, assured, and entirely at odds with the chatter on deck. Their southern plunge was no voyage to the Indies at all, but a deliberate feint, a great looping arc meant to slip past the British patrols guarding the direct northern passage to New England.

He kept this to himself. Let the others guess; he had no intention of betraying what he was never meant to hear.

The tension broke on May 28th. At noon, signal flags snapped up the mizzen of the *Duc de Bourgogne*. The order was relayed from ship to ship, a quiet ripple of confirmation that became a roar of understanding. The helm was put over, and the entire convoy, as if on a single, invisible pivot, began its long-awaited turn to the west.

A collective exhale seemed to pass through *Le Pluvier*.

"There," Siméon said, pointing at the wake now curling directly behind them. "Now we are going to America."

Vincent clapped him on the shoulder, grinning. "I knew it all along."

"You did not," Fleur laughed, the relief clear on his face. "You bet me your wine ration for a week we were bound for the Caribbean!"

"Just keeping up your spirits, Fleur, my boy!" Vincent said without missing a beat.

Siméon leaned against the rail. "Wherever we are bound, I pray the sea will deliver us there."

With the new course set, a renewed sense of purpose settled over the fleet. When the winds cooperated, the trade winds filled their sails and carried them westward with steady speed. The sea settled into a deep blue rhythm, the days marked by the harsh noon sun and the progress logged by the pilots. The men, convinced at last that America lay ahead, now faced the vast, empty expanse of the Atlantic with a single goal: to cross it.

The turn west did not bring immediate progress. The first days of June were marked by light, fickle winds that slowed their advance to a crawl. The sea itself changed, becoming carpeted with long trails of golden-brown seaweed drifting in vast mats. The sailors called it *raisin de mer* (sea grapes) for the small bladders that kept it afloat. The heat intensified as the sun climbed higher each day, until it stood almost directly overhead at noon.

Across the fleet, sickness spread. The *Conquérant*, serving as the hospital ship, had taken on sixty men from ships across the convoy, a floating infirmary where the sounds of coughing and delirium drifted through the gun decks. Siméon tried not to think about it. Louis's cough was nothing. Just the close quarters.

Le Pluvier was an old ship, broad of beam, slow to turn, but strong in her bones and tempered by years at sea, her timbers hardened by salt and time. There was nothing elegant about her, yet her crew spoke of her with a rough affection. She rode low in the water, burdened with guns, wagons, and powder, but she was steady and sure. Siméon thought better an old ship with scars than a new one untested by the sea.

Life aboard was a test of endurance. Below decks the problems multiplied quietly. Hammocks swung above barrels of biscuit already softening with weevils, and casks of water turned sour long before mid-voyage. In the heat trapped between decks, men weakened quickly, and sickness moved through the close-packed ranks with an ease that no drill could counter.

They scrubbed the decks with vinegar and seawater, aired their bedding in the sun, and burned powder in small pans to sweeten the air. The memory of the previous summer was still fresh. That lesson had been learned in blood.

This time, the precautions were constant and enforced. Under d'Aboville's command, cleanliness became discipline, and discipline saved lives. Across the entire convoy, fewer than sixty men were lost before landfall, a grim tally, yet an astonishing one by eighteenth-century measure.

Still, the living suffered. Scurvy haunted many, and foul water carried fevers through the holds. Even with fewer dead than on most crossings, the shadow of illness remained among them nonetheless, silent and patient in the dark.

When a man died, there was no ceremony. The body was sewn into canvas, weighted with a round shot, and slid over the side at night with a few prayers from the ship's Chaplain. The splash was lost almost at once to the dark sea. Few spoke of it afterward. "Better to let the sea keep them," Sans Soucy murmured when Vincent whispered about a boy from Dijon who had died two hammocks over. "We have no room for ghosts."

Siméon nodded but prayed quietly for each one, tracing the sign of the cross in private.

All of them fell ill at one time or another. Even Captain Bonnay was not spared. For seven days he stayed in his small cabin, weakened by fever brought on by heat and confinement below decks. Men lowered their voices when they passed his cabin. A sick officer meant uncertainty, and Bonnay was the one who held the company together. When he finally emerged, thinner but upright, a quiet cheer moved through the gun deck. If the captain could outlast the crossing, then so could they.

Louis's cough had begun in the later days on the Channel Coast, but now, in the ship's stifling belly, it deepened. At first they teased him, saying his bark could drown out the creaking hull.

"It is nothing," Louis insisted between fits. "Just the sea air." By the fourth week, his laugh had thinned to a rasp. He ate little, and the lamplight revealed pale hollows beneath his eyes.

"You should see the medic," Fleur d'Épine urged one night.

"They will toss me in the hold," Louis muttered. "Or feed me their vinegar brew and call me cured."

He went anyway. The surgeon's mate gave him a *flasque* of fortified wine and a spoonful of syrup that smelled of pitch and camphor, muttering that his lungs were turning to water. It did little good. The cough grew thick and wet. None of them knew the word *pneumonie*, but they recognized its grip.

Sans Soucy watched him in the dark one night as the ship rolled under the northern stars. "You are not dying," he said quietly, more a promise than a comfort. "Not yet. Tell me if the pain reaches your back."

Louis nodded once. "I will."

After that, the cough became part of their world. It was steady, human, and inescapable.

The days aboard *Le Pluvier* fell into a pattern so fixed it no longer required notice.

One afternoon, in a rare patch of shade on the foredeck, a small circle of soldiers formed as a scrap of worn sailcloth was spread as a gaming board. The stakes were not coin, but the last shreds of a tobacco twist, broken into precious nubs.

"Your roll, Breton," Fleur d'Épine said, his sharp eyes fixed on Vincent.

Vincent cupped the bone dice and blew on them for mock luck. They clattered onto the canvas. A four and a two.

"Ha!" Fleur leaned forward, grinning. "You see that? The four landed on its edge and tipped. That's a five, not a four."

"The deck is moving, you fool," Vincent shot back, more amused than angry. "The dice move with it. That's a four."

"A moving deck is a cheat's best friend," Fleur insisted, tapping the disputed die.

The argument was edging toward a quarrel when a familiar voice cut through the circle.

"A problem with geometry?"

Sergeant Sans Soucy stood at the edge of the men, no longer an observer but an arbiter. The soldiers straightened. His attention was on the dice, not on them.

Fleur held up the die. "It tipped, Sergeant. Four or five?"

Sans Soucy turned the bone cube slowly in his fingers. "The pips are shallow. The center of mass is unstable on a rolling deck." He set it on the sailcloth and nudged the cloth with his boot, mimicking the ship's roll. The die rocked, then settled on four. "Under these conditions, the original call stands. Chance favors the four."

He handed it back to Vincent. "Continue."

Relieved laughter rippled through the circle. The verdict was the real entertainment. The tobacco was forgotten.

As the days stretched on, life aboard *Le Pluvier* shrank to such small contests and comforts carefully rationed. Stories of home wore thin. Sour wine followed water already gone bad. At night the ship rolled gently under the stars, and Siméon and Fleur traced constellations in chalk on the deck, pretending they were astronomers instead of soldiers.

Through it all, the small circle of friends, *Le Trio Infernal* and its Thornflower, remained bound together. They shared unspoiled fruit, a dry scrap of cloth, a whispered joke in the dark.

The monotony was broken on June 12th when their frigates captured a small English cod-fisher. From its crew came welcome news: the British ship *Defiance* had been wrecked, and Charles Town[47], that city whose fate had haunted every council and rumor since Brest, still held against siege. A cheer went up across the deck. Perhaps they would arrive in time after all.

The hope lasted six days.

"Unknown sails to leeward!" The call rang out on June 18. The admiral dispatched *Neptune* and *Éveillé* to investigate. By four o'clock the frigates had closed the distance and returned escorting a captured British brig, newly departed from Charles Town.

This time the news was current and grim. The city had surrendered on May 12, more than a month earlier. With it fell nearly the entire Southern Continental Army, thousands forced to lay down their arms in the greatest American defeat of the war. The cod-fisher's news had been wrong, or weeks out of date. It no longer mattered.

"Settle your bets, lads," someone muttered. No one smiled.

A strange quiet settled over *Le Pluvier*. Some cursed softly. *Le Trio Infernal* stared at the wake curling past the hull, as if the sea itself had shifted beneath them.

---

[47] **Charles Town**, the colonial name of the city in South Carolina, was officially renamed Charleston in 1783 following the American Revolutionary War.

"Five thousand men," Vincent said at last. "Prisoners. The whole Southern army."

Louis leaned on the rail. "So who are we reinforcing now?"

Siméon hesitated. "Washington still has his army in the North. The war isn't over."

"No," Vincent said. "But it's a different war now."

No one argued.

That resolve was tested on June 20. A new squadron appeared. This was no merchantman. The signal from *Neptune* confirmed a powerful British force, ships of the line with a frigate in support.

The drum beat to quarters. Men rushed to their posts. Siméon and the gunners stood by their pieces, the air thick with slow-match.[48] Across the water the French line shifted, placing itself between the convoy and the enemy. Signal flags climbed the rigging of *Duc de Bourgogne*. Then the French hoisted the English flag, a ruse to draw the enemy closer.

It worked.

Cannon fire opened at long range, a deep boom that shuddered through the timbers. Pale flashes winked across the horizon as the two lines felt for each other in the swell. One English ship pressed forward, but French vessels surged to block her and forced her back.

From *Le Pluvier*, the soldiers watched, hearing the thin whine of shot passing high overhead. The engagement remained cautious. Admiral de Ternay held the line, protecting the convoy rather than seeking a decisive battle. When *Neptune* edged forward, eager to close, she was signaled back.

After a quarter hour, the English withdrew into the dusk. Relief washed through the ship, tempered by frustration at having stood so close to the fight without joining it.

By morning only scattered enemy frigates remained in sight before turning north. Later the men learned they had faced the squadron of

---

[48] **Slow match** was a slow-burning cord, typically treated with saltpeter, used by artillerymen to ignite gunpowder charges. Kept smoldering while at quarters, it allowed cannon crews to fire quickly when action commenced.

Captain William Cornwallis[49], returning to England from the West Indies.

Only when the French line resumed its course did the murmurs return, low and uncertain. "The Admiral did right," some said. "He spared the convoy."

Others muttered that the English should have been sunk outright.

The convoy resumed its course.

In the days that followed, heavy fog closed around the ships. Courses were changed again and again to avoid unseen shoals or enemy sails. Word passed quietly that a council of war had met. The fleet would not sail for Boston after all. Newport had been chosen instead, guided by winds, tides, and danger.

Siméon's thoughts drifted far from the journey ahead. He saw instead Laure Hudel's hand pressing a folded blossom into his palm, her kind eyes and her smile. The memory steadied him more surely than the deck beneath his feet.

<hr>

When storms came they brought howling, sky-shattering tempests that rocked the convoy and snapped spars like kindling. Cannons were lashed down, men tied their hammocks together, and even the heaviest equipment was secured against the bulkheads. Lightning flashed over the mountainous black water, illuminating faces pale with nausea or fear. On one terrible night, Siméon and the rest of his eight-man gun team fought to anchor a cannon that had broken loose. Shoulders met iron, ropes cut into bleeding palms, and the air filled with the roar of wind and waves. A few men from other crews cowered in the hold, frozen by terror. Siméon spent the night repeating the Our Father and praying silently to see the next dawn.

He held tightly to the flower she had given him, now pressed flat between the pages of the small volume of Voltaire that Fleur d'Épine had

---

[49] **Captain William Cornwallis** (1744 – 1819), younger brother of General Charles Cornwallis, commanded a returning squadron consisting of two seventy-four-gun ships of the line, Lion and Hector; two sixty-four-gun ships, including Ruby; one fifty-gun ship; and the frigate Niger, totaling six vessels after operations in the West Indies. His encounter with the French convoy is noted in Rochambeau's correspondence to the prince de Montbarey, June 23 – July 12, 1780, Source: *Benjamin L. Huggins, ed., The Papers of George Washington, Revolutionary War Series, vol. 27 (Charlottesville: University of Virginia Press, 2019), 53n4.*

gifted him before Grand-père's funeral. Around his neck hung the rosary beads from his mother, and in his pocket rested the knife his grandfather had carried for decades.

What followed was a quieter, crueler torment. On the first, the pilots announced they were in the latitude of the Chesapeake. A cheer went up, only to die as the leadsmen hauled their lines, shouting, "No bottom!" Currents and faulty longitudes had deceived them. The land was a phantom. The only certainty was death, as another scurvy-ridden soldier was slid through a gunport into the deep.

Two more days passed like this. "No bottom!" became a grim refrain that chipped steadily at hope. The voyage was already long. The sick were everywhere. Frustration moved through the ranks.

Then, on the fourth of July, the mood aboard *Le Pluvier* shifted on a knife's edge. The *sondeur* cried out, *"À la marque de vingt-deux!"* Twenty-two fathoms. The news raced through the decks. America was at last beneath their feet. A ragged cheer rose.

Signals to prepare for anchorage climbed the rigging of *Duc de Bourgogne*. Soldiers rushed the rails, straining to glimpse the coastline through the failing light. The end felt close enough to touch.

Then voices cut through the haze.

"Sails!"

The light was nearly gone. No one could tell friend from foe.

Orders snapped across the convoy. To the soldiers' disbelief, the great ships tacked away from the land. Frigates hoisted warning signals. An unknown fleet was near. The wind, as if sharing their dismay, fell to nothing, leaving the ships drifting helplessly in the dark.

Le Pluvier's timbers shuddered with each small swell. Men listened to the night, convinced English ships were sliding among them.

"He manoeuvres like a coward," a sailor muttered. "We should have closed to see their strength."

Lights flickered across the water. Voices carried through the mist. A warning gun boomed, sending fear rippling deck to deck.

"Are they among us?" Vincent whispered.

Captain Bonnay stood at the rail, coat drawn tight against the damp. "Pray the wind returns," he said quietly.

The fleet hung in stillness for hours. Every sound sharpened. Men imagined ladders scraping hulls, orders shouted just beyond sight. Even officers spoke in low voices, unwilling to break the fragile quiet.

Dawn finally revealed the truth. The unknown sails belonged not to ships of the line, but to British transports returning from Charles Town, guarded by only two frigates, carrying thousands north toward New York.

With the first breath of wind, the French gave chase, but the transports ran before it and soon slipped beyond reach.

"What a pity," the sailor grumbled. "We might have taken the lot."

The moment vanished as quickly as it had come. It cost them a night of terror and a day's progress. As the convoy turned north once more, word passed that one transport, *l'Isle de France*, had been lost in the fog, three hundred and fifty men of the Bourbonnais regiment gone with her.

It was a cold reminder of how narrow their margin had become.

At last, on the evening of July 11, 1780, the coast of America rose again through the fog. Before dawn they had raised anchor, only to drop it again when the mist thickened into a white wall. For hours they waited while bells rang at intervals, each sound swallowed by the damp air. Sea and sky fused into a single gray curtain through which *Le Pluvier* crept blind.

At eight the fog thinned. Slowly, faint shapes emerged. Sand. Rocks. The rise of a distant headland. When it parted for a moment and revealed the gentle curve of a bay, a ripple of relief passed along the deck. The officers had judged correctly. They were approaching Rhode Island. After nearly ten weeks at sea, battered by storms, slowed by shifting winds, and worn down by the long route, the men braced themselves for landfall.

Then a shout rose from the bow.

Two flags snapped faintly in the breeze, each planted on a different stretch of shoreline just visible through the haze. Both were French.

"That is Lafayette," Bonnay said, his voice low but certain. "He kept his word to Washington. It seems the English are gone, for now. There will be a second signal tomorrow, then we will be more certain."

A quiet ripple moved through the ranks. The thought that the British might no longer hold the island felt like salvation.

With pilots from Newport guiding them through the narrow channels, the transports crept forward. The one who climbed aboard *Le Pluvier* was a stout man who declared himself a friend to everybody, "neither royalist nor continental." With a calm that bordered on indifference, he called for a bottle of rum and began barking orders, guiding the weathered *flûte* as if it were a Sunday skiff.[50]

The fog opened and closed again like a giant hand. When it finally parted at midday, Newport lay before them, its harbor sheltered and calm beneath a sky turning slowly to gold. But the distance was still too great and the channels too complex. As dusk fell, the order came to anchor for the night, the town's lights a taunting promise across the water.

There was no cheer, only a long breath drawn and held. The voyage had cost them more than any of them cared to admit. Scurvy had swept the decks relentlessly. Swollen gums bled at the lightest touch. Limbs stiffened. Men who had crossed oceans before could no longer stand without help. Between six and seven hundred soldiers, and nearly a thousand sailors, were on the sick lists.

Siméon felt it himself. His legs trembled as he gripped the railing. His mouth tasted of iron.

"We are here," Vincent said quietly.

"If the time at sea were any longer," Siméon muttered with bleak honesty, "it would have finished me."

Fleur wiped sweat from his brow. "At least the earth does not sway. I have prayed to feel solid ground again."

Louis, also pale and weak, leaned just far enough to peer at the shore. For the first time in days, a spark lit his eyes.

---

[50] **Claude Blanchard** recorded a similar encounter aboard the *Conquérant*, where a pilot from Martha's Vineyard described himself as "neither a royalist nor insurgent, but a friend to everybody." Source: *The Journal of Claude Blanchard, Commissary of the French Auxiliary Army Sent to the United States During the American Revolution, 1780 – 1783, trans. William Duane, ed. Thomas Balch (Albany: J. Munsell, 1876), 39.*

"Land," he whispered. "I swear I can smell it."

That evening they anchored at last.

Morning brought an even thicker fog, a damp shroud that muffled every sound and clung to wool and skin. Out of this haze appeared small boats with silent rowers. Fresh local pilots climbed aboard, men who knew the hidden shoals and narrow channels of Narragansett Bay. With their guidance, *Le Pluvier* moved forward, cautious and slow, her weathered timbers straining toward land as if eager to end the voyage.

Five hours before sunset, the fog opened like a curtain. Newport lay before them.

Houses rose close together along the slope above the wharves. The scars of British occupation were visible even from the water. Pilings stood charred and uneven, docks lay half ruined, and several stores sat deserted. They anchored, the routine of the sea finally stilled. Now, the men could only wait for nightfall.

Then, just as Captain Bonnay had said, the second signal came. As night descended, the citizens of Newport illuminated their houses. One by one, then all at once, windows blazed golden along the hillside. Lanterns shone in the narrow lanes until the whole town seemed to shimmer against the dark, a silent, brilliant confirmation of their welcome. The promise of the flags was now a spectacle of light. A final, collective sigh of relief passed through the soldiers on deck. The long voyage was over, but no ship weighed anchor, and no man slept deeply that night.

The next morning, the French returned the gesture with a thirteen-gun salute, a formal acknowledgment of friendship and respect, answered from the shore by signal guns along the harbor.

They had crossed an ocean. They had reached America. And the war waited, close enough now to be felt.

The men of the Régiment d'Auxonne had half expected a hero's welcome. Instead, once daylight returned and the formal signals faded, a guarded stillness lingered over the town. The inhabitants showed neither the satisfaction nor the trust the soldiers had expected. Shops remained closed, shutters drawn tight, and merchants watched from their doorways with folded arms, wary of yet another occupying force. Years of British control had left deep wounds, and the arrival of Catholic soldiers from another distant monarchy stirred its own quiet unease. Faces appeared in windows and doorways, some curious, many cautious.

Whispers moved along the shoreline. Would the French behave like the British garrisons before them: drinking, brawling, and bullying the townspeople? Would their strange language and unfamiliar manners threaten the disciplined New England order? For years, the British had warned them what Frenchmen were: dwarfish, pale creatures who lived on frogs and snails, effeminate dancing masters reeking of perfume, papists who wanted not to help America but to seize her land for themselves. Few in Newport had ever seen a Frenchman except over the barrel of a musket.

So perhaps it was not surprising how many local families only came out accompanied by American officers, as they needed reassurance before venturing close. It was only in the presence of these friends and allies that they began to come near French soldiers and to have some confidence. Without the American military escorts the townspeople might have offered no welcome at all.

This was not a city ready to celebrate its rescuers. It was a community wary, wounded, and determined to protect what little peace remained.

Still, the arrival carried a fragile promise, a narrow bridge between allies who needed one another more than either wished to admit.

Disembarkation proved slow and exhausting. Newport had been an American-held town since the British deliberately abandoned and sabotaged it the previous October, after the Great Hurricane of 1779, one of the most powerful of the century, devastated their fleet at anchor. As foreign troops, the French required formal permission from the American commander, General William Heath, and Rhode Island authorities. This led to an express prohibition against landing on the twelfth.

Permission finally arrived around four o'clock in the afternoon. Then a second problem emerged: too few transports and a critical shortage of small boats. The troops were forced to borrow craft from islanders to ferry men and supplies ashore. Piece by piece, the artillery of the Auxonne regiment landed on the rocky beaches, each cannon pulled from the ships with care.

Rochambeau's first concern was securing a defensible position.

After surveying the island, he placed the main camp to the south of the town. The troops disembarked on the thirteenth and fourteenth and formed their lines in strict order. Bourbonnais and Deux-Ponts held the right. Soissonnais and Saintonge held the left. The artillery shielded headquarters. Lauzun's Legion advanced a mile ahead to watch the coastline and cover any approach.

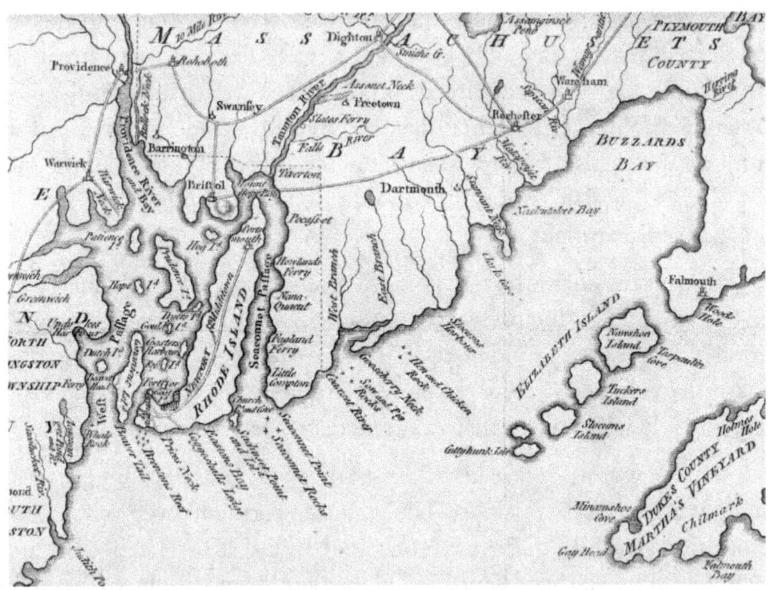

Detail from a 1780 map of New England showing Martha's Vineyard at lower right and Newport on the left side of Rhode Island. (New York Public Library)

A quiet relief moved through the camp on the 15th when the transport l'Isle de France, separated in the fog off the Chesapeake more than a week prior, sailed unharmed into Narragansett Bay. Her three hundred and fifty men of the Bourbonnais regiment came ashore to join their comrades, the last of the division to reach America.

The army had scarcely pitched its tents before the real work began. Old British earthworks were reinforced. New trenches were dug. Redoubts rose along the shoreline. Under the direction of Colonel d'Aboville, the artillery was brought ashore and assigned methodically, each piece placed according to a larger plan rather than reactive haste.

Then, on the 21st, came the alarm that froze every man in place. A lookout shouted that sails were approaching from the southeast. He counted nineteen of them.

"They are English," someone said. An enemy assault could undo the entire expedition. The French were ashore but not yet fortified, and only a handful of field pieces had been landed, a moment of maximum vulnerability.

Rochambeau reacted instantly, not with bravado, but with the settled determination of a man who had already decided that retreat was unthinkable. The few guns already on the beach were hauled to the most vulnerable points. The French fleet moored broadside to block any attempt by the British to force the channel. Captain Bonnay told the men that General de Rochambeau had said publicly that he wished that the English would attempt it.

For days the enemy hovered offshore, studying the French lines, while the French studied themselves, counting guns, counting men, and wondering whether they would be tested before they were ready. By the 23rd, lookouts could see there were eleven large vessels, the rest frigates or transports. Finally they turned away and disappeared beyond the horizon.

Artillery wagons rolled steadily from the beaches as the gunners placed each piece in its new position. The cannons formed a web of defenses across the island. Batteries rose on Goat Island, Rose Island, Brenton Point, Coasters Harbor Island, and Conanicut Island, each commanding a different reach of the bay. To Newport's citizens it must have seemed as though the very shape of their island was being reforged into a fortress.

Camp life that followed tested discipline and patience, unfolding against a backdrop of persistent illness. Within days of landing, reports showed that more than seven hundred of the army's five thousand men were on the sick lists. The German regiment of Deux-Ponts suffered most, many already weakened by the long Atlantic crossing before a single tent had been raised. Hospitals filled quickly as surgeons struggled to stabilize men whose strength had been spent at sea. Meanwhile, couriers rode constantly between Newport and Washington's headquarters, carrying cautious hopes, revisions, and urgent questions about a joint campaign that might yet strike a decisive blow.

Slowly, trust grew between the French and the people of Newport. As that trust took root, Siméon began to notice small signs of the country they were helping to defend. One afternoon, not far from the harbor, he paused before a flag he did not yet understand: red and white stripes, thirteen white stars scattered across a field of blue.

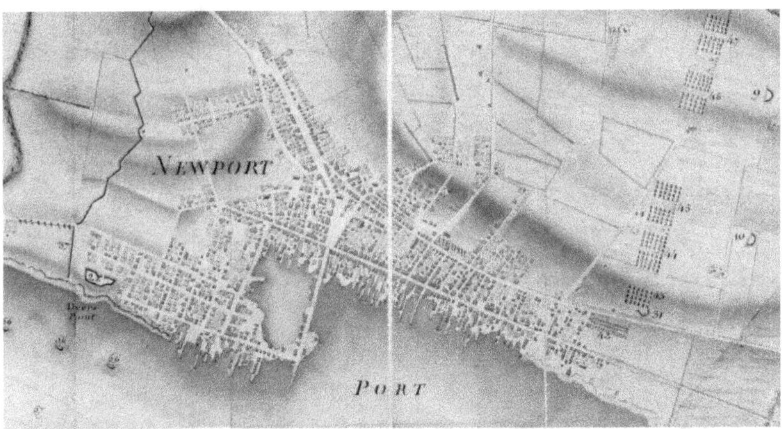

This French engineer's map of the French encampment at Newport depicts the town and the disposition of Rochambeau's forces during their first winter in America in 1780–1781. Each numbered position corresponds to a distinct unit. **The camp of the Regiment d'Auxonne is marked as number 31 in the lower right.** Two infantry regiments bordered them closely: number 43 identifies the Saintonge Regiment, and number 42 the Bourbonnais Regiment. Together, these camps formed one of the most active and disciplined sections of the French line. (Library of Congress)

When he asked about it, an American explained that Congress had ordered it four years earlier, and that it was often said that General George Washington himself had once described its meaning. The stars, the man said, were taken from heaven. The red came from the old mother country, separated by white to mark the break, with liberty carried forward for those yet to come.

Siméon did not know whether the words were true. What struck him was that the Americans repeated them because it mattered.

With each passing week the soldiers repaired fences, rebuilt damaged homes, and restored properties they would later leave in better condition than they found them. Every repair and every purchase was paid for in coin, and French currency revived a town starved of real money. Soldiers and civilians worked side by side. The French soldiers saw that the land was rich, sown with flax and maize. To Siméon's eye, the oxen and cows were as handsome as any he remembered from Rosières-sur-Mance. Even the reserved clergy softened when they saw the conduct of the army.

While this quiet work of alliance-building continued, the larger machinery of war and diplomacy turned on. Admiral de Ternay kept vigilant watch on the British squadron offshore, a mutual observation that stopped short of engagement.[51] At the same time, Rochambeau and his officers worked to navigate the complex diplomatic landscape of the new world, maintaining communication with American authorities and seeking to understand the disposition of various Native American nations, whose alliances and enmities could become important to understand.

Against this backdrop, Louis's strength ebbed like a tide.

His cough, which had never fully left him since the Channel Coast and had worsened aboard ship, grew deeper and more ragged. He still found ways to joke, insisting he felt better and the worst was behind him.

By the last week of August, he slept whenever he could.

One evening, Michel pulled Siméon aside. His voice was low.

"Is it the pox?"

Siméon felt the question like a blow. He had not let himself think it. The ships had been crowded. Sickness had swept through the fleet. Men had died of things no one could name.

"I do not know," he admitted.

Sans Soucy, who had overheard, said nothing. He crossed to where

---

[51] **Naval forces in the 18th century** routinely tracked enemy movements through visual observation, flag recognition, and ship positioning. Admiral Arbuthnot's British fleet maintained a watchful presence off Newport but did not impose a sealed blockade, leaving the French able to sail when circumstances allowed. The situation was one of contested waters and constant vigilance, not sealed containment.

Louis lay and crouched beside him. For a long moment he studied Louis's face, his neck, his hands. He lifted the blanket and looked at his chest. Louis stirred but did not wake.

When Sans Soucy stood, his expression was unreadable.

"It is not the pox," he said quietly. "I know the pox."

The others looked relieved. Only Siméon understood the weight behind those words. He remembered the fireside, the story of Charlotte and Lucie, and knew that Sans Soucy had learned to recognize the disease by watching it take everything he loved.

Not the pox. Louis would recover. He had been sick before, on the coast, and had come through. He would come through again.

"He needs a medic," Siméon said one morning when they woke to find Louis still asleep, his breathing now shallow and his chest rising only by effort. "I will find one."

He returned a short while later. "Rest," he told them. "Rest and time. That is what they said."

They stayed close to him each evening as he shivered and wheezed, telling stories, sharing jokes, and keeping the fire alive. Louis smiled at their worst attempts at humor. Some color returned to his cheeks. Fleur declared he looked better, and no one disagreed.

Then, one night, Louis stopped breathing.

Siméon woke suddenly, startled by the silence. He had grown used to the rhythm of Louis's labored breaths, and its absence filled the tent with dread. He lunged for the spot where Louis lay, calling his friend's name, though he already knew. Gently, he brushed the hair from Louis's forehead and remembered how, on the day they first reached America, Louis had leaned at the rail, insisting he was fine and breathing in the smell of land. The hope in his eyes then made the stillness in his face now almost unbearable. He whispered a prayer before waking the others.[52]

They all knew he was unwell, but he still laughed and argued.

"We should tell Sans Soucy," Siméon said.

---

[52] **Louis Bayrettes**; died August 28, 1780, at Newport, Rhode Island. Source: *Les combattants français de la guerre américaine, 1778 – 1783 (Washington: Imprimerie Nationale, 1905), 355.*

"I will go," Vincent answered. He stepped outside and, before reaching the sergeant's tent, leaned against a post and vomited.

Fleur d'Épine sat silently beside Louis, head bowed, one hand on his shoulder, whispering a German prayer while tears ran down his cheeks.

Vincent soon returned with Sans Soucy, and behind him came Captain Bonnay, fastening his coat as he approached. Bonnay rarely visited the enlisted tents at night, and his presence made the small space feel suddenly still. He knelt beside the body and drew the blanket up to Louis's chin, smoothing it as if tucking him in for one last night. Sans Soucy traced the sign of the cross over their friend.

Bonnay spoke only once, his voice low enough that only those nearest heard him. "He served with honor. I will see to the death report."

Then he stepped outside with Sans Soucy, and together they stood by the fire as the sergeant coaxed the dying embers back to life. Behind them, the tent remained quiet, its grief shared in a silence that needed no words.

"We will see that he is buried with honor," Sans Soucy said quietly. "Not in that ragged coat. Louis deserves better."

Goodbye, My Friend

They kept that promise.

The next evening, the regiment's chaplain gathered a few of the men on the rocky shore. Salt spray mingled with tears that no one cared to hide. The priest's words were simple, speaking of courage, friendship, and rest after toil. He sprinkled holy water over the canvas shroud and blessed the ground where Louis would lie. One by one, the men pressed a stone or a handful of soil into place with solemn care.

Vincent had carved a small wooden cross with hands that did not waver until the work was done. He pressed it carefully into the earth above their friend. Fleur d'Épine stood beside him, whispering German prayers that barely rose above the wind; the language of his childhood, summoned now when French felt too thin for grief.

When it was done, most drifted back toward camp in silence. Siméon remained behind.

He stood beneath a wide, indifferent sky as the stars rose above the black horizon. A cool wind tugged at his coat. He reached into his pocket, fingers finding the small book he carried. Between its pages, kept safe, lay the flower Laure had given him. He did not open it, but its presence alone was a talisman.

Chapter Ten: General Washington

September 1780 to May 1781

On the morning of his nineteenth birthday, Siméon woke to boots stamping mud and Vincent's voice rising in a bawdy marching song. Fleur d'Épine was dancing, if one could call his graceless hopping a dance.

Sans Soucy appeared with a tin cup. "No cake, lad," he said, pressing it into Siméon's hands. "But at least it is hot."

The coffee was bitter and thin, a rare luxury in camp, but Siméon wrapped both hands around the warm tin and grinned.

That night they sat close to the fire with weak wine. Sans Soucy raised his cup. "Dix-neuf ans."

"To nineteen." Vincent echoed.

"To Louis."

The fire cracked. No one spoke. They drank again.

Later, Fleur d'Épine said quietly, "He always shared his bread with me. Even when there was not enough."

Vincent nodded. "He would have made a joke about this wine."

Siméon stared into the flames, imagining what Louis would say. The space where his voice should have been pressed against them like the cold beyond the fire.

The camp settled into a rhythm of readiness. The British fleet hovered offshore, testing resolve. Batteries lined the shores; redoubts were manned. Rochambeau declared he wished the English would try.

Supplies remained scarce. The Americans had little to offer, and attempts to communicate dissolved into a muddle of accents.

Beyond the lines, the island revealed rich soil and old field boundaries beneath neglect. What startled them most was the treelessness: the British had taken the last stands, leaving the land flayed.

Along the water, a different world endured. Fishermen hauled in cod with such abundance that even Breton sailors stared. Oyster skiffs rowed between the ships; for a few coins a man could eat better than in months. Fresh fish, vegetables, cherries: scurvy began to loosen its grip.

Illness remained a constant threat: smallpox, typhus, dysentery, marsh fevers. At its height, the hospitals held eight hundred sick. Quarantine held. Inoculations were enforced. Fewer than two hundred soldiers died in Rhode Island, leaving Rochambeau's force largely intact.

The men kept fever at bay with bark tea, drills, and Fleur's whispered prayers. Siméon felt his strength return.

Vincent organized their work with steady clarity. Jean-Baptiste made sure everyone ate. Fleur channeled grief into poetry he shared with no one. Divertissant's jokes came less often but still landed. Michel and Pierre remained inseparable: Michel repairing, Pierre at the magazines, saying little, missing nothing. Jean Soriol, who had enlisted shortly after Siméon, took Louis's place. In time, he became one of them.

Conditions improved. Rochambeau's silver revived trust. Farmers returned, shopkeepers reopened. Newport became the most welcoming of American towns to the French.

Catholics in a Protestant town, the French earned admiration through courtesy and quiet devotion. Each Sunday, regiments filed into a great canvas chapel where altar cloths and candles brought from France transformed the interior. The sight of battalions kneeling in prayer, swords at their sides, left New Englanders quietly moved.

Invitations followed. Officers attended dinners and dances, their bright uniforms contrasting with the plain coats of their hosts.

The calm of the island, the rebuilding, the drills, and the loss of Louis pressed Siméon inward. He thought often of Laure, of his grandfather's words, and of the vineyard soil he hoped to see again. The more he turned those words over, the more he understood that his grandfather had not spoken only of grapes or soil.

On September 18, word spread that Rochambeau and de Ternay had departed for Hartford to meet Washington.

For days, the camp talked of little else. A sergeant claimed he heard an officer say it was time "to think of making some use of our troops." The phrase moved like a promise.

Siméon allowed himself to hope. They all did.

When the generals returned on the 24th, no orders followed. Drills continued. Patrols continued. Whatever had been decided did not include them.

Officers spoke of Washington in fragments: "Easy and noble bearing," "extensive and correct views." The words meant little to men who had never seen him, but the tone carried weight.

Some muttered the Americans were too cautious. Others said Washington did not trust them enough to commit.

The alliance, it seemed, would be built slowly. Trust did not arrive with a treaty. It had to be earned, day by day, in the silence between orders.

At the end of September, the frigate *La Gentille* arrived with news that stunned the camp: Benedict Arnold had attempted to hand West Point to the British. Exposed, he escaped to New York.

For the French, this was no distant scandal. Their camp sat within sight of enemy ships, among towns where Loyalists still lived quietly. If a man trusted by Washington could turn traitor, who could be trusted? Patrols stiffened. Watches doubled.

The first frost came early that year, a brittle glass over the puddles that cracked beneath their boots before sunrise.

One night, fueled by too much wine and haunted by thoughts of Louis, Siméon and Vincent nearly succumbed to the fever of recklessness. They were on the verge of joining a half-planned raid against a farmstead rumored to shelter Loyalists, the kind of impulsive action that could shatter the fragile local trust. Fleur d'Épine, sensing the trouble, quietly fetched Sans Soucy, who intercepted them as they buttoned their coats.

"Do not throw yourselves away," he said, his voice low but cutting through the night air. "That is not vengeance. It is waste."

Siméon let out a long, visible breath. Vincent stared at the ground, his fists clenched. They both knew he was right.

"*Oui, mon sergent.*"

In the morning, Sans Soucy's disappointment was a colder, more potent force than the frost. He summoned them without ceremony, letting the silence stretch until it was its own reprimand.

"If this foolishness were heard beyond this tent," he said, "the consequences would be public, permanent, and severe. This matter goes no further. Your conduct was reckless and unbecoming. Consider this your final warning."

Both men straightened to attention.

"*Oui, mon sergent,*" they answered, their voices steady now.

Early in October, a handful of officers received long-delayed letters. For the enlisted men, there was only silence. Siméon watched them read by lantern light and felt the distance sharpen.

A week later, something far worse than silence arrived.

On the night of October thirteenth, a storm tore across the island with unexpected violence. Wind rose in a sudden howl, ripping through rows of tents. Canvas snapped loose. Poles collapsed. Cooking fires scattered sparks across the mud. From the heights above the harbor, lanterns swung wildly aboard the French ships at anchor, the vessels straining against their cables. A merchant vessel was not so fortunate: at dawn, its shattered hull lay jammed against the shoreline, beyond hope of salvage. By morning the island was littered with splintered wood and scattered belongings. The men rebuilt quickly, joking that nothing in America was as dangerous as the wind.

No private letters had left the harbor since landing. The few packets that sailed carried only official dispatches.

Then, one evening, a ripple moved through camp as Captain Bonnay stepped into the company street and called the men to attention.

"The frigates *Amazone* and *Hermione* will sail for France in late October," he announced. "Their captains have agreed to carry a limited number of personal letters. Write now. Seal your letters and deliver them on time. There will be no second chance."

The murmur that followed was low and unguarded. Some men exhaled as if they had been holding their breath for months. Others closed their eyes, imagining faces they had not seen in years.

He wrote first to his father, describing the crossing, the sickness aboard ship, and the moment the American coast rose from the sea. He assured him that he was safe, that the officers were just, and that he kept the household in his prayers.

When he reached Louis's name, his pen stilled. Those pages he folded separately and returned to his satchel.

By candlelight he began another letter, this one addressed formally to Monsieur Julien Hudel. He thanked him again for his kindness in Rennes and asked after the family's health. He added a few lines meant for Laure, if Julien thought it proper: that the voyage had been long but safe, that he thought often of home, and that he remained constant in his intentions. Nothing more.

He sealed the letter carefully and handed it to the officer collecting the mail with a quiet nod.

The letters would take months to cross the Atlantic, if they arrived at all. Many never did. In Newport, men learned to measure distance not in leagues, but in unanswered words.

November brought little beyond cold and routine. The days blurred into a gray sameness until only after dark did the men pause, hands stretched toward the fire, grateful for an hour when the sameness loosened its grip.

With little visible movement, rumor became its own occupation.

On the morning of December 15, 1780, somber news swept through the French camp at Newport. Admiral Charles Henri Louis d'Arsac, Chevalier de Ternay, commander of the fleet that had carried them across the Atlantic, was dead. The surgeons named typhus, the putrid fever that had claimed so many sailors since the summer. Others whispered that strain and disappointment had hastened the end, though no one could say. The loss struck the camp with quiet force. Even soldiers who had never spoken to him understood that without his seamanship the crossing itself might not have succeeded.

From the hour of his death, the flagship *Duc de Bourgogne* fired a cannon every half hour. The deep boom rolled across the harbor through the day and into the night. Even townspeople paused at the sound.

At dawn on December 16, funeral preparations began. The procession formed at the Hunter House on Water Street, where the Admiral had lived. Nine Catholic chaplains led the way. Behind them, sailors from the *Duc de Bourgogne* bore the casket on their shoulders, escorted by senior officers of the fleet. Rank after rank of infantry, artillery, and marines followed. One officer wrote simply, "The whole army was paraded for his funeral."

Siméon stood in formation with his company, Captain Bonnay at their head. The captain's face was set in a hard, composed line. He gave a single nod down the ranks, steadying them in a way no speech could have done.

The cortège wound slowly through Newport's narrow streets, past Long Wharf, along Thames Street, then turning toward Church Street and the Common Burying Ground beside Trinity Church.

As the casket came into sight of the *Duc de Bourgogne* at anchor, the flagship fired a fifteen-gun salute. The sound shook the harbor. Siméon felt it in his ribs, a final tribute from the ship that had been the Admiral's command.

Funeral of Admiral de Ternay in Newport

American troops stood alongside the French by order of General Washington. Although Trinity Church was Anglican and its burial ground unconsecrated in Catholic eyes, the chaplains performed a full service at the graveside. Latin prayers rose into the gray December air while the French ranks stood motionless. Newport's residents watched in respectful silence.

Siméon felt the beads of his rosary press into his palm. The cold stung his face. He marched beside Vincent and Fleur behind Bonnay, each step an echo of the crossing they owed to the man now laid to rest.

The distance between past and future, between France and whatever lay ahead, had never felt sharper. He prayed that the Admiral would find peace, and that the living might yet be carried safely through what remained.

That night, as the harbor winds cut through the tents, Siméon prayed long after the others slept. Then the guns aboard the fleet finally fell silent.

The first Christmas away from France was a quiet, almost wordless affair. In Puritan New England the day passed with little notice. Shops remained open, work continued as usual, and the ordinary rhythm of labor sharpened the homesickness. The French observed the feast as they could. Mass was celebrated in the great canvas chapel, the chaplains' voices rising in prayers the townspeople would not have recognized. There were no carols sung aloud, no decorated church, no feast waiting afterward. A few men shared extra rations or passed a bottle of wine saved for the occasion, but the celebration felt small and guarded, a flame cupped against the wind.

Christmas Day, Newport, 1780

After Mass, Siméon and Vincent walked toward the small military hospital, hoping to visit the Auxonne men carried there during the autumn fevers. A sentry barred the door. Strict orders, he said. No visitors.

Siméon tried to explain that they wished only to bring Christmas greetings. Before the guard could answer, a hospital orderly appeared behind him, his apron marked with the work of the ward. He looked at them without unkindness.

"Quarantine," he said. "Men with the fever inside. No one enters and no one leaves until it is lifted. Not today."

They turned back toward camp in silence.

It snowed that afternoon, a fine dust settling over the frozen ground where Louis lay. Vincent knelt beside the wooden cross he had carved months before; it had tilted in the late autumn storms, battered by wind and rain. He straightened it with hands stiff from cold and pressed the earth firm around its base. Siméon and Fleur d'Épine stood beside him in silence. In the moment, the war felt blessedly distant.

But there was no time to linger. Their patrol rotation came due, and Sans Soucy was waiting near the eastern batteries, stamping his boots against the cold. He greeted them with as much warmth as the day allowed, his voice low and steady.

"Come on, lads," he said. "Let us walk the line. The cold will not wait for us."

They fell in beside him and trudged along the batteries as the harbor wind cut through their coats. Salt spray carried inland, crusting their sleeves.

As they walked, Siméon fell a few steps behind. The cold had settled deep into his bones, and his thoughts drifted far from Rhode Island. He saw his mother's kitchen in Rosières, warm with hearthlight. He imagined Laure in Rennes, arranging winter greenery at a window, her breath fogging the glass. Chestnuts toasted over the fire. Midnight Mass prayers rose in familiar cadence. It was a France of warmth and certainty.

When he returned to himself, only the grey Atlantic wind remained, sharp and indifferent. He quickened his pace and closed the distance to Vincent and Fleur, saying nothing.

CULTURAL NOTE: CHRISTMAS IN PURITAN NEW ENGLAND

In 1780, New England still carried the legacy of Puritan laws that had once banned Christmas outright. In 1659, the Massachusetts Bay Colony fined anyone who celebrated the holiday, calling such observances "superstitious." Although the law was repealed in 1681, its cultural influence persisted: December 25 was an ordinary workday, shops remained open, and churches held no special services. For French soldiers accustomed to Midnight Mass and public celebration, the silence was jarring. Rochambeau's chaplains celebrated Mass in the military chapel, but Baron Ludwig von Closen, aide-de-camp to Rochambeau, noted the muted season, recording that local customs centered on simple meals rather than the elaborate festivities of Catholic France. Sources: *Massachusetts Bay Colony Law of 1659; Evelyn M. Acomb, ed., The Revolutionary Journal of Baron Ludwig von Closen, 1780 – 1783 (Chapel Hill: University of North Carolina Press, 1958).*

Winter tightened its grip: frozen ground, grey skies, a cold that clung.

Officers attended dinners in warm houses, Bonnay among them on occasion. He returned with little more than a polite remark, never dwelling on comforts his men could not share.

Newport became a waiting room. The troops patched uniforms, repaired harnesses, tended guns, drilled on frozen fields. Morale shifted by the day.

Twelfth Night passed without fanfare, no Kings: no cakes, no music. January 5th, the eve of Epiphany, fell heavily on Siméon. At home, his family would honor his name day, opening the first bottles of the 1779 Gaugien red. He saw it: his mother setting a candle, his father testing the vintage, Colas judging it like a Parisian merchant. The distance sharpened the memory.

The bitter months passed with fewer deaths than predicted. Quarters were kept separate from townspeople, limiting illness and temptation.

Discipline carried its own cost: boredom.

Gossip endured. A grenadier swore he saw an officer stealing brandy. A drummer insisted their colonel courted a Newport widow. A soldier caught sneaking to see a sweetheart became, within nights, a legendary rogue who had seduced a governor's daughter and escaped through a second-story window.

February arrived without mercy. Worse than the cold was the waiting.

Then the rumors changed.

News came in fragments and whispers, carried by officers' servants, by sailors, by men who had overheard more than they were meant to hear. The traitor Arnold was no longer merely in Virginia. He was burning it. Foundries destroyed. Magazines blown apart. Public buildings and private stores reduced to ash. Even the Americans, it was said, had been caught off guard. For the first time that winter, the camp grew quiet in a different way.[53]

Ships that had sat idle were suddenly tended with care. Stores shifted at odd hours. Crews boarded without ceremony. No orders were posted, but the work spoke for itself.

Then, one by one, the ships slipped their moorings and vanished beyond the bay. Among them were *Éveillé*, the frigates *Gentille* and *Surveillante*, and a small cutter called *La Guêpe*. There were no farewells. No explanations. Only absence.

For weeks, no one knew what had become of them.

When word returned, it came in pieces. The squadron had reached the Chesapeake, but the water ran too shallow to follow Arnold's transports. After days of waiting, they turned north.

Off Cape Henry, they encountered the British frigate *HMS Romulus*, alone and outmaneuvered. She struck her colors. When the captured vessel

---

[53] **Governor Thomas Jefferson**, lacking reliable intelligence regarding Benedict Arnold's intentions, was unable to organize effective resistance to the British raid of January 5 – 6, 1781. Arnold sailed from New York on December 20, 1780, with approximately 1,600 troops, landed at Westover on January 4, and marched roughly twenty-five miles inland in a single day. His forces destroyed the Westham foundry, public records, military stores, and significant quantities of tobacco, rum, and salt. The raid exposed Virginia's vulnerability and underscored the strategic importance of control over the Chesapeake. Source: *Thomas Jefferson to George Washington, January 10, 1781, Founders Online, National Archives, The Papers of Thomas Jefferson.*

returned under French colors, the harbor stirred with cautious pride. Arnold had not been destroyed, but blood had been drawn.

Almost at the same time, word came of Cowpens: General Morgan had shattered the British, taking hundreds of prisoners. Men repeated the name under their breath. If the Americans could win such a victory, perhaps the war was turning.

The cold did not ease. The wind did not soften. But something in the camp had shifted. For the first time, the waiting felt different.

It no longer felt like endurance alone.

News from home arrived near the end of the month when a French frigate reached Boston with packets of letters. Only a handful reached the camp at Newport, but the effect was immediate.

Siméon received a small folded sheet in his father's handwriting. He wrote that everyone at home was well, that his mother sent her love, and that Colas had taken to lingering at the cobbler's shop more than was strictly necessary. The girl there, his father noted, seemed to welcome the attention.

That was all that was said. But Siméon understood it well enough. The news was already months old by the time he read it, yet it warmed him more than the fire at his feet.

Vincent teased him for reading it twice before speaking, and Fleur declared himself personally offended that the letter was so short.

Fleur received a letter too, a narrow envelope marked with a careful hand. Before he could open it, Vincent snatched it with a laugh and squinted at the lines. He frowned and turned it sideways, then upside down. The words made no sense to him, since he did not read German. Fleur plucked it calmly from his fingers and tucked it into his coat without comment. Vincent complained that it was unfair for a man to receive a letter written in a language no one else could pry into. Fleur only smiled and stirred the fire.

Then the unexpected happened. Sans Soucy was handed a letter of his own. A cheer went up around him before he could protest. Within an hour the camp invented a dozen explanations. Some said it was from a secret wife. Others claimed he had left a mistress in Metz. One soldier swore he had a child somewhere near Nancy. Even Captain Bonnay paused, his eyebrow lifting in mild amusement.

Sans Soucy ignored it all. When the excitement faded, he read the letter alone in the firelight. It was from his aging aunt, the last of his mother's sisters. The truth would have disappointed the gossips, so he kept it to himself. The story grew larger in their hands, and he let it.

Between rumors and drills, the days crept by. Vincent, Siméon, and Fleur d'Épine played dice, tossed quilles, and invented tall tales to chase off boredom. Even stickfighting, once good for a laugh, was played out.

He wrote letters he knew he could not send, trying to keep his memories alive in ink. Some nights, unable to sleep, he walked the outer line of camp alone, his boots crunching on the frost, haunted by Louis's laughter, by Laure's smile, and by the distance that winter seemed to stretch wider each day.

Liberty, he thought, had never felt so far away, somewhere beyond the sea.

Newport, Rhode Island — March 1781

By March, the harbor ice had broken. Supplies improved. Uniforms were patched, boots replaced. Rumors of a spring campaign moved through camp like fire.

The squadron, including the captured Romulus, was readied with sudden urgency. Supplies rolled to the docks. Regiments received orders to prepare.

"Something is moving," Vincent said, watching soldiers march toward the waterfront.

Fleur nodded. "By sea."

Rumors multiplied. Some said New York; others whispered the Chesapeake. The men packing said nothing.

On March 5, the purpose swept through camp: Benedict Arnold. The traitor remained in Virginia, and the French fleet was sailing to trap him.

Lafayette had already marched south. Washington himself had ordered it.

On March 6, official orders struck the camp before sunrise. Captain Bonnay rode down the gun line himself, cloak whipping in the wind, calling for every man to assemble at once. The French regiments were to form for review. General Washington was on his way to Newport.

The camp snapped awake.

Siméon gulped down his ration of bread and hurried to the gun line. Every man moved with the same urgency. Brass fittings were polished until they shone like mirrors. Wheels were oiled. Gun carriages scraped clean of salt and frost. The Auxonne prided itself on precision, and even on short notice, the regiment became a perfect line of gleaming metal and blue coats.

Down at the harbor, the embarked soldiers waited on crowded decks, their departure now only days away. The entire fleet was preparing to sail, including the captured *Romulus*, now armed and flying French colors, ready to turn her British guns against her former masters.

By noon, Washington arrived. He crossed the bay by ferry from Jamestown, Rhode Island. The harbor guns welcomed him with a salute that rolled across the thawing hills.

"Mon Dieu," Vincent muttered. "They say he is taller than any of us."

Fleur d'Épine watched the approaching riders with undisguised anticipation. "A Roman hero. I cannot wait to see him."

A stir ran through the ranks. Heads tilted. Someone whispered, "Here they come."

"Garde à vous." Captain Bonnay's voice rang across the company. Rammer heads touched the ground. The men straightened, eyes fixed ahead.

Two riders emerged through the haze of smoke and sunlight. Rochambeau rode first, brilliant in blue and gold. Beside him came the figure every soldier strained to see.

Washington.

General Washington Visits Newport

He was taller than rumor, and somehow quieter than expected. He rode with an ease that made the horse seem an extension of his will. His coat was plain. His expression unreadable. Yet his presence drew every eye. The camp did not fall silent because of orders. It fell silent because something in the air shifted.

The ranks stood at rigid attention. The drums settled into a steady, reverent beat.

Washington passed so close that Siméon could see the worn stitching on his gloves and hear the soft clink of the horse's bridle. Nothing about him suggested show or vanity. He looked like a man shouldering a load that belonged to thousands.

"He looks as if he carries the whole war," Fleur said.

Vincent nodded. "And he still sits straight."

Siméon said nothing. A farmer in a general's coat; a man who had worked land before he commanded armies.

Washington did not dismount. He returned their salute with a slow, deliberate motion, acknowledged the line, and continued. No words. No flourishes. Only the calm, exact movements of a commander who knew what was at stake and carried no illusions about glory.

All afternoon he toured the camp and visited the ships in the harbor. Washington urged an attack on New York. Rochambeau argued the army was not ready. Reinforcements were still at sea. None of this reached the enlisted men directly, but Siméon sensed it in the way officers rode past with tight jaws and in the way Washington had studied the guns so carefully. Captain Bonnay spoke briefly with the lieutenants and then with the sergeants, his tone clipped but steady.

When the two generals rode back toward town and the last salute echoed across the water, Siméon let out a slow breath. His hands were raw from polishing brass. Seeing Washington and Rochambeau together made the alliance feel alive.

On the evening of March 8, the fleet prepared to sail. Siméon watched from the heights as signal flags rose aboard the *Duc de Bourgogne*. One by one, the great ships turned into the wind. Canvas unfurled like distant thunder.

The *Conquérant, Neptune, Ardent, Provence, Jason, Éveillé*: each vessel heeled slightly as it caught the breeze and began to move.

The *Romulus* sailed with them, no longer British but French, her former allegiance erased by new colors at her mast.

More than a thousand men sailed that evening: grenadiers and chasseurs, infantry from each regiment, artillerymen with their guns lashed to the decks. Baron de Vioménil commanded the expedition; Admiral Destouches held command at sea.

Siméon watched until the last sail disappeared. The wind smelled of salt and winter's end. Somewhere beyond the grey horizon, Arnold waited.

That night, the camp fell quiet. Men played cards or wrote letters they might never send. This was not the waiting of idleness but of men who had sent their brothers toward uncertain fate.

Washington remained in Newport for several days after the fleet sailed, in constant council with Rochambeau. When he finally departed on March 13, the questions of where and when to strike remained unresolved.

Days passed. A week. Then another.

Rumors moved through the camp like smoke. Someone claimed a merchantman had seen the French fleet engaging British warships off the Virginia Capes. Another swore the expedition had already landed and taken Portsmouth. A third said Arnold had fled upriver and the whole affair was finished.

No one knew. The officers said nothing.

Then, on the afternoon of March 26, sails appeared on the horizon.

The fleet was returning.

Siméon joined the men gathering along the shore as the ships entered the harbor one by one. They moved slowly, carefully, and even from a distance something looked wrong. Rigging hung in tatters. Sails were patched with raw canvas. The *Conquérant* listed slightly, her mizzen mast jury-rigged with spare timber.

The *Duc de Bourgogne* fired no salute. The flags hung at an angle that spoke of damage, not celebration.

By evening, the wounded began to come ashore.

Men with bandaged heads, arms in slings, legs splinted with broken oars were carried on litters or in the arms of shipmates. The hospital tents filled quickly. Surgeons worked by lantern light. The smell of blood and powder smoke clung to the men like a second skin.

Siméon stood near the landing and watched them pass. He recognized a few faces: grenadiers from the Bourbonnais, chasseurs from Soissonnais. They looked at no one, their eyes fixed on some middle distance, seeing something the men on shore could not.

One of the wounded, a young fusilier with a bloodied coat, paused long enough to catch his breath. Vincent offered him water from a canteen.

"What happened?" Vincent asked quietly.

The fusilier drank, wiped his mouth, and stared back toward the ships. "The English were waiting for us. Off Cape Henry. We fought them ship to ship."

"Did we win?"

The fusilier shook his head slowly. "We fought. That is all I can say."

He moved on, and Vincent looked at Siméon. Neither spoke.

The truth came in pieces over the following days, carried by sailors and soldiers who had been aboard the ships, stitched together in the quiet spaces between drills and duties.

The French fleet had reached the Chesapeake on March 14 and sighted land at Cape Henry. But the British fleet had arrived first. It was commanded by Rear Admiral Mariot Arbuthnot, a sixty-nine-year-old officer more tolerated than respected, even within his own navy. Eight British ships of the line, including the massive *London* with her three tiers of guns, had been waiting.

Admiral Destouches had tried to avoid engagement, but the British closed fast. The battle began at two in the afternoon on March 16. The wind was against the French. The seas ran high.[54]

The *Conquérant*, leading the French line, had taken the worst of it. She fought three British ships at once, trading broadsides with the *London* at point-blank range. Her decks were swept clean. The wheel was shot away. The tiller shattered. Seven steersmen died at their posts. The ship drifted, helpless, while British guns pounded her hull.

---

[54] **The Battle of Cape Henry**, fought March 16, 1781, pitted Destouches' eight ships of the line against a British squadron of similar strength under Rear Admiral Mariot Arbuthnot. Then sixty-nine years old, Arbuthnot was widely regarded as one of the least competent flag officers in British service; contemporaries described him as a coarse, blustering bully who owed his command largely to the refusal of more capable officers to serve under the Earl of Sandwich. His handling of the battle bore out these assessments: he allowed his three lead ships to be badly mauled by the concentrated French line while the remainder of his squadron failed to engage effectively. Despite this, the tactical stalemate favored British strategic aims, as Destouches withdrew without landing his troops. Sources: *Tilley, The British Navy and the American Revolution, 182 – 184; Larrabee, Decision at the Chesapeake, 89–94.*

The *Neptune* and *Duc de Bourgogne* came to her defense, but the damage was done. At least seventy French sailors and soldiers lay dead; more than a hundred were wounded. The British suffered less. Their ships were larger, their position better. When the guns fell silent and the fleets drifted apart in the failing light, Arbuthnot controlled the bay.

Destouches called a council of war the next morning. The *Conquérant* could barely steer. The *Ardent* was damaged. Supplies were low. Without control of the bay, landing the troops was impossible. Arnold's fortifications at Portsmouth remained untouched.

The fleet turned north and sailed for Newport.

Siméon stood on the heights above the harbor three days after the fleet's return and watched the carpenters working on the *Conquérant*. Her hull was scarred with shot holes. Her masts were wrapped in makeshift cordage. She floated low in the water, listing slightly to starboard, as if even at anchor she carried the memory of what she had endured.

The men who had sailed away full of purpose had returned with empty hands. Arnold remained free. The Chesapeake was still in British control. The victory everyone had hoped for had slipped away in smoke and splintered wood.

For the first time, the French had met the British fleet in open battle and held the line. The *Conquérant* had fought three ships and survived. The men had not broken. The alliance, tested by fire and failure, had not shattered.

Siméon thought of the wounded fusilier's words. *We fought. That is all I can say.*

The thaw had come. The ground was starting to soften. And though the long wait continued, the waiting now carried a different weight. They had tested themselves, and they had not been found wanting.

HISTORICAL NOTE: WASHINGTON'S MARCH 1781 VISIT TO NEWPORT

George Washington arrived in Newport on March 6, 1781, to an artillery salute, his visit coinciding with final preparations for a French naval expedition to the Chesapeake intended to trap Benedict Arnold in Virginia and reinforce Lafayette. The fleet, commanded by Chevalier Destouches, sailed March 8. A British squadron under Admiral Arbuthnot intercepted the French off the Virginia Capes, engaging them at the Battle of Cape Henry on March 16. The British retained control of the Chesapeake; Destouches withdrew without landing his troops. Arnold remained secure. Washington stayed in Newport until March 13, meeting repeatedly with Rochambeau, with Lafayette serving as intermediary between the allied commands. Washington pressed for an attack on New York; Rochambeau urged patience until naval reinforcements arrived. The question of where and when to strike remained unresolved. Sources: *George Washington to Major General Lafayette, March 8 and 11, 1781; George Washington to Samuel Huntington, March 11, 1781, Founders Online, The Papers of George Washington.*

Chapter Eleven:
Arrival at Yorktown

May – Late September 1781

In early May, command of the fleet passed to Comte de Barras. Sailors moved with sharper purpose; officers spoke his name more often. Something larger than patrol duty was underway.

Later that month, Rochambeau met Washington in Wethersfield, Connecticut. The news spread faster than any dispatch. Officers gathered in tight circles; soldiers looked up from their drills.

This was no cautious consultation like Hartford the year before. The tone was charged, decisive. Most assumed the target was New York; others whispered of the south. Nothing definite reached ordinary ears, but everyone sensed it: something major was in motion.

What the men did know was this: the coming campaign would be decisive, and the fleet would shape its outcome. Still, a phrase drifted quietly through a few officers' tents, spoken like a promise. *Le coup décisif.* The decisive blow.

When Rochambeau returned to Newport, anticipation surged through the ranks. Campfires burned late into the night. In the tents of the Regiment d'Auxonne, voices rose in bursts of excitement. Some swore they would march beside Washington. Others dreamed of glory or simply an end to the monotony of garrison life.

When the orders were read, enthusiasm dimmed. Only part of the Artillerie d'Auxonne would march with Rochambeau. Siméon's section was ordered to remain behind: to tend the fires of a ghost army, guard the warehouses, and keep the camps looking full.

Captain Bonnay stood rigid, his jaw tightening before he masked it. He had expected to march. They all had.

Washington's own notes later revealed that only limited French detachments were formally assigned to guard the supply depots and hospitals across Rhode Island. Everything else, from the maintained tents to the tended hearths, was a deliberate illusion meant to deceive British observers across the water.

Auxonne's divided role reflected that strategy. Their comrades marched south toward whatever destiny awaited them. Siméon and the others were left to hold the stillness, keeping alive the appearance that the French army remained at Newport when in truth its heart was already on the road.

The guns were far too valuable to move without careful timing, and the commanders revealed nothing until the moment was right. In the meantime, the Auxonne in Newport could only stand their post, maintain the illusion, and wait.

The news struck hard.

"Marvelous," Vincent said. "They chase glory. We watch campfires."

"At least fires do not shout," Fleur offered.

Sans Soucy snorted. "Wait until you polish bronze for weeks and the only ones admiring your work are the cannons."

"The siege hinges on the guns," Siméon said. "If we are not marching beside them, this is still our part of the fight."

"Feels like the half with all the splinters," Vincent muttered.

A few muted laughs.

For Siméon and his comrades it became a different kind of courage: to stand still while others marched toward the heart of the war. They understood the value of the ruse and the weight placed on their shoulders; yet understanding did not always quiet the ache.

Duc de Lauzun's Legion Leaving Newport

On June 9th, Lauzun's Legion departed, stirring new speculation. Cavalry did not ride out lightly.

The next morning, the great march began by sea. As troops prepared to board, word spread that two officers had fought a duel south of camp.

Sans Soucy had the tale. "The Marquis du Bouchet was told he would stay behind. He took it badly."

The details emerged over days. Du Bouchet had dined with General de Choisy and a young aide, Lauberdière, who was marching south. During the meal, Lauberdière offered to buy du Bouchet's horses; a man stuck in Newport would have no use for them.

Du Bouchet heard it as an insult. Words were exchanged. An hour later, Lauberdière returned with a second and demanded satisfaction.

"They fought with swords," Vincent said. "The count took two cuts. Du Bouchet caught a blade in the chest. His collarbone saved him."

"Over horses?" Fleur asked.

"Over honor," Sans Soucy said. "The horses were the spark. The fire was already burning."

The story spread: du Bouchet walked back to town wrapped in a greatcoat, bleeding, unnoticed until his landlord's daughter found him shirtless and covered in blood. She fainted. The surgeon had to revive her before tending his wounds.

The men laughed, the nervous laughter of soldiers who understood.

"He preferred a sword in his chest to staying behind," Siméon said.

No one answered.

Du Bouchet survived. Lauberdière rode south. Before the month ended, de Choisy forced a reconciliation over dinner.

But the story lingered like smoke. A man had nearly died because staying behind felt worse than dying. The gunners knew what that meant.

On the morning of June 11th, drums and fifes lifted over the rooftops. Newport's residents lined the streets, shoulder to shoulder, to watch.

Regiment after regiment passed, white coats bright in the sun, standards rippling. Nearly four thousand Frenchmen moved through the town toward the harbor, boarding boats for Providence.

Siméon and his section stood at attention near their camp. As the battalions marched past, the artillerymen removed their hats in silence. They had drilled beside these men, shared bread and winter hardships. Watching them leave stirred pride and ache.

Children ran alongside, waving. Women held handkerchiefs. The drums did not slow.

Siméon watched until the last colors disappeared. A long, heavy silence followed.

"The camp already feels smaller," Fleur murmured.

Sans Soucy's gaze stayed on the harbor. "The heart of it is heading south."

Vincent tried to smile. "Then we had better keep the rest of it alive until we rejoin them."

Siméon did not answer. The emptiness stretched across the parade ground, quiet and solemn as a church after the congregation had gone.

Through June and into July, Newport became a stage, and the men left behind became its masters of illusion.

Captain Bonnay gathered his artillery crews on the first morning after the main force departed. His voice was low but carried clearly.

"We are now keepers of a necessary fiction," he said. "The army marches toward a purpose we are not yet permitted to know. Our task is to ensure that purpose remains hidden. You will drill as if the full regiment stood beside you. You will light fires as if a thousand men required warming. You will raise dust on the roads as if columns were moving. The British must not know."

They walked back toward the gun park in silence.

"We are scarecrows, my boys," Vincent said. "Scarecrows with drums."

No one laughed. The words stirred something none of them wanted to name.

The force that remained numbered only a few hundred: gunners to guard the siege train, details to tend the hospitals and warehouses, enough men to maintain the illusion but not enough to defend it if the illusion failed.

Siméon saw it in Vincent's face first, the way his jaw tightened, the way his eyes moved toward the harbor where the remaining ships rode at anchor. Two summers past, they had stood on the Channel Coast and watched infantry file toward boats while the artillery stayed ashore. They had cursed their luck then, furious at being denied the invasion of England. And then the waiting had begun, and the dying, and by September they understood that being left behind had saved their lives.

Now they were left behind again. The irony was not lost on any of them.

"Different this time," Vincent said quietly, as if reading Siméon's thoughts. "This time, those who march are marching toward something. Not rotting on ships."

"We hope," Fleur said. His voice carried none of its usual lightness.

Sans Soucy's words from that terrible summer echoed in Siméon's memory: *It is not the war that kills most soldiers. It is the waiting.* Whether this waiting would save them as it had before, none of them could say.

The rhythm was exhausting in its precision. Before dawn, details lit cooking fires in patterns suggesting full occupation, fires spaced as a real encampment would have them, smoke rising from empty company streets. Siméon and Vincent drew this duty twice weekly, moving through grey light with slow matches and kindling.

"How many fires today?" Vincent muttered.

"Same as yesterday. Same as tomorrow."

"We light fires for ghosts and raise dust for phantoms."

After the fires came the drums. The morning call sounded at its usual hour; the evening tattoo rolled across the harbor at sunset. Regularity was the soul of the deception.

At midday, small columns marched out the main gate with deliberate noise, boots striking packed earth, sergeants calling cadence. They followed the road south for a mile, looped through woods, circled back, and reentered camp, three circuits of the same mile.

Siméon's crew hauled an empty caisson to add weight.

"We are marching in circles," Fleur observed. "Like oxen at a mill."

"Oxen do not complain," Sans Soucy said. "Act like it."

Fleur wiped his brow. "If the English see us coming, they will surrender just to avoid carrying this."

"If hauling bronze wins wars," Vincent said, "we will all be marshals by Christmas."

Siméon smiled. "You would settle for marshal of the tavern."

"Only if they pay in cider."

The humor faded. These men had trained for battle, not performance.

"At least we are marching," Vincent said quietly. "On the coast, we waited and men died." They completed the circuit in silence.

One evening, cleaning equipment by lantern light, Fleur broke the silence.

"Do you think they know? The army marching south, do they know we are here, playing at being an army?"

"Bonnay knows. Rochambeau knows. Washington knows. That is enough."

"But our friends in Newport. Do they think of us at all?"

"They think of the road ahead," Siméon said. "We think of the road behind. That is our burden."

Vincent looked up from the gun. "When we were left behind on the coast, we thought ourselves unlucky. We envied the men who boarded the ships." He paused. "Then we learned there is good service in waiting."

No one argued.

The harbor added its own layer to the illusion. Admiral de Barras's ships rode at anchor, their crews visible on deck, small boats moving between the vessels and the wharves with purposeful regularity. The activity suggested preparation for a naval operation, perhaps a thrust toward New York, perhaps something else entirely: anything except what was actually happening, an army slipping south by land while the fleet waited to follow by sea.

Soldiers guarded the warehouses with conspicuous vigilance. Others tended the hospital wards where the sick and wounded still convalesced.

The great bronze siege guns remained on the wharf, covered against the salt air, their presence a silent argument that the army had not truly departed. Who would leave such weapons behind if they intended to fight?

In the evenings, lanterns were lit in officers' tents, their glow suggesting conferences and correspondence. Laughter rose from the remaining soldiers, deliberately louder than natural, carrying across the water to wherever British ears might listen. The taverns stayed open, and French soldiers were encouraged to frequent them, spending freely, talking easily, behaving as men behave when they expect to remain in place for months to come.

Amid this calculated theater, small moments of genuine peace survived.

Newport itself had grown fond of the French. One merchant, a quiet man from Portugal with sun-worn hands, kept a small shop near the waterfront and tended a few rows of hardy vines behind his house. He had planted them years earlier from cuttings he carried across the Atlantic. The vines were hardly more than a family garden, yet he cared for them with the patience of a man remembering a different coast.

On warm afternoons, when the dust-raising marches had ended and the evening fires were not yet due, Siméon sometimes helped him prune or tie the shoots to their posts. The work absorbed him completely. Each tendril he guided reminded him of Colas and the family rows in Rosières-sur-Mance. The scent of bruised leaves, the rasp of the twine, even the shape of the soil beneath his nails brought him back to those quiet mornings on the slope above the Mance. For a little while, the war felt impossibly far away.

The merchant spoke little French, and Siméon spoke no Portuguese, but the language of vines needed few words. When a young shoot threatened to chafe the cane, Siméon showed him the knot his father had taught him, looping the twine under so it would hold without cutting. The man watched, tried it himself, and nodded. A shared silence as they surveyed the rows together. When they finished, the man would give him a look that held something like gratitude. Siméon would return to camp with a calmer heart, ready to resume his role in the great deception.

In the streets, children still followed the French soldiers, delighted by brass buttons and foreign words. On warm evenings, townsfolk and soldiers shared the taverns, where fiddles played and laughter mingled with the smell of tobacco and salt air. The townspeople did not know they too were part of the performance, their ease with the French soldiers another argument that nothing had changed.

Even Sans Soucy sometimes allowed himself a weary smile at these gatherings. But when the laughter faded and the men walked back to their tents through the summer darkness, the weight of their strange duty settled over them again.

"Two years ago," Sans Soucy said one night, as they passed the silent gun park, "I told you that waiting was its own burden." He paused, looking at the covered guns. "I did not know then that waiting could also be a weapon."

He walked on without explanation.

Each fire, each drum beat, each dusty circuit of the roads purchased time for an army they could no longer see.

They kept their posts. They lit their fires. They beat their drums.

By mid-August, the wait broke. Orders came. The camp snapped awake. Wagons clattered, sailors' calls echoed, and the bronze guns swung over the decks.

Siméon and the others worked until their arms trembled. Vincent leaned on a coil of rope, breathless but grinning. "So this is it. Our march to glory, by sea."

Sans Soucy clapped his back. "May you keep your morning meal through the first storm."

Fleur rolled his eyes. "If he does not, I will throw him over myself."

"I would like to see you try."

As the last gun disappeared below, Siméon felt the same tight stirring he had felt when Washington rode past months earlier. At last, they were moving.

On August 25, 1781, Admiral de Barras's squadron raised anchor from Newport Harbor: eight ships of the line, four frigates, and eighteen transports carrying the French siege guns, engineers, powder, and the artillerymen of the Régiment d'Auxonne.

Siméon stood at the rail of the *L'Aigrette* as Newport dissolved into gray haze.

"Strange to leave so quietly," he murmured.

"Quiet departures make loud arrivals," Vincent said.

Fleur sniffed the wind. "Loud enough if the British find us."

Captain Bonnay rested a hand on the rail, his eyes on the thinning coast. "Pray they do not. This voyage is won by silence, not glory."

The men straightened, absorbing his steadiness.

Their orders were simple but perilous: guard the siege guns bound for Virginia. The British Navy patrolled the coast, eager to seize the guns that might tip the war's balance. If found, the siege of Yorktown could fail before it began.

Barras refused to hug the coast, steering wide into the Atlantic, arcing south and east before turning west. Days passed with nothing but horizon, emptiness that makes men imagine sails where there are none.

The frigate's sleek hull handled the ocean well, but below decks was close and airless. Two hundred sailors, plus artillerymen, engineers, powder crews, and siege equipment left no room to breathe. Hammocks swung so close men brushed shoulders in sleep. Powder barrels and shot were lashed into every corner. The August heat turned the lower deck into a furnace.

Water tasted of wood. Hardtack crumbled like chalk. Salted meat was softened in broth when the cook was generous. Sweat clung to timbers. Tar dripped from seams in thin black threads.

Fleur turned to Captain Bonnay at the rail. "Captain, may I go aloft? If I stay on the mast, I can see everything coming. Nothing will catch us unawares."

Siméon laughed. "Ah, Fleur, *toujours en haut* like some great sea bird. Careful, if you stay up there too long you will grow feathers."

"Is that worse than growing mildew down below?" Vincent asked.

Captain Bonnay's voice, calm but authoritative, stopped Fleur before he reached the shrouds. "A moment, soldier. You are an artilleryman. Your post is with your gun."

"I know, sir. But in the quiet watch, my eyes are sharp. It may help."

Bonnay gave a slow, considering nod. "I will speak with the ship's captain."

Later that day, he found Fleur again. "The captain has agreed. You may go aloft when there is room. The instant the drum beats to quarters, you come down. Is that clear?"

"*Compris, mon capitaine,*" Fleur said, a quick glint of appreciation in his eyes.

"Keep your eyes sharp, Fleur," Bonnay added. "The sea may hide us, but it can also betray us. I know you stay alert; I think you will be helpful there."

Siméon laughed softly as Fleur climbed the mast, calling after him, "Ah, Fleur, you have your freedom in the sky. Do not try to fly away!"

The soldiers were told little. Course changes came suddenly, sometimes late at night, with whispered commands sending sailors scrambling. Lanterns flashed from ship to ship like blinking eyes in the dark.

Siméon noticed everything: the captain pacing at dawn, officers scanning the horizon, the tension in each signal flag.

Rumors slipped between decks: de Grasse not yet at the Chesapeake, the British massing at sea, Barras setting a trap or being hunted.

Fleur watched from the mast with a seriousness that silenced even Vincent's teasing.

At night, men lay awake listening to the creaking hull. Siméon stared at the constellations, praying not for victory but for strength, for a glimpse of France again.

"Will you sleep?" Vincent asked.

"Not until this ends."

"Then none of us will sleep," Fleur muttered.

Sans Soucy made his rounds, checking lashings, knotting ropes, his steady presence keeping fear at bay.

They were alone in the vast Atlantic: no escort, no rescue, only the guns of Auxonne and the hope that the sea might keep them hidden.

Time lost its shape. Powder crews checked barrel straps each dawn. Fleur took every watch he could on the mast. Vincent sang low songs to quiet the men around him. Sans Soucy kept them working, hauling, polishing, repairing, anything to keep fear at bay.

Siméon wrote letters he would never send, describing the sky at dawn, the stars over the rigging, the ocean breathing beneath the hull. He folded the pages and tucked them into his pack.

Discovery at sea offered no refuge: only open water and British sails that could appear without warning.

At last, a change came. The wind softened, the swells eased. Flecks of green appeared in the water, vegetation carried far from shore.

A gull circled overhead. Fleur spotted it from the mast. "We are close to land!"

Men surged to the rails. Hours later, a faint smudge appeared on the horizon. Fleur slid down, breathless.

"We made it," he whispered.

Vincent gripped the rail. "Not a British sail in sight."

The convoy angled toward the Chesapeake, the air warming. Somewhere ahead lay the admiral they hoped to join and the battle whose outcome they could not yet know.

Siméon watched the shoreline sharpen: trees, marsh, river glints. After a year in New England, Virginia looked impossibly lush.

"Do you smell that?" he asked.

"Land," Sans Soucy said. "And work."

They had reached the gateway to Virginia alive.

On September 5, while they were still days from knowing it, fate was decided at the Chesapeake. De Grasse had won. His fleet of 24 ships of the line and four frigates had driven off the British and seized control of the Chesapeake, closing the bay to enemy ships at last. Virginia Governor Thomas Nelson Jr. confirmed the details in a letter dated September 11, writing that a British fleet had appeared off the capes, drawing out de Grasse, and that after a sharp engagement the British fled and were pursued by the French.[55]

But that was not all they heard.

Word followed quickly, passed in lowered voices among officers and aides, that the American army itself had nearly failed in the days before. There had been no money. No pay. Discipline fraying to the edge. Another delay, another march without coin, and Washington might have arrived with nothing but intent and an empty line.

The crisis, they were told, had been answered at the final hour when George Washington himself called for Philadelphia financier Haym Salomon[56], who then raised the funds needed to hold the army together and set it in motion.

Without command of the sea, the siege could not be supplied. Without money, the army could not have stood. Without both, Yorktown could never have begun.

---

[55] **Thomas Nelson Jr.** to Governor Thomas Burke, September 11, 1781, Source: *Letters of Thomas Nelson, Jr., Governor of Virginia (Richmond: Virginia Historical Society Publications, New Series, no. 1, 1874), 16–17.*

[56] **Haym Salomon** (1740 – 1785), a Polish-born Jewish merchant and financial broker, supported the American Revolutionary cause after immigrating in the 1770s. Working with Robert Morris, Superintendent of Finance, he helped convert foreign loans into usable cash and broker bills of exchange for the Continental Congress. In 1781, during severe financial strain on the army, he assisted in securing funds that supported ongoing military operations, including those associated with the Yorktown campaign. Between 1781 and 1784, he was involved in raising more than $650,000 for the war effort, much through personal credit and financial intermediation. He died in Philadelphia on January 6, 1785, his estate insolvent. Source: *Eli Faber, "Haym Salomon," Immigrant Entrepreneurship: German-American Business Biographies, 1720 – 1920, German Historical Institute, last modified 2014, https://www.immigrantentrepreneurship.org/entries/haym-salomon/.*

Haym Salomon, Financier of the American Revolution;
commemorative stamp issued by the U.S.
Postal Service (1975)

In the days that followed, Admiral de Barras entered the Chesapeake unopposed. His ships joined de Grasse's victorious fleet at the mouth of the York River. Between them, the two fleets had brought the full weight of French artillery: the siege train from Newport aboard Barras's transports, and additional heavy guns from the West Indies in de Grasse's warships. The York River lay closest to the siege, but its crowded waters left little room for sustained unloading. The James River, farther south, offered the space and stability needed for the heavier work ahead.

Within days of anchoring, urgent orders arrived: General Washington would review the combined French forces at Williamsburg on September 15. Siméon's detachment was among the first called forward, ordered to march inland immediately, leaving the heavy guns aboard ship under naval supervision.

By the time they reached the outskirts of Williamsburg and made camp, they had only days to prepare for inspection. The previous rain had passed, leaving the air heavy and clean. Coats were brushed, queues tied, and brass buttons caught the new light.

The men of Auxonne stood shoulder to shoulder as General Washington rode slowly before the French line, his buff and blue coat dusted from the march, his face calm and grave. Rochambeau followed beside him, with the young Marquis de Lafayette and Baron von Steuben, the Prussian whose name Fleur had spoken beside the fire at Auxonne so often. Siméon caught the change in Fleur's expression as he finally saw the man himself. Riding just behind them was Marquis de Saint-Simon, commanding the French troops newly arrived from the West Indies under Admiral de Grasse. Their horses moved with the measured rhythm of ceremony, hooves pressing softly into the damp Virginia clay.

For a long moment no one spoke. This was no diplomatic visit. This was the full allied command assembled on the eve of the decisive campaign.

Bonnay's voice carried low along the line, barely above a whisper. "Heads high, mes garçons. You will remember this day." It was not an order so much as a promise, and the men straightened instinctively.

To see the commanders of two nations united here, before the siege had even begun, was to feel history drawing tight around them. Even Fleur fell quiet, his expression solemn and proud.

The Commander in Chief spoke little, yet his presence carried the weight of every hardship endured and every hope yet to come. When he paused before their company, the line fell silent. He nodded once, and the muskets rose in salute, sunlight flashing along their barrels like fire along a fuse.

In the days that followed, information flowed through the allied command with unusual clarity. Cornwallis's strength, his shortages, his dispositions along the York were known with a confidence that surprised even seasoned officers. What mattered was that the enemy's position was understood, his movements anticipated, his options already narrowing. Somewhere beyond the reach of uniforms and ranks, unseen hands had carried word across the lines.

HISTORICAL NOTE: SPIES IN YORKTOWN

Among the most crucial intelligence sources at Yorktown was James, enslaved by William Armistead of New Kent County, Virginia. Posing as a runaway, he gained access to British headquarters under Cornwallis, delivering reports invaluable to allied planning. Throughout the war, enslaved and free Black men and women gathered intelligence, their service largely unrecorded. What distinguishes James's case is its survival in the archive. Learning in 1784 that James remained enslaved despite his wartime service, Lafayette submitted a testimonial to the Virginia General Assembly certifying that his intelligences "from the enemy's camp were industriously collected and faithfully delivered." In 1786 the Assembly granted James his freedom. In gratitude, he took the surname Lafayette. Sources: *Michael Kranish, Flight from Monticello (2010); Lafayette's testimonial, November 21, 1784.*

After the review, the artillery companies returned to their ships, which had repositioned to the York River anchorage, close to where the siege lines would soon be drawn. Some ships anchored directly off Yorktown; others positioned along the river approaches where the heavy guns could be brought ashore nearest to the battlefield.

There the long, grueling labor began: unloading the siege train, hauling powder and shot, and lowering the immense Gribeauval guns by block and tackle. Men strained at ropes and levers, their linen shirts clinging to their backs.

Siméon had shed the heavy outer garments of his uniform and, like the others, stripped to his work clothes: linen shirt, sleeves rolled, breeches and boots streaked with grime. He braced a cannon as it swung from the rigging, the ropes creaking under strain. Fleur, still in his vest and jacket, had been assigned watch with another soldier from their regiment, Nicolas Fole, on the upper deck. Fleur's gaze fixed on a frayed line above. As he stepped forward to shout a warning, the lashing snapped with a sound like a musket shot.

The cannon lurched. A hauling line whipped around Siméon's waist-belt, yanking him off his feet and toward the ship's side. He had time only to gasp before the world turned black and cold as he plunged into the water. Vincent, standing behind the gun, shouted as Siméon vanished beneath the surface.

The York River closed over him. Rigging bit deep into his belt, pulling him down. His lungs seared. He tried kicking himself free, but the weight of the cannon was inexorable, dragging him into darkness.

A figure plunged after him. Fleur had witnessed the entire event and, without hesitation, threw his musket to the deck and dove in, short sword flashing silver as he plunged toward Siméon. In the blur of bubbles and tangled rigging, his hand found the rope. One desperate tug of the blade, and Siméon was released.

Siméon burst to the surface, gasping for breath. Faces leaned over the rail, shouting. He reached for a rope, looking for his rescuer. He made eye contact with Vincent, who yelled, "Fleur!" Clinging to the rope, Siméon scanned the cold current. "Fleur!" he shouted, searching the froth and bubbles.

But Fleur d'Épine did not rise.

Nicolas Fole, a seasoned soldier with eight years of service, saw what had happened from his post and cast himself into the water, grasping at the fast-disappearing ropes. Yet the river had its own merciless grip. Weighted by sodden clothing and boots, dragged by the plunging gun, he was pulled into the depths. In moments, both Fleur d'Épine and Nicolas Fole were gone. Men dove again and again, came up for air, and went down once more. Nothing came. Only widening circles marked where the water had swallowed them.

Above, the tackle creaked. The next gun swung out over the side.

Siméon stood on shore after the others had been ordered back to work, his hand pressed against the place on his belt where the rope had bitten through. He could not stop touching it. There was no time for ceremony. No time for grief. There would be no recovery of the bodies, no burial. Two men from Bonnay's own company, lost on the same afternoon, with nothing left to mark their passing but the river closing smooth above them. One of them had saved his life.

That evening, as the campfires glowed low across the shore, the men of their regiment gathered in a small circle. They had requested one of the ship's chaplains perform a brief service, a memorial for the two young men who had vanished beneath the water.

Vincent, Sans Soucy, and the others sat in silence, their faces drawn. The chaplain spoke softly, reminding them that it was the Feast of Saint Matthew the Apostle, a day that marked the moment when a man was called without warning from his ordinary life into service beyond himself. He commended Fleur d'Épine and Nicolas Fole to God's mercy, and to the prayers of those who remained.

A quiet nod, a muttered prayer, a hand on a shoulder passed among them.

Partway through the chaplain's soft Latin, Captain Bonnay approached. He did not interrupt or stand before them. He removed his hat and remained just behind the circle, head bowed, saying nothing. When the prayer ended, he moved into the group and rested a hand briefly on Siméon's shoulder, a gesture more grounding than any order.

Loss on the York River

"They served with honor," he said quietly. "We will remember them."

Sans Soucy, beside him, said nothing for a long moment. Then: "In all our time together, we have never lost two in a single day." He did not say it as complaint or accusation. He said it the way a man states a fact that must be spoken aloud before it can be carried.

Then, just as quietly, Bonnay stepped back into the shadows, leaving the moment to the men themselves.

Siméon could not meet Vincent's eyes. Fleur and Nicolas were gone, not to cannon fire, but to a rope and a river that did not distinguish between the brave and the rest. Ahead lay Yorktown. He could feel its weight already, and the knowledge that two men had paid its first cost for him.

HISTORICAL NOTE: GREAT LOSS WHILE PLANNING FOR VICTORY

The deaths of Jacques-Cristianne Closset, known as Fleur d'Épine, and Nicolas Fole are recorded in Les combattants français de la guerre américaine, 1778 – 1783 with the notation: "noyé dans la rivière d'York le 21 sept. 1781" (drowned in the York River on September 21, 1781). That same day, General Washington and Rochambeau were offshore aboard Admiral de Grasse's flagship Ville de Paris, anchored at Cape Henry, finalizing siege plans. Washington's diary records his return to Williamsburg on September 22. Sources: *Les combattants français de la guerre américaine (Washington: Imprimerie Nationale, 1905), 355; George Washington, Diaries, vol. 3 (Charlottesville: University Press of Virginia, 1978).*

The days that followed moved the way grief does when war will not permit it to settle. There was ground to cover, equipment to move, and no time to stand still with what the York River had taken. Siméon marched because marching was the order, and because stopping would have left him alone with a silence that had no bottom.

The meadows near Jamestown held the largest encampment the regiment had ever seen. The French lines stretched with mathematical precision: white tents in neat rows, banners trimmed in gold, artillery on freshly tarred carriages, supply wagons painted red or yellow: the discipline of a professional army.

The Americans nearby were a different picture: uneven, improvised, alive with noise. They could not hide the want that had shadowed them through the war: shortages in shoes, coats, paint. Yet they had pressed on with a resilience that needed no polish.

Their wagons told the same story: Conestogas, patched powder carts, "little chariots painted red." Some gun carriages were newly painted with French stores; others were weathered by long marches. Equipment revealed hardship, not neglect.

Some American units wore new blue coats from French depots; others wore homespun hunting shirts repaired too many times. A few militia companies arrived with little uniformity and fewer arms, mocked by British officers as "barefoot rabble."

But Siméon saw something else: farmers, tradesmen, boys scarcely grown, brought together not by royal command but by conviction. They carried hunting muskets, old fowling pieces, pikes fashioned from farm tools. Their formations were uneven, their officers uncertain, but beneath the chaos ran a firmness of purpose no polish could manufacture. The contrast revealed the strength of both.

The encampment buzzed with the hard focus of men readying for battle. Across the open fields, artillery trains rolled in with a rhythmic creak of harnesses and wheels. The air was thick with the smell of horse sweat, tobacco, and hot iron from the traveling forges, which clanged day and night. Blacksmiths hammered repairs and wagoners swore in every tongue. Over a thousand horses and oxen strained against harnesses, hauling the lifeblood of the siege: guns, powder, and the promise of the final blow.

Among this hum of motion, the men began to mix. French soldiers wandered curiously through the American lines, where ragged Continentals traded tobacco for wine or scraps of bread. Siméon watched as a group of Americans offered rough salutes, their accents thick but their smiles genuine. A few words bridged the gap: *liberté*, America, King George no more. Laughter followed, awkward but real.

At night, when the campfires glowed across the plain and the smoke drifted low under the stars, the two armies looked out across the same horizon. French and American, polished and ragged, noble and hungry.

For the first time, they were not strangers sharing a cause, but comrades sharing a field.

As Siméon turned in his blanket, the sounds of Jamestown merged: the metallic ring of a forge, the low murmur of Frenchmen singing, the hoarse American laughter around a fire.

The ships had repositioned from the York River to the James, and the regiment with them. After days of unloading at Trebell's Landing and preparing the siege train for transport, the work slowed and then paused. Wagons stood idle in the heat, horses and oxen drooped in their traces. Soldiers sweated and waited, unaware that miles away in Williamsburg a dispute over Spanish silver was delaying the next stage of the march inland.

The air above the James River hung thick and still, heavy with the dust of the barren, sandy country. Powder and tar scented the landing, but beneath it was the gritty dust that coated their mouths and clung to sweat-dampened skin. The men still spoke of Fleur and Fole, who had disappeared in the York River a week before. No one forgot, and no one was going to swim in the York. The waiting pressed on every soul until grief itself seemed to give way to the heat.

Trebell's Landing

Vincent, a strong swimmer who never missed a chance to be in the water, saw an opportunity and felt nothing could be lost by asking. He nodded toward Captain Bonnay, and when he had the captain's attention, he called out loudly enough for all to hear,

"*Mon capitaine*, perhaps the men could swim while we wait?"

A few laughed at his boldness. Bonnay regarded him for a long moment before giving a small nod. "*Oui, messieurs, vous pouvez nager.*" Yes, men, you may swim.

The permission was hardly out of his mouth before cheers and laughter broke out and boots began to fly.

The men stripped quickly, pale backs gleaming in the sun as they ran down the muddy bank and plunged naked into the river. The first splash drew a cheer, then another, and another, until the James River rang with laughter. They swam like boys, floating on their backs and kicking up the brackish current that sent sunlight dancing across the surface, calling out to one another in French, Breton, and the rough accents of Burgundy. Even the oxen turned their heads at the commotion. For a little while the heat and monotony vanished, replaced by the simple joy of cool river water and comradeship. Bonnay smiled at last, shaking his head as Vincent surfaced laughing, water streaming from his hair.

The spell broke at the sound of a distant bugle. They scrambled back to the bank, dripping and laughing, pulling on shirts that clung to wet skin. Within minutes they were back in ranks, the smell of damp wool and river mud rising as they queued for *souper*.

The guns still waited on the wharf. The animals still stood tethered. French Quartermaster Claude Blanchard, charged with the custody of royal funds, had become locked in a dispute with American Quartermaster General Timothy Pickering over payment for wagons and transport. Blanchard refused to release the money. For several critical hours this disagreement halted the movement of the siege train.

By morning, word spread that the dispute had been resolved. Teams were hitched before sunrise. Sailors and gunners heaved the great cannons onto their wagons, and the movement inland began again, dirt and dust flying from the wheels.

Only later would the men hear fragments of a further tale involving the Spanish silver from Havana entrusted to the French quartermaster, Claude Blanchard. In his own later account, Blanchard recorded a striking detail: the sheer weight of the silver in his charge caused the floor of the room adjoining his to collapse during the night. The silver survived intact, though his servant, who slept in that room, narrowly escaped injury.

Among the veterans who remembered the Channel coast, the news prompted darker humor. "At least this time they sent something that arrived," Vincent said, and no one laughed.

The others said nothing. Last time Spain had promised ships and soldiers. This time Spain sent silver, heavy enough to break through a floor. But it arrived.

Every man knew they had lost precious time. Yorktown was waiting.

HISTORICAL NOTE: MATERIAL WEIGHT OF THE REVOLUTION

The logistical dispute between Quartermaster General Timothy Pickering and Intendant Claude Blanchard is documented in their own records; administrative friction over funds briefly halted the campaign's momentum. The collapsing floor, caused by the weight of Spanish silver entrusted to Blanchard, is recorded in his journal. The silver, approximately 3.5 tons (800,000 livres), was raised in Havana in a single day by Spanish Commissioner Francisco de Saavedra, providing the hard currency needed to pay troops and secure supplies: the vital and often overlooked Spanish financial contribution to American independence. Sources: *"To George Washington from Timothy Pickering, 5 October 1781," Founders Online; Claude Blanchard, The Journal of Claude Blanchard (1876); James Giesler, "Francisco de Saavedra's Role in Securing the Independence of the United States," Queen Sofia Spanish Institute (2022).*

Chapter Twelve: The Siege of Yorktown

Late September – October 19, 1781

The last of September and first days of October were spent not in battle but in relentless preparation. The entire army turned to forests and fields, hands busy with axes and knives, weaving the sinews of the coming siege: fascines, gabions, and the long, sausage-like saucissons that would protect the men in the parallels to come.

For Siméon and the Régiment d'Auxonne, the duty was more direct. The Bonnay Company continued to work on the James River, nine miles from camp, assisting in the back-breaking work of landing the heavier siege guns. Artillery from Newport and the West Indies converged here, each bronze colossus a hope and a promise of thunder, hauled from the riverbank onto waiting carriages for the final journey to Yorktown.

Even here, far from the main lines, the war reached out. Word passed through the ranks that an American patrol had been wiped out a day prior by a single, horrific shot that killed four and left a fifth wounded.

On October 3rd, news crackled through the camp from the opposite shore at Gloucester. The Duc de Lauzun, at the head of his hussars, had charged Tarleton's dragoons, driving them back in a sharp, successful skirmish. It was a small victory, but it felt like a sign: the noose was not yet drawn tight, but the cord was in their hand.

The morning of the fifth broke under a light, lingering rain; welcome news for the men who would soon be digging the first parallels, since softened earth would yield more easily to the spade. For the artillery, it meant a day of mud and struggling wagons. Drums beat the call to move, and soon the air was alive with motion: harnesses rattling, wagon wheels groaning under the weight of bronze and powder.

Siméon shouldered his pack in silence. Sans Soucy checked the traces on a team of horses with practiced efficiency, while Vincent muttered under his breath about the dirt they would eat before the day was out. Fleur d'Épine's absence rode with them, a silent passenger in the space he should have filled. His name lived now only in glances and in the silence between words, heavy with a comment he would have made, the wry observations now unshared. At every halt, Siméon caught himself looking for his friend's lopsided grin before the memory, cold and sharp, returned. Ferréol Millot[57] fell into line beside them, a Comtois like Siméon, transferred from another gun team to fill the gap Fleur had left: quiet, watchful, still finding his place among men bound by shared grief. Michel, Jean-Baptiste, Pierre, Soriol, and Divertissant followed, each man casting a glance down the road that stretched southward into the haze.

The heat rose swiftly, the air a suffocating blanket of humidity. They marched slowly, making frequent halts, but the sun was relentless. Men began to falter, stumbling out of the column to collapse in the dust; comrades dragged them to shade, poured water when they had it. Twice Siméon saw a man fall and not rise, carried away on a wagon, his war ending not with a musket ball but with sunstroke on a Virginian road.

For those hauling the siege train, it was nothing but hardship. The roads turned slick and rutted, wagons sank to their axles, and every hill became a test of strength and will. The supply of bread was measured in days, the land stripped bare, the English having captured vessels carrying vast quantities of their flour.

---

[57] **Ferréol Millot**, born 1761 in Recologne, Franche-Comté; enlisted in October 1779 in the Régiment d'Artillerie d'Auxonne and was assigned to the Compagnie Bonnay de la Rouvrelle; served alongside Siméon Gaugien in the French Expédition Particulière under the command of Jean-Baptiste Donatien de Vimeur, comte de Rochambeau, during the American War of Independence. Source: *Les combattants français de la guerre américaine, 1778 – 1783 (Washington: Imprimerie Nationale, 1905), 355.*

By evening, both men and cannon had reached Yorktown, the great guns finally in position, ready for their place in history.

Grand Battery, French Artillery Park, Yorktown

For Siméon and his comrades, this was the moment their long journey from France to America had promised. The artillery massed like coiled thunder in what the engineers were already calling the Grand Battery[58]. He looked down the line at the silent, dark-mouthed barrels of the Gribeauval field pieces, his own twelve-pounder among them, alongside their larger brothers, the sixteen-pounders and twenty-four-pounders. More than forty French pieces in all, the largest concentration the regiment had ever assembled.

On the eve of the siege, Captain Bonnay gathered his company. He had sailed from France with forty-nine men assigned to his command. Now, forty-one stood before him, strong, seasoned, and ready. The officers confirmed what the men suspected. The allied force now numbered approximately 16,000 men, roughly 8,000 Americans and 7,800

---

[58]**The illustration depicting the Grand Battery**, French Artillery Park, Yorktown, was commissioned to correct documented inaccuracies in the painting currently displayed at the site by the National Park Service. French Army artillery carriages were light blue with bronze barrels; Navy carriages were red with iron barrels; Quartermaster wagons were a brighter red: a departmental color-coding system established before 1750 that allowed soldiers to identify ownership of materiel at a glance. For a full accounting of the original painting's errors, including harness design and limber placement, see *Karl G. Elsea, "Artistic License and the French Artillery Park at Yorktown: A Case Study," Emerging Revolutionary War, October 8, 2021, https://emergingrevolutionarywar.org.*

French, facing an estimated 8,000 British and Hessian troops entrenched at Yorktown, with the Royal Navy held at bay by Admiral de Grasse. The numbers were the architecture of a trap, now sprung.

That night the order came. The siege would begin.

October 6, 1781: First Parallel

Under a sky so black it seemed to swallow the stars, the allied army began to move.

From the woods and ravines came the low shuffle of boots and the muffled clink of shovels. Thousands of men filed forward in silence toward the British lines at Yorktown.

Then the digging began. Spades bit into the Virginia earth, each scrape and grunt a heartbeat closer to discovery. The First Parallel took shape beneath the very muzzles of British guns, stretching from the York River across the fields to the woods beyond. They worked in silence, knowing discovery meant cannonade.

Siméon, Vincent, and their crew from the Régiment d'Auxonne stood ready at the edge of the works, watching as French Marines and infantry dug with frantic urgency. The Marines' anchor-marked buttons flashed whenever a flare rose from the British lines. The Marines moved with shipboard precision, their discipline steady as the tide: France united, sea and land together with their American allies, one purpose, one resolve.

The labor was brutal. Men sweated and cursed softly in the heat, while above them, British flares hissed and musket fire cracked. Twice, a sharpshooter's ball struck home, each shot followed by a low, dreadful thump and the swift, hushed efforts of the stretcher bearers. Still, the trench crept forward through sandy soil, a raw scar in the pitch black, facing the enemy's teeth.

By dawn, the First Parallel was born: a line of earth and sweat, fragile yet defiant.

October 9, 1781

Siméon's crew stood ready at their twelve-pounder in the heart of the Grand Battery. Moments before the signal, Sergeant Sans Soucy had stalked down the line, his voice cutting through the tense quiet. "Range to the redan: eight hundred yards. Elevation at two degrees. Make it count."

The numbers were not abstract. They were a recipe for destruction. Siméon's hands moved automatically, adjusting the quoin under the barrel, his mind converting the sergeant's command into the physical tilt of iron. Eight hundred yards: a flat, brutal sprint for a man, a fleeting arc for their shot. He checked the sightline, the enemy wall a dark smudge beyond the churned field. The calculation was complete; now the gun would speak it.

"Silence abruptly gave way to thunder."

The signal came at mid-afternoon. General Washington himself stepped to the first American gun, a gesture both ceremonial and defiant. The Commander in Chief laid the match to the touchhole. The cannon roared, its report rolling across the field like a crack of doom, and silence abruptly gave way to thunder. Moments later, Colonel d'Aboville raised his hand, and the French batteries answered in coordinated fury.

French and American batteries erupted in unison, shaking the ground with flame and smoke.

To the left, under Baron de Vioménil, the Régiment d'Auxonne manned the heart of the Grand Battery. Orders passed quickly down the line, batteries firing in disciplined volleys that hammered specific sections of the British works with relentless precision. Across the field on the right wing, General Henry Knox's American batteries added their thunder, with Colonel Lamb's regiment at the fore. The air itself seemed to tear apart.

Still they worked. The sky was never clear of smoke. Each man moved by instinct now, half blind and half deaf, bodies carrying on through muscle memory alone. The sponge plunged. The cartridge rammed. The lanyard pulled. Again. Again. Again. Heat radiated off the iron until the gun could not be touched without pain. Their ears rang constantly, a high, endless shriek that would never truly fade.

Vincent wiped sweat from his face and glanced toward the British works. "They're slowing," nodding toward the enemy batteries. "Heavy old pieces. Ours fire twice for every one of theirs."

Sans Soucy grunted, already calling the next elevation. "Gribeauval knew what he was doing."

Swinton's Map: Siege of Yorktown, 1781

Across the field[59], British works splintered, earth and timber flying skyward. The air was thick with powder smoke and the smell of burning

---

[59] **William Swinton's Map**, "Siege of Yorktown, 1781," in *First Lessons in Our Country's History* (New York: Ivison, Blakeman, Taylor & Company, 1872).

pine. Adrenaline pumped through him, and then a cold, professional focus took hold: all Siméon could think about was where the next shot would hit. The Gribeauval system's standardized parts and lighter carriages meant his crew could serve their piece with a speed the older British guns, mired in soft Virginia earth, could not match: reposition when needed, maintain the relentless rhythm that was breaking Yorktown's defenses one measured blow at a time.

Beside him, Sans Soucy barked corrections, his voice rough but steady. Vincent, covered in grime, cracked a joke between bursts about cannon grease making good boot polish. Somehow, the humor eased the men around him.

When night fell, the crews rotated in shifts, each gun pausing just long enough for the men to scrape mud from their boots and gulp down hardtack with powder-blackened hands. "Barely time to swallow," Vincent remarked one evening, staring at the red horizon.

"Long enough to remember what we're here for," Siméon replied.

October 11, 1781: Second Parallel

Under cover of darkness, work began on the Second Parallel, now a mere 400 yards from the enemy lines. Closer. Always closer. The men dug as cannonballs whistled overhead, the air thick with freshly turned earth and spent powder. Fragments of iron rained down. A shovel blade shattered.

Then it was their turn. The order came down the line: move the guns forward. No longer sheltered by the massed fire of the Grand Battery, Siméon's crew became targets in the open ground between the parallels. Their world narrowed to the weight of the carriage, the scream of shot overhead, and the suck of the mud underfoot. Every muscle burned with the effort to keep the wheels turning, to not stall, to not become a still target in the killing zone. They did not look up; they leaned into the ropes, boots sliding in the churned muck, each man trusting the next to keep pulling. It was a gauntlet measured in heartbeats and yards.

The work was a deadly calculus: dig fast and risk exposure, or dig slow and endure the fire. They chose speed.

The bombardment never ceased. Day folded into night folded into day. The guns spoke. The trenches crept forward. Yorktown's walls crumbled stone by stone.

October 14, 1781: Thirty Minutes of Hell

The order came at dusk: Redoubts 9 and 10 must fall. Without them, the Second Parallel could not be completed. With them, Cornwallis would be trapped.

All afternoon, Siméon's battery had pounded Redoubt 9, tearing at its parapets and silencing its light guns. When the order came to cease fire, the sudden quiet was unnerving. In the stillness, he could hear the clink of axes, the low murmur of officers issuing final instructions. The silence felt more dangerous than the bombardment.

As night settled, the redoubt took shape against the gloom: earthen walls eight feet high, crowned with palisades, fronted by a ditch choked with abatis, felled trees sharpened and interlocked into a barrier as dense as a hedge of iron. Inside waited a garrison of 120 British and Hessian soldiers, muskets leveled, bayonets fixed.

From their position in the Grand Battery, two hundred yards behind the assault line and slightly to its left, Siméon and his crew watched the columns assemble. The French would strike Redoubt 9 directly ahead; Redoubt 10 lay further right, where Hamilton's Americans waited in the dark. Word had passed that Hamilton had ordered his men's muskets left unloaded. The attack would be made with cold steel alone, a mandate for silence and absolute commitment. Whether the French column had received similar orders, Siméon did not know, but the faces under Baron de Vioménil's command showed no less resolve. Yet a tension hummed in the French ranks: the fascines and scaling ladders meant to bridge the ditch and scale the wall were conspicuously few. The tangled abatis before Redoubt 9 waited, undisturbed and ominous.

At the signal of three shells, or was it six? Shortly after eight o'clock, the night shattered. "Vive le Roi!"

The French column surged forward into chaos. The abatis was a deeper, more vicious thicket than anyone had gauged. Men scrambled to hurl their few fascines into the ditch, but where were the ladders? Shouts for them were lost in the din. A few appeared, hoisted by stumbling men who became instant targets for the muskets above. British fire flashed from the parapet. The first French soldiers were cut down, their bodies snagging in the sharpened branches. What was meant to be a swift rush stalled into a bloody, grinding brawl at the redoubt's foot. Jacques Crevoisier, whom Siméon had known as a boy in Jussey, charged with the Régiment de Gâtinais, musket clenched like a spear. The night collapsed into close-quarters fury: bayonets thrusting, musket stocks swinging, men shouting and dying in French, German, and English.

French Troops Storm Redoubt 9

To the right, across the dark field, a different fury unfolded. Lt. Colonel Hamilton's Americans advanced in near-total silence. Among them moved soldiers of the 1st Rhode Island Regiment, men who had been enslaved and won their freedom through service. The watchword was "Rochambeau." In the dark, spoken quick and hard, it became its own command: Rush on, boys! The name of a French general turned into an American cry. They hit the abatis before Redoubt 10 with axes and bare hands, tore through with a speed that left no time to answer, and flooded the ditch. The defenders reeled under the silent, sudden avalanche. Within minutes, resistance collapsed.

For a moment before the cheer, something impossible seemed to happen.

At the parapet of Redoubt 10, where no ladder could be seen, a dark figure surged upward, lifted by unseen hands. He stood exposed for a heartbeat, shouting orders in English, his voice sharp and commanding, then vanished forward into the work.

"Who is that?" Vincent said.

Someone near the guns answered, uncertain. "Hamilton?"

A sharp, triumphant cheer erupted into the night.

Siméon and his crew watched, helpless, their guns silent. Every man strained to see through the smoke and darkness.

Vincent grabbed Siméon's arm. "They took it!"

Moments later, a figure climbed atop the captured parapet. A voice carried across the field, Lafayette calling toward the French still locked in their desperate struggle.

"*Monsieur le Baron!* How goes it with you?"

The reply came back, strained and edged with the frustration of a fight not yet won: "Tell the Marquis I shall be there in five minutes!"

Some of the gunners laughed, the tension cracking. Vincent grinned. "The Americans were quicker."

Sans Soucy did not lower his spyglass. "Different ground," he said quietly. "Different fight. Both redoubts are ours. That's what matters."

He was right. Even as he spoke, the resistance at Redoubt 9 finally collapsed. A final surge of French troops crested the parapet, and the scattered musketry was swallowed by the dark mass of their advance. The fighting ceased.

Both redoubts had fallen in under half an hour. The French, after a brutal struggle, captured all 120 defenders of Redoubt 9. The Americans, in a swift, surgical strike, took some seventy prisoners from Redoubt 10.

The men of the Gâtinais and the soldiers of the 1st Rhode Island had earned their place in that victory.

By morning, both redoubts would join the allied lines, their guns turned against their previous owners.

Between the smoke and river haze, French masts showed beyond the town, dark and still.

The Expelled

Movement behind the British lines drew attention along the allied works. At first, Siméon thought a sortie was forming. Figures emerged from Yorktown in loose groups, too many for a patrol, too slow for troops. Then he saw women. Children. Bundles carried low against thin bodies.

The line wavered as the truth became clear.

They were being driven out.

British sentries followed at a distance, muskets leveled, not escorting so much as herding. When one of the figures turned back, a red-coated soldier stepped forward and raised his bayonet. The column lurched on again, away from the town, away from shelter, toward the open ground between the armies.

"What are they doing?" Vincent asked quietly.

Sans Soucy raised his spyglass. He watched for a long moment before answering. "They are pushing black people out," he said. "The people who ran to them."

He did not say why. He did not need to.

The procession reached the edge of the open ground between the armies. Some stopped entirely, looking back toward the town they had been forced to leave, then forward toward the silent allied lines. No one advanced to meet them. No orders were given. The ground between the armies remained empty, watchful, indifferent.

A woman sank to her knees. A child began to cry, the sound carrying thinly across the distance.

Ferréol shifted beside the gun. "They fought with us last night," he said, not quite a question. "Men like that. With the Americans."

No one answered him.

Siméon looked at the people between the armies and could not reconcile the two images: the Black soldiers moving in silence at Redoubt 10, bayonets fixed, their place in the line unquestioned, and this.

Sans Soucy held the glass steady, watching longer than seemed necessary. When he lowered it, his face had changed.

"Some of them are sick," he said. "The way they move. The way they hold themselves."

He stared into the middle distance for a moment. Then, his voice low: "It is the pox."

No one spoke. Siméon watched Sans Soucy's face and saw something old move behind his eyes. Charlotte. Lucie. The knowledge that never leaves.

"They know," Michel said. His voice was flat. "The British know what they are sending out."

Sans Soucy did not answer. He raised the glass again, as if looking away from the men beside him was easier than letting them see his face.

By midday, the expelled began to make camp where they stood. They gathered scraps of wood, torn canvas, anything that might serve as cover. Fires appeared, small and uncertain, flickering in the open ground.

The guns did not pause. Shot and shell continued their arc, passing overhead or striking beyond them. The camps existed in the intervals of thunder, in the spaces between targets.

On the third night, Siméon saw a burial party leave the allied lines and stop short of the open ground. They did not cross it. They turned back, empty-handed.

Whatever promises had been made to these people by the British, they were not honored.

HISTORICAL NOTE: THE EXPELLED AND THE BLACK SOLDIER AT YORKTOWN

In 1775, Virginia's royal governor Lord Dunmore promised freedom to enslaved people owned by rebels who reached British lines. This strategic offer targeted Patriot plantations alone; Loyalist slaveholders were protected. Throughout the war, thousands risked escape on that promise. By the siege of Yorktown, an estimated 2,000 men, women, and children were inside the British garrison. As supplies ran out, Cornwallis ordered them expelled; beginning October 15, nearly all were forced into the open ground between the armies. The precise numbers were never recorded; that absence is itself part of the tragedy. Neither side accepted them. This expulsion came one day after Black soldiers of the 1st Rhode Island Regiment helped capture Redoubt No.10. Baron von Closen recorded that the regiment was "the most neatly dressed, the best under arms, and the most precise in its maneuvers." On the same ground, within hours, Black soldiers proved themselves among the finest in the American army while Black refugees who had trusted the British were cast out to die. Sources: *Sylvia R. Frey, Water from the Rock (1991); Cassandra Pybus, Epic Journeys of Freedom (2006); Baron Ludwig von Closen, Revolutionary Journal (1958).*

October 15, 1781

At first light, Siméon saw the Americans already at work. Through the lifting smoke, crews from General Knox's artillery were manhandling field pieces up the captured slope of Redoubt 10, their shirts stained dark with sweat. Some worked barefoot, feet caked in the same Virginia mud that clung to his own boots.

"Look at them go," Vincent muttered, following his gaze. "Not a moment's pause."

Sans Soucy watched a crew muscle a gun into place without a word of complaint. He gave a slow, approving nod. "That is how you earn a nation."

Their own orders came before the sun was fully up. "Haul forward," Sans Soucy said, his voice stripped of all humor. "Into the parallel behind Redoubt Nine." All along the Grand Battery, other crews were receiving the same command. The heavy siege mortars remained in place, their deep thunder uninterrupted, but the field pieces were shifting forward. Siméon and his crew dragged their twelve-pounder through the communicating trench, the iron wheels sinking into earth still littered with the debris of the night's assault. When they locked the carriage into its new emplacement, the sergeant gestured toward the dark shape of Yorktown. "Four hundred yards, by the engineers' measure. They can see us breathing now."

October 16, 1781: The Abercromby Sortie

By morning, the captured redoubts had been absorbed into the Allied siege lines. French and American gunners hauled their pieces forward into the newly completed second parallel, dragging iron through earth still torn from the night's assault.

The French batteries resumed their relentless work. The guns were so close now that Siméon could distinguish figures moving along Yorktown's ramparts, men ducking and vanishing behind shattered parapets. There was nowhere left for the British to withdraw except into the town itself.

The crews worked in shifts, day bleeding into night and back again. On the night of October 15, Sans Soucy kept watch at the battery with Jean-Baptiste and Pierre, maintaining the guns and standing ready should the enemy attempt a sortie. The others slept in the earthworks just behind the position, close enough to reach the guns in seconds.

Siméon had fallen into an exhausted sleep with his coat bundled beneath his head, Vincent snoring softly beside him, when the world shattered.

At about four in the morning, musket fire cracked through the predawn darkness. A sentry shouted a warning and was abruptly silenced.

Then Sans Soucy's voice cut through the chaos.

"To the guns! The British!"

Siméon came awake instantly, seizing his musket. Vincent was already on his feet. They scrambled over the parapet and plunged into confusion.

British light infantry swarmed the battery.

In the dim light, Siméon saw Jean-Baptiste locked in a brutal struggle with a grenadier, both men wrestling for control of a bayonet. Pierre swung a handspike like a club, driving two attackers back from the carriage. Sans Soucy stood beside their twelve-pounder, blood streaking his sleeve as he bellowed orders and thrust his bayonet into a British soldier at arm's length.

"Protect the guns!" he roared.

Ferréol burst in at Siméon's left, still clutching the sponge staff he had seized in his rush from sleep. He swung it like a quarterstaff, striking an attacker across the jaw with a crack that sent him reeling. Michel and Soriol rushed from the flank, muskets raised but useless in the press, unable to fire without striking their own men.

A British soldier lunged at Siméon with fixed bayonet. He barely raised his musket in time to deflect the thrust. They grappled, boots sliding in churned mud, the man's weight forcing him backward until Divertissant appeared out of the darkness with a rammer clenched in both hands and drove it hard into the attacker's ribs, throwing him against the parapet.

"Not this one!" Divertissant bellowed. "Not our gun!"

Even as the French crews fought to hold their position, other attackers moved methodically from gun to gun. One pulled a metal spike from his belt and tried to hammer it into a vent, only to find it too large. He cursed, then rammed his bayonet into the touch-hole instead, twisting violently until the blade snapped, wedged deep inside the cannon's vent.

"Drive them out!" Sans Soucy shouted.

The gunners surged forward with renewed fury, striking with handspikes, rammers, and musket butts. The British, their work done, withdrew as quickly as they had come, falling back under covering fire from their lines.

The entire *sortie* had lasted perhaps ten minutes.[60]

In the sudden stillness, Siméon became aware of the blood on his hands. His breath came in ragged pulls. Around him, the crew checked one another by voice and touch. Jean-Baptiste clutched a deep gash in his forearm but remained standing. Pierre leaned against the carriage, pale but whole. Vincent wiped blood from a split lip. Ferréol still gripped his sponge staff, knuckles white.

Gunners from neighboring crews lay motionless in the mud. The wounded groaned as the sky began to pale. Hundreds of men had attacked, yet fewer than a dozen French or American guns in the battery were successfully spiked.

Sans Soucy moved through the wreckage, his expression set, blood running down his arm. He did not slow.

"Clear the vents," he ordered. "Now. Michel, Divertissant, the drill bits. The rest of you, stand guard. They may try again."

They worked as dawn spread across the works. Michel and Divertissant bored into jammed metal while Siméon, Vincent, and Ferréol stood watch with loaded muskets. Pierre organized powder with trembling hands. Soriol bound Jean-Baptiste's arm and returned to the line.

Siméon took his turn at the twelve-pounder, easing a broken blade free millimeter by millimeter. The metal was still warm from the violence of the twist.

Within the hour, the twelve-pounder spoke again. Then another. One by one, the battery returned to life, thunder rolling across Yorktown.

Siméon looked down at the shattered blade in his hand. The gamble had failed. The guns were speaking again.

Sans Soucy came by last, inspecting each man in turn: Siméon,

---

[60] **Lieutenant Colonel Robert Abercromby** led the pre-dawn sortie of October 16, 1781, consisting of approximately 350 British troops drawn from the Royal Guards, elements of the 80th Regiment of Foot, and light infantry and grenadier detachments. Their objective was to spike the guns in the Allied second parallel. Several cannon in both French and American sectors were temporarily disabled, often by driving bayonets into the vents after prepared spikes proved too large; Allied artillerists cleared the obstructions by morning. George Washington later observed that the spikes "were easily extracted." Sources: *Jerome A. Greene, The Guns of Independence: The Siege of Yorktown, 1781 (El Dorado Hills, CA: Savas Beatie, 2005); and Baron Ludwig von Closen, The Revolutionary Journal of Baron Ludwig von Closen, 1780 – 1783, ed. Evelyn M. Acomb (Chapel Hill: University of North Carolina Press, 1958).*

Vincent, Ferréol, Michel, Jean-Baptiste with his bandaged arm, Pierre, Soriol, Divertissant. Filthy, bloodied, shaken, but standing. All eight.

"You held," he said quietly. He gestured toward the twelve-pounder, already firing once more. "The gun is yours. You earned it."

Then, almost as an afterthought: "Rest when you can. But not yet."

He turned his gaze toward Yorktown.

"We finish this first."

October 17 – 18: Parley

By the next morning, an uncanny quiet had settled over the lines. After days of constant thunder, the sudden absence of sound pressed in. Soldiers lay in the trenches with their boots still on, unable to rest, waiting for the world to exhale. It was not peace; it was suspense, drawn tight as a drumhead.

Rain fell before dawn, a steady drizzle that turned the trenches to mud and muffled the usual sounds of camp. By mid-morning it had ceased, but fog rolled in behind it, thick and clinging, softening the edges of the battlefield. Earthworks and shattered cannon wheels faded into pale silhouettes. There was still fear, yes, but also something neither side dared name aloud. Hope.

Vincent moved among the wounded, carrying water, cracking jokes that made even the stretcher-bearers grin. Sans Soucy hauled planks and gabions for the engineers without a word, his shoulders bowed but steady. Siméon worked beside him in silence, his hands blistered and muscles aching, his thoughts on what might come next.

Bonnay walked the battery line as he had each evening. He looked down at the men slumped beside the guns, blackened and spent. "Fifteen thousand rounds," he said quietly. "That's what we've fired since we opened the batteries." No one answered. The number explained the ache in their arms better than words.

Then Michel stiffened. "Look," he hissed, nudging Siméon. "Look there."

A speck of white flickered against the grey, waving faintly from the British lines.

Then the fog thinned, and they saw it clearly: a lone British drummer boy stepping forward, the dull thud of his drum carrying across no-man's-land. He picked his way across the scarred ground, through the crowded makeshift camps of those the British had cast out days before: the sick, the starving, the expelled. Beside him walked an officer, a white handkerchief tied to the end of his sword, raised high. The sight froze the trenches. Men stopped mid-motion. Even the groans of the wounded fell quiet.

The drummer kept beating the slow rhythm of parley, each stroke echoing through the valley like a heartbeat. Soldiers stood on their parapets, peering through the drifting fog. Disbelief gave way to awe.

"Mon Dieu," someone breathed. "A flag of truce."

"They want to parley," another voice said, louder now.

The British officer was blindfolded and led forward into the American lines, disappearing into the fog. No one knew yet what message he carried, but the meaning was unmistakable. After nineteen days of siege, Cornwallis was ready to negotiate.

Then Vincent exhaled, long and low, and clapped Siméon on the shoulder.

"Well, my friend," he said, a grin breaking across his tired face, "better polish those boots." He winked. "You'll want to look your best when we participate in history."

October 18, 1781: Negotiations

All day, rumors swirled through the encampments like smoke. Some said Cornwallis himself would come to meet Washington. Others insisted he would not show; that he'd never face his conquerors. Men speculated over every messenger that passed, every mounted officer seen crossing the lines. The air buzzed with restless anticipation, the kind that made soldiers forget to eat, or laugh too loudly at half-formed jokes.

Siméon stayed near the artillery depot, polishing tools; the scent of oil and gunpowder still heavy in the air. Around him, the camp had taken on an uncanny stillness, a great machine wound tight, waiting. The fighting was done, but not yet finished. The final word, the ink on the page, had to come first.

By midmorning, the word spread: negotiations were underway at a small house between the lines. General Cornwallis had not come himself; he had sent Lieutenant Colonel Thomas Dundas and Major Alexander Ross in his place. The allied officers, Viscount de Noailles and Lieutenant Colonel John Laurens[61] representing France and the United States respectively, met to decide the fate of thousands.

"The Redcoats are wrangling over their pride," one American joked nearby. "Still can't bring themselves to say surrender."

Another replied, "Let 'em wrangle. They'll march out tomorrow all the same."

The French soldiers, more restrained, spoke quietly among themselves. Their discipline showed even now: uniforms brushed, muskets gleaming, the battery crews at their posts, cannons silent but ready. Vincent leaned on a cannon wheel, watching an American unit pass with mismatched coats and bare feet. "If not for our artillery," he murmured to Siméon with a faint grin, "these brave fellows would still be digging trenches."

Siméon chuckled softly. He knew it was true.

By afternoon, word rippled through the camp: the surrender was agreed upon. The formal ceremony would take place the next day, October 19.

That night, the men sat by their fires, passing bottles and talking in low voices. Some laughed about how they'd tell the story back home, how they had seen a great empire bow. Others simply stared into the flames, too drained or too humbled to speak.

Vincent broke the silence at last. "Tomorrow," he said, tipping his cup toward the stars, "we will watch history happen."

Siméon raised his cup. "To history."

---

[61] **Viscount Louis-Marie de Noailles** (1756 – 1804) and **Lieutenant Colonel John Laurens** (1754 – 1782) represented the Allies at the surrender negotiations held at Moore House on October 18, 1781. Because Cornwallis declined to attend in person, he sent Lieutenant Colonel Thomas Dundas (1750 – 1794) and Major Alexander Ross (1742 – 1827) in his place. Sources: Jerome A. Greene, *The Guns of Independence: The Siege of Yorktown, 1781* (El Dorado Hills, CA: Savas Beatie, 2005). Biographical details are drawn from *Dictionary of National Biography* (London: Smith, Elder & Co., 1885 – 1900), s.v. "Dundas, Thomas" and "Ross, Alexander (1742 – 1827)."

October 19, 1781: The Surrender

That morning dawned clear and windless, the kind of stillness that felt almost sacred after weeks of thunder and fire. Across the fields of Yorktown, the allied armies assembled in perfect ranks. French soldiers, immaculate in gleaming white coats, the dark blue of the artillery, and polished brass, stood shoulder to shoulder with the ragged Americans whose patched uniforms bore the marks of years of hunger and endurance. Their banners lifted in the crisp air: the Stars and Stripes and the white Bourbon flag of France fluttering side by side, emblems of a unity that had finally broken an empire.

From the opposite ridge, the British emerged in silence. Red-coated columns advanced with slow precision, their colors cased and dipped in defeat. The faces of the soldiers were hollow, eyes fixed straight ahead. They moved with the rigid dignity of men trying to hold on to what pride remained. Cornwallis himself was nowhere to be seen, still pleading illness; he sent his second-in-command, General O'Hara, in his place. Washington, maintaining his own quiet balance of honor and reproach, responded in kind: he too sent his second, General Benjamin Lincoln, to receive the surrender.

Siméon stood with Vincent and the rest of their gun crew at the edge of the French batteries. Together they watched the long, red line of British soldiers march forward and stack their muskets, the metallic clatter echoing faintly across the open field. The drums beat a hollow rhythm: steady, mournful, and final.

The ceremony itself was restrained, almost cold in its formality. The British sword was presented and received, the symbol of surrender sealed before thousands of watching eyes. Then the order to dismiss was given. From the American lines, a roar of cheers burst forth, rolling like a wave down the ranks. Formations dissolved into a flood of activity as soldiers broke ranks, celebrating. An American soldier grabbed Siméon in a rough embrace, laughing through tears, shouting words he could barely understand. Around them, the sea of white and blue and makeshift uniforms seemed to merge, French and American joy erupting as one.

The British Surrender at Yorktown, October 19, 1781

Somewhere, it was said later, the British band played a final tune as their men marched away: *The World Turned Upside Down*. Whether it truly happened or not, the story endured, because on that day the order of things had indeed been reversed. When the defeated British turned their faces toward the French, refusing to acknowledge the Americans they had once dismissed as rabble, Lafayette is said to have ordered his fifes and drums to strike up *Yankee Doodle*, the very tune the Redcoats had used to mock their colonial subjects. Now it was a victory song. The contemptible rabble had won.

The British Empire's power in America had collapsed. The war had not yet ended everywhere, but there in Virginia, they had decided it.

As the last British column passed and the surrender drums fell silent, Siméon felt. The weight of victory settled: not light, but immense, like the still air after a storm.

Fleur d'Épine and Louis should have been there. Siméon could imagine Fleur leaning against a gun carriage, grinning at the absurdity of the ceremony after the violence and chaos, and Louis teasing Vincent about his crooked cravat. The image brought no comfort, only the ache of absence.

In the hours that followed, the release was palpable. The American soldiers, their superiors, and townsfolk swept the French allies into an unplanned celebration. Laughter rose, awkward at first, then warm and unrestrained. Strangers clapped them on the shoulders, pressed mugs into their hands, and toasted with a vigor that needed no translation.

Siméon was jostled by the crowd and turned, half annoyed, only to find Antoine Porcherot staring back at him in disbelief. The last time Siméon had seen him, Antoine was marching toward Jussey with the recruiters while Siméon stood rooted to his father's vineyard. For a heartbeat they simply looked at one another, then Antoine laughed and pulled him close, a hard, wordless embrace that said everything neither could. They broke apart grinning, each suddenly aware of how close things had come to ending differently.

That night, barrels of hard cider and rum rolled into the streets. Roasted meat was passed from hand to hand, and awkward toasts in broken French and English turned to laughter. "*Vive la France!*" echoed beside "God bless America!" Songs rose, some familiar, some strange, until they mingled into one chorus of victory.

For a few hours, the war felt like it was finished. The streets were filled with music, the glow of lanterns, and the mingled voices of two nations who had fought side by side. It was the first night in weeks where the stars looked clear instead of veiled by powder smoke.

But French discipline prevailed. Orders came: the men were to return to camp. As they walked back in the cool night, their steps were slower than usual, not from weariness but from the weight of what they had just lived through.

Later, by the fire, they raised their cups with reverence, not to the victory alone, but to all who had been lost along the way.

"To our brothers lost," Sans Soucy said, his voice uncharacteristically soft. "Gone too soon, but never gone from us. Rest well, brothers."

They drank, the simple cider a sacrament carrying both the weight of loss and the fragile hope that the war's ending was near, into the quiet night.

HISTORICAL NOTE: THE SIEGE OF YORKTOWN

General George Washington and Lieutenant General Jean-Baptiste Donatien de Vimeur, Comte de Rochambeau, led a combined force of approximately 16,000 soldiers, roughly equal parts American and French, against Lieutenant General Charles Cornwallis at Yorktown from September 28 to October 19, 1781. Admiral de Grasse's fleet blockaded the Chesapeake, severing British escape and reinforcement. The allied armies advanced behind successive parallels, their artillery reducing Yorktown's defenses with systematic precision. Cornwallis, his position untenable, requested terms on October 17. The formal capitulation followed two days later. Washington had spent six years holding an army together through defeat, hunger, and desertion. Rochambeau had crossed an ocean and subordinated his command to an ally. De Grasse had won the battle that made the siege possible. At Yorktown, everything they had endured and risked arrived at the same moment. The Treaty of Paris in 1783 confirmed what the guns had already decided. Source: *United States Congress, Senate Document No. 234, Serial Set No. 9347 (1976).*

PART IV
VICTORY TO LEGACY

Chapter Thirteen:
After Yorktown

October 1781 – December 1782

WWhat had begun as thunder and smoke upon the bluffs of the York River dissolved into a silence so profound it unnerved the men who had grown accustomed to the constant roar of cannon. Word spread unevenly, drifting through campfires and taverns, across muddy roads and winter villages: Britain had yielded.

The formalities of victory unfolded around them. On October 21st, two days after the surrender, Cornwallis dined aboard the *Ville de Paris* with Admiral de Grasse, General Washington, and the French commanders. The same Cornwallis who had claimed illness too severe to attend his own surrender was apparently recovered enough for French wine and conversation. Junior officers and soldiers who worked the dinner carried fragments of conversation back to the camp, and soon rumors spread of what Cornwallis had written to General Clinton in New York. He had called their guns "an immense train of heavy artillery, perfectly well manned." He admitted the allied fire silenced every British cannon; by the end they could not answer with a single gun. Some said he spoke directly to Colonel d'Aboville, acknowledging that French artillery had broken his defenses.

The artillerymen of Auxonne received such gossip with quiet pride. They had served those guns. They had hauled them from France fed them powder and shot through the long nights, and kept them firing when the British tried to answer. Now even the enemy's commander was forced to admit what they had done.

The camp buzzed with talk, much of it echoing the sharp satisfaction of their own commissary, Claude Blanchard, who had been heard to re-mark on the British: "All their pride and arrogance, and for what? Beaten by a bunch of almost-naked peasants they claimed to despise."

Vincent, ever ready with a pointed quip, repeated it with a grim smile. "He is not wrong. All their fine clothing and high manners, disarmed by men in rags. It is a new world, my boys."

Then, on October 28th, word came that Cornwallis had signed his parole and would be permitted to return to England. The news landed differently than the men expected.

"They let him go," Michel said flatly, staring into the fire. "The coward who would not face Washington at the surrender. And now he sails home to his manor while his men rot in prison camps."

"That is how it works for lords," Sans Soucy replied, his voice even. "The officers go free. The common soldiers stay behind."

Siméon thought of the British troops he had seen marching out of Yorktown, their faces pale and drawn, some weeping, others throwing down their muskets in fury. They would remain prisoners until exchanged or paroled, perhaps for years. But Cornwallis, the man who had command-ed them, would be received warmly in London.

Word came that Admiral de Grasse was preparing to depart. By November 4, the French regiments from the West Indies had re-embarked.

For Siméon, Vincent, and the rest of Captain Bonnay's artillery com-pany, there was no voyage home. That week they entered winter quarters. Their eight-year enlistments still bound them to the King's service, and Williamsburg became their assigned station.

Garrison life brought small frictions. The first came when Siméon and Vincent went into town for a whetstone and tobacco.

A merchant, his cart nearly empty, raised a hand. "No French today. Orders. Americans only."

"We have coin," Vincent said.

"It's not the coin," the man replied, nodding toward a group of Continentals sorting through worn shoes. "They're paid in paper worth almost nothing. You carry silver. If I sell to you first, there'll be nothing left."

Siméon looked at the Americans, coats threadbare, feet wrapped in cloth. They had stood in the same trenches and won the same victory, but with almost nothing.

Vincent's anger eased. "They've been fighting for years," he said. "Paid when they can be. Shod when there are shoes."

"And they are still here," Siméon answered.

He guided his friend back toward camp. "Today we can wait."

It was a small concession, but as the ragged soldiers clutched their purchases, the fairness of the order was plain. The French would manage. The Continentals had endured years of want.

Yorktown lay scarred and largely deserted. Williamsburg, by contrast, retained its colonial grace, broad streets, brick houses, taverns alive with talk, church bells marking the day. After months of marches and sieges, it felt almost like peace.

While winter in Virginia gave Siméon a vision of a new world, it was the men of his regiment who gave him continuity. Without the pressure of war, they came to know one another differently.

Vincent, irreverent as ever, became the camp's storyteller, spinning tales, some true, most invented, of Paris taverns and women undone by French artillerymen. Jean-Baptiste foraged and fished, returning almost daily with something useful. Michel tended the camp kitchens with priestly care, insisting that victory should taste like something, and mending whatever broke. Pierre, the glassworker from Lorraine, sketched the camp, the river, and the faces of his comrades with the same precision he once brought to the magazines. Divertissant's singing carried across clear nights, lifting spirits as reliably as his jokes had on the march. Soriol, no longer the nervous merchant's son, kept careful inventory of powder and supplies. Ferréol, quieter than Fleur, maintained their equipment and sometimes hummed the old songs of Franche-Comté that stirred Siméon's homesickness.

Charcoal Sketch at Yorktown.

Sans Soucy watched over them all, offering correction or approval with undiminished vigilance. He, Siméon, and Vincent remained constant. They had fought and mourned together, and now shared the steady rhythm of peacetime duties: patrolling quiet roads, escorting wagons, attending church, drilling, cleaning cannons that would never again fire in anger on American soil. Like soldiers everywhere, they waited for orders to return to France.

It was on a grey afternoon, the kind where the cold settled into your bones and would not leave, that Siméon found the poem again.

He had been reorganizing his trunk. The small Voltaire volume sat atop the pile, its leather cover darkened from many months of handling.

As he lifted it, he noticed a folded paper that had slipped free and drifted to the bottom of his trunk.

He picked it up slowly, recognizing Fleur's careful script visible through the thin paper even before he unfolded it. The poem. He had tucked it into the book and forgotten it in the chaos of preparation, the march to the coast, the ocean crossing, the siege.

He sat down on the edge of his cot and unfolded it.

The verses were in French, simple and direct, but below them, in Fleur's neat handwriting, was a recipe, with little notes crowding the margins.

Mutti Closset's Wildzwiebelsuppe

For when the cold settles in your bones

> *Clean and chop two handfuls of wild onions, bulbs and greens both. Melt butter in a heavy pot and cook the onions slowly until soft and sweet, not brown. Add good broth, enough to fill the pot, and simmer until the onions are tender. Tear day-old bread into pieces and stir in at the end. Salt to taste. Serve hot.*

Siméon stared at the recipe. Annotations dotted the page: "Mother's way: If it smells like onion, it IS onion," read one note. "Don't let Michel add too much salt," warned another, followed by a tiny sketch of Michel's scowling face. At the bottom, in smaller script: "Best shared with brothers."

His throat tightened.

"What is that?"

Vincent stood in the doorway, shaking cold rain from his coat.

"Fleur's soup recipe."

Vincent was quiet a moment. "I had forgotten he gave you that."

"So had I."

Then Vincent straightened. "We should make it."

"What?"

"The soup. We should make it." Vincent gestured toward the paper. "He wrote it down for us. We have time now. It is what Fleur would want."

"Yes, we should."

By evening, word had spread through the barracks. Michel appeared first, reading the recipe with the gravity of a scholar examining scripture. "Wild onions in December," he muttered. "In Virginia. This will be interesting."

Jean-Baptiste overheard and grinned. "There is a clearing near the old stone wall, south-facing, where the sun warms the ground. I have seen wild onions there, even this late. Small, but they are there."

Sans Soucy contributed a heavy iron pot and a knowing look.

The next morning, they went foraging. The plants were small, stunted by the cold, but unmistakably onion. Michel pulled one, and held it to his nose. "Wild onions," he confirmed. "We will need twice what Fleur's Mutti Closset called for."

Siméon pulled out Grand-père's pocket knife. He dug carefully around the cluster, loosening the soil, the way Grand-père had taught him.

"Leave some behind," he said. "So they grow again next year."

They gathered what they could, both the white bulbs and the tender green tops, and carried their harvest back to camp.

Soriol met them at the barracks with a loaf of day-old bread. "The recipe calls for it," he said with a shrug, as if he had not walked half a mile in the cold to find it.

The preparation took the better part of the afternoon. Michel commanded the fire. Vincent cleaned and chopped the wild onions. Pierre sat near the fire, sketching the scene with quiet concentration. Sans Soucy also contributed butter. Siméon carefully measured out the ingredients according to Fleur's notes.

"More salt," Michel insisted.

"Fleur specifically says not to let you add too much salt," Vincent countered.

"Fleur was seventeen and knew nothing about cooking."

"And yet he left instructions warning about you and salt."

Divertissant leaned in from his seat by the door. "If Fleur wanted us to follow his mother's recipe, we follow it. Germans know about soup!"

Charcoal sketch of Mutti Closset's Wildzwiebelsuppe

Despite the bickering, or perhaps because of it, the soup came to-gether. The barracks filled with the sweet, sharp scent of onions cooking in butter, the aroma mingling with woodsmoke and the earthy smell of bread softening in broth.

When it was finally ready, Michel ladled it into whatever vessels they could find.

In the firelight, nine men made the sign of the cross, and Divertissant murmured the familiar words: *"Bénis-nous, ô Dieu, et bénis ces dons que nous allons recevoir de Ta générosité, par le Christ, notre Seigneur. Amen."*

"Amen," they answered.

Ferréol hung back at the edge of the circle. "You are one of us," Vincent said quietly. "Fleur would have wanted you here."

"To Fleur d'Épine," he said, "who gave us this."

"To Fleur," they echoed.

The soup was simple: sweet and warm, nothing fancy, the kind of thing a German mother might make on a cold evening. It tasted like the kind of comfort a good friend would bring.

"He would have made fun of us," Siméon said, his voice rough. "Sitting here weeping into our soup like a bunch of children."

"He would have," Michel agreed. "And then he would have asked for thirds."

They laughed, the sound breaking through. And for a little while, in the warmth of the fire and the taste of Mutti Closset's recipe, it felt as though their friend was there with them, grinning in that way he had, pleased that they had finally figured out what the paper was for.

When the pot was empty, Siméon carefully folded the recipe and returned it to the back cover of Voltaire, tucking it beside Laure's pressed flower. Two kinds of love, preserved between pages.

The soup became a ritual after that. Whenever the cold grew sharp and the wait felt too long, they would make it again; never with ceremony, but always together. It was their way of keeping Fleur with them through the long Virginia winter.

The fire burned low.

Though mail was scarce after the siege at Yorktown, a letter eventually reached him from his father. It carried the familiar rhythm of home. He added, in his careful way, that his mother sent her love and Colas seemed happy these days, still seeing the cobbler's daughter from time to time.

Siméon kept the letter in his trunk beside his most treasured belongings; fragile as they were, these few things held his world together, anchoring him when he wondered if he would ever see Laure's face, or the soft light of the French countryside again.

On rare occasions, duty carried them beyond Williamsburg. During one upriver escort, Siméon met Pamunkey guides hired to navigate the bends of the York. They showed him how to draw fish from beneath the ice, their movements precise and unhurried. The encounter lasted only an afternoon, but it lingered.

More often, they dealt with Virginians: a farmer grateful for French protection, a tavern keeper who introduced Siméon to the sharp bite of corn whiskey, children trailing the soldiers and calling out broken French learned at home.

In Williamsburg, officers met by candlelight, trading dispatches and rumor: campaigns near New York, a return to the Caribbean, perhaps a voyage home. For the common soldier, the future remained unread.

In January's deep cold, the frigate *La Sibelle* anchored in the Chesapeake with two million livres. The army would be paid. Relief nearly eclipsed news from Boston: Lafayette had sailed for France on Christmas Day aboard the *Alliance*, carrying word of Yorktown to the King.

Around their fires, the men spoke of him with quiet pride. Nobility though he was, he had shared their mud and danger, leading from the front when it mattered.

"He will make them understand," Vincent said, breath rising in the cold. "The court, the ministers. He will make them see."

Sans Soucy nodded. "Young enough to charm them. Brave enough to be believed. And at Washington's side."

Siméon remembered the Marquis riding the lines before the assault on the redoubts, face alight as before battle. Now he crossed the grey Atlantic, carrying their victory like a torch.

Word also arrived from Versailles: the King and Queen had welcomed a son, the Dauphin[62]. France had an heir. The men raised what cups they had and drank to the prince, to the King, to victory, to home.

Yet for Siméon, the warmest news came with the courier who brought the mail.

When his name was called, his heart quickened.

The letter bore the careful hand of Julien Hudel of Rennes. Inside were a few lines reporting that Laure remained in good health and proper circumstance. At the close, Julien added a brief passage sent with her knowledge and consent.

---

[62] **Louis Joseph Xavier François, Dauphin of France** (1781 – 1789), was born on October 22, 1781, three days after the surrender at Yorktown. News of his birth reached French forces in America in the weeks that followed, and formal celebrations were delayed until the army could observe the occasion appropriately. The elaborate festivities held in Philadelphia in the summer of 1782, including the pavilion commissioned by the chevalier de La Luzerne, marked the most visible expression of this rejoicing. The Dauphin died on June 4, 1789, at the age of seven, shortly before the outbreak of the French Revolution. Source: *Antonia Fraser, Marie Antoinette: The Journey* (New York: Doubleday, 2001).

She asks that you be assured of her continued remembrance. She prays for your safety and commends you to God's protection. She hopes you remain in good health.

Siméon read the lines twice, then folded the letter and placed it inside his vest.

The spring of 1782 passed slowly. Then in June came word that stopped men mid-sentence: the Ville de Paris, Admiral de Grasse's flagship, the great ship that had held the Chesapeake and made Yorktown possible, had been captured by the British. Whatever hopes they held of an easy peace faded. The war at sea was not over.

Weeks later, the Williamsburg camp stirred with the unmistakable industry of an army preparing to move. Wagons were inspected, chests opened, axles greased, harness repaired. No proclamation had been read, but the camp spoke for itself.

That afternoon, Captain Bonnay gathered his men beneath the trees.

"Be ready," he said. "The army marches north, through Maryland and Pennsylvania, back to the sea. Pack your gear and oil the axles. We wait only on final orders."

A murmur moved through the company, relief edged with regret.

Soriol lingered. "Do you think we will fight again, Sergeant?"

Sans Soucy shrugged. "If the diplomats fail, perhaps. For now, it is the road and the drum."

Written orders soon arrived from General d'Aboville's staff. The army would march. The Régiment d'Artillerie d'Auxonne would again be divided. One hundred fifty men would remain behind.

A groan rose as the roster was posted.

Captain Bonnay's company was named among the Auxonne 150, assigned to West Point, Virginia, to guard the siege artillery until it could be sent by sea. Newport again: still guns, the duty of waiting while others took the road. Siméon scanned the list and found the expected names:

Vincent, Michel, Pierre, Soriol, Ferréol, Jean-Baptiste, Divertissant. Sans Soucy. All staying. All together.

Vincent kicked a stone. "Babysitters for the guns. Again."

"At least this time we know the children," Sans Soucy said, drawing weary chuckles.

On the morning of July 4, 1782, they watched the infantry brigades roll out of camp. The guns they had prepared remained silent. The road north passed the burned remains of Gloucester Point and the fields of surrender.

The days dragged. The air lay heavy with flies and impatience. The detachment drilled, shifted camp, and waited for orders that never came.

One afternoon, Siméon and Vincent sat in the narrow shade of a storehouse, tin cups in hand. Sans Soucy lounged nearby, hat tipped low. Michel and Pierre lingered a few yards off, Pierre carving at a stick. Divertissant attempted a card trick for Soriol. Jean-Baptiste and Ferréol argued quietly.

The silence between Siméon and Vincent was easy.

"How many times have we waited?" Vincent asked.

"Four," Siméon said. "If you count the coast as two."

"I do."

Sans Soucy grunted. "The coast. Newport. Now this."

"At least the guns are real," Vincent said. "At Newport we lit fires for ghosts."

A faint breeze stirred.

"Do you remember what you said on the coast?" Siméon asked. "That it is not the war that kills most soldiers. It is the waiting."

The sergeant lifted his hat brim. "I remember."

"I understand it now."

Sans Soucy studied him. "Took you long enough."

Vincent leaned back. "First time, I thought we were cursed. Second, forgotten. Newport, punished." He shrugged. "Now I think this is what it means to serve the guns."

"The guns go where they are needed," Sans Soucy said. "And they wait. So do we."

Siméon raised his cup. "To waiting."

Vincent touched his cup to it. "And to knowing why."

Sans Soucy lifted his without ceremony. "To the guns. And to the fools who tend them."

The others joined, cups and canteens raised against the heat. They drank in silence. The road shimmered. And they sat in the shade, letting the hours pass.

In mid-August, orders finally came. The detachment broke camp and marched to West Point, the head of the York River, which opens into the Chesapeake. The siege guns waited on the wharf, loaded onto transports under sailors from La Villesbrunne's squadron[63].

At the end of the month, they sailed up the Chesapeake and rejoined the army in Baltimore.

The city's welcome felt personal. Much of Baltimore was home to Acadian families[64], exiles of another war, who watched the soldiers of their ancestral land pass with reverence. French voices rose from the crowd, praising their bearing and the strength they still carried after Yorktown. It was a thread of shared language and loss stretched across an ocean.

Siméon leaned toward Vincent without breaking step. "Do you hear that? It feels strange, being noticed after all this time."

Vincent gave a low laugh. "Strange? It feels glorious. Two years in America, and I thought we would return like ghosts."

---

[63] **François-Louis de Saillans, comte de La Villesbrunne**, comte de La Villesbrunne, commanded a French naval squadron operating in the Chesapeake in 1782, coordinating transport of artillery and troops after the Yorktown campaign. Source: *W3R-US*, *"1782: Global Naval Warfare," W3R-Archive*, w3r-archive.org/history/hist-1782.htm.

[64] **The Acadians** were French settlers expelled by the British from Nova Scotia beginning in 1755; some resettled in Maryland and Baltimore, where French language and Catholic traditions endured.

Siméon smiled. "Well, they see us now."

"Aye," Vincent said, standing a little taller as another cheer rose. "For once, they do."

From Baltimore, the Auxonne 150 joined the final march north. The artillery corps were granted the honor and burden of leading, rolling out a day ahead of the infantry. The route carried them to White Marsh Forge, then Lower Ferry, and north to the wide Susquehanna at Head of Elk. Ferrymen guided wagons and cannons onto rafts as families gathered along the banks. Children cheered when the dripping horses clambered ashore, stamping and snorting.

HISTORICAL NOTE: THE AUXONNE 150

Following Yorktown, roughly 150 men from the Régiment d'Auxonne were assigned to guard the siege artillery. In August 1782, protected by La Villesbrunne's squadron, they sailed to Baltimore, then marched north as the Franco-American army repositioned while the British fleet remained active along the coast. The allied forces later passed in review near New York. Sources: *Lee Kennett, The French Forces in America, 1780 – 1783 (Greenwood Press, 1977), 1782: Global Naval Warfare," Washington-Rochambeau Revolutionary Historical Archive, w3r-archive.org/history/hist-1872.htm.*

"We look like a parade," Vincent said, shaking his head.

"Better than a funeral," Sans Soucy muttered.

The march carried them through Delaware and Pennsylvania, through Trenton, Princeton, and the long fields of New Jersey. Townspeople brought food and waved flags.

Philadelphia was the grandest stop of all. The city had been preparing for weeks to celebrate the birth of the Dauphin. Siméon and his comrades saw little of that splendor directly. Their camp lay on the outskirts, far from the magnificent open-air pavilion the Chevalier de la Luzerne had commissioned, far from the seven hundred guests who filled the ballrooms, far from Generals Washington and Rochambeau raising their glasses among members of Congress and Philadelphia's leading families.

For the soldiers, it was quieter. Small fires. Shared rations. A toast to their commanders and the new prince. Violins drifted on the summer air, mingling with laughter and occasional celebratory musket fire.

The Dauphin's Fête, Philadelphia, July 15, 1782

When the fireworks began, the men fell silent. Red, gold, and white bursts rose above the skyline, reflecting in the river and flickering across their faces.

"Imagine," said Vincent, "such splendor for a baby's birthday."

"Our future king," Siméon answered. "Their way of saying thank you and farewell."

Vincent watched the sparks fade. "We crossed an ocean for war, and now we watch fireworks for an infant we will never meet."

"A prince," Siméon corrected quietly. "One day he will be king. And we will tell our children we toasted his birth on the far side of the world."

They remained seated as the last rockets dissolved into darkness. In the distant pavilion, generals and ministers toasted alliance and victory. In the grass beside a cannon, two young artillerymen from Auxonne did the same.

After crossing the Hudson, the army formed on the plains of Verplanck's Point in a grand line of battle, deliberately staged within sight of the British garrison across the river. The masts of their ships pierced the sky, now silent spectators.

This was no ordinary review. Word had passed: this would be the last time the allied armies stood as one. After three years of shared hardship and victory, the alliance was ending. The French would march to Boston and sail home. The Americans would return to their posts. The two commanders who had forged the partnership would part, perhaps forever.

On September 14, Rochambeau and Washington met to review the troops.

The men of Auxonne stood in perfect ranks, uniforms brushed spotless, bronze guns gleaming in the autumn light. Along the line, French and American soldiers stood shoulder to shoulder: Bourbonnais in white faced with crimson, Royal Deux-Ponts in sky blue, Continentals in worn buff and blue. A living mosaic of two nations united one last time.

Siméon felt the surge of it, pride edged with something heavier. He fixed on the two figures riding slowly down the line. Washington sat tall on his gray horse, composed and reserved. Beside him rode Rochambeau, weathered and resolute, surveying the men who had followed him across an ocean. Behind them, standards lifted in the river breeze.

As they neared, Siméon studied Washington, once a whispered hope, then a rallying cry, now a promise fulfilled. He fixed every detail in memory: the steady bearing, the slight inclination of the head toward each regiment, the authority that required no display.

When they reached the Auxonne, Washington reined in and raised his hand in salute.

"France has done us a great honor."

The words settled deep within Siméon.

Across the field, Baron von Steuben commanded the Continentals through their maneuvers, voice sharp and clear. The regiments moved with crisp precision, every wheel and column drilled to perfection. Siméon felt a pang for Fleur, who had not lived to see this day, nor to witness von Steuben's discipline made manifest.

When the review ended, the two generals dismounted and faced one another before the assembled armies. For a moment they stood, two men who had gambled on an audacious march south and won. Rochambeau extended his hand. Washington clasped it.

A rolling feu de joie erupted, musket fire cascading down the Franco-American lines like thunder. The volleys echoed across the water toward the British garrison, a final declaration.

The British did not answer. There was nothing left to say.

That evening, campfires lined the Hudson like embers of shared triumph. Siméon and his chosen brothers sat near their cannon, the river dark before them.

"Strange," Vincent said softly, "the enemy so close, and no shots fired."

"Because," Siméon replied, eyes drifting from the British tents to the stars, "we have nothing left to prove."

Sans Soucy nodded. "They watched us today. They know what it meant."

"It meant we won," Michel said.

Silence followed. Across the river, British campfires mirrored their own.

Siméon thought of Washington's salute, Rochambeau's handclasp, the thunder of the *feu de joie*. Of Louis. Of Fleur. Of the others who would never see home.

The march east through Connecticut carried them through Ridgefield, Danbury, Hartford, and Windham. At every stop, townspeople came out to greet them. Fireworks flared above village greens. Old men raised their hats. The sharp autumn air turned the woods from Chesapeake green to New England red and gold.

The road wore on them. On the third day out of Hartford, Michel noticed Alexis Le Bru falling behind.

Alexis was twenty-one; he had enlisted in December, crossed the ocean with them, endured Newport, marched to Yorktown, and fired his gun alongside the rest. But he had remained quiet, never fully part of bonds forged before his arrival.

Now he walked with his head down, pack slipping from one shoulder, boots dragging.

Michel slowed until he was beside him. After a few steps, he lifted the pack from Alexis's shoulders and swung it onto his own broad frame.

"I can carry it," Alexis said, voice thin.

"I know," Michel answered. "But I want to."

Pierre moved to Alexis's other side without a word. The three walked on together, oak and reed bracing the one who faltered.

"How far to Newport?" Alexis asked.

"A few days," Pierre said. "We will get there."

"I just need to rest. When we arrive, I will rest."

Michel and Pierre exchanged a glance but said nothing.

That evening, Michel gave Alexis bread from his own ration. Pierre spread his coat near the fire. No fuss. Only what needed doing.

Across the flames, Siméon watched. Michel and Pierre had carried each other from the beginning. Now they carried Alexis too. That was what brothers did.

When the first cool winds of October came, the regiments arrived in Rhode Island. The Régiment d'Auxonne took up familiar quarters near the sea. Drills resumed each morning: drumbeat, brass in pale light. They maintained the batteries, cleaned the guns, prepared matériel for transport.

On October 6, without warning, Alexis Le Bru collapsed during drill. They carried him to the surgeon, but nothing could be done. The cold and the long march from Yorktown had taken what strength remained. He would be the last of Bonnay's Company to die in America.

They buried him in Newport, far from Granges-le-Bourg. Siméon stood at the grave with Vincent, Michel, Pierre, Jean-Baptiste, Ferréol, Soriol, Divertissant, and Sans Soucy. The chaplain's Latin prayers carried on the October wind. Michel's broad shoulders bowed. Pierre wept beside him.

Alexis had survived the crossing, Newport, Yorktown. He would never see France again.

As they returned to quarters, Siméon counted the names of those who had begun the journey with them, and the graves that would remain in foreign soil.

Before leaving Newport for the last time, Siméon and Vincent walked to the rocky shore where Louis lay buried. The wooden marker had weathered in the salt air, but it still stood.

They did not speak. Vincent placed a stone on the grave. Siméon traced the sign of the cross and whispered a prayer.

Then they turned back toward camp, leaving their friend to the sea and the sky he had crossed an ocean to find.

General Rochambeau marched out for Providence in the first week of November. The departure from Newport was staggered; Auxonne and its cannons arrived the following week. There was little respite. Sixty acres of woodland were felled for 1,681 cords of firewood. The steady ring of axes signaled an army digging in, not for battle, but against the cold.

In the cramped, smoky barracks they built, the mood turned somber. Philadelphia's distant music had faded, replaced by the long anticipation of departure.

They remained encamped through November. On the twenty-seventh, the Rhode Island General Assembly formally thanked Rochambeau, calling him "the Protector of the rights of mankind." It was a fine phrase, but it did not warm their bones.

On the first of December, word spread through camp: the General was leaving. Not with the fleet for France, but overland to Newburgh to bid Washington farewell before taking ship from the Chesapeake. Heavy snow fell as he prepared to depart.

The regiments assembled in the cold, breath rising in pale clouds. Rochambeau rode slowly past the ranks, face grave beneath his tricorn. He paused before each regiment, offering a word, a nod, a raised hand. When he reached the artillery, Siméon snapped to salute with the others, holding it as he watched the man who had led them from Newport to Yorktown and back again.

Rochambeau said nothing grand. He looked at the men who had hauled his guns across an ocean and a continent, and he saluted.

"God keep you," someone murmured as his horse turned toward the road. Snow swallowed the sound of hooves. Then he was gone.

They would not see him again.

In the days that followed, orders finally came: the army would march to Boston, where Admiral Vaudreuil's fleet waited to carry them home.

The march took less than a week, but the cold was punishing. On December 5th, they camped at Dedham, the last stop before the city. Private Flohr of the Royal Deux-Ponts later called the cold "almost unbearable." The men of Auxonne would have agreed.

In Boston, they were quartered in vacant houses and barns, a city of closed doors and watchful eyes. The camaraderie of the campaign endured, now edged with uncertainty.

For Siméon, the waiting was its own torment. Letters received, letters written but unsent, a pressed flower, the memory of her promise. Anchors of the soul, and ballast too.

Then a letter came in his father's careful hand.

> *My son, we trust this finds you in health. The winter here is mild so far. The vines are pruned and sleeping. Your brother has repaired the stone wall by the lower field. He works from dawn to dusk and speaks of you often. Your mother lights her candle each evening without fail. We have had no news since summer. Send word when you can. We pray for your safe return.*

Your father.

He read it aloud to the others, his voice steady until the final line.

Chapter Fourteen: Peace Beneath a Poisoned Sky

December 1782 – Spring 1784

Orders arrived at last: embarkation would begin within the week. Admiral Vaudreuil's fleet lay at anchor in the harbor, waiting to carry them to the West Indies. Not home, not yet, but away from this frozen shore.

The final evening before departure, Siméon walked the line of the guns as he had done countless nights before. The muzzles were tarred, the touchholes sealed, the bronze cool beneath his fingers. He stopped beside a twelve-pounder he knew as one might know a comrade: the same piece that had stood with him through Yorktown.

"How many times did she save our skins?" Vincent said quietly, coming up beside him.

Siméon smiled. "Enough to make me superstitious. I used to tap her twice before a fight. It felt like a promise. We looked after her; she looked after us."

Vincent laughed softly. "Superstition or not, she never missed when you aimed her. You and that cannon are bonded."

Siméon ran his palm over the breech one last time. "She made me what I am. My hands, my back, my hearing, they all remember her noise and weight."

Vincent grinned. "That is one way of looking at it."

Not all men would return to France. Pierre Stenietz, the skilled craftsman, announced his intent to stay. His term of service would not end until spring, but his officers had granted early discharge for valorous service rather than transporting a man who had already found his future. Opportunities abounded for a craftsman of his skill, and he had found both work and affection with a local lady, a combination that made the New World worth the gamble.

Michel Caillet stood apart as the farewells were made, his face unreadable. He had years yet to serve on his re-enlistment and would sail with the regiment, but something in him seemed to break at this parting. The Oak and the Reed had bent together through every storm and every hardship since Auxonne. Now one would root in foreign soil while the other returned to France.

Pierre approached him slowly. For a long moment neither spoke. Then Michel extended his hand, and Pierre took it, and what began as a handshake became a firm embrace between brothers whose bond would not break even as they both knew these were their last moments together.

"Every happiness," Michel said roughly, stepping back. "And many children."

Pierre could not answer. He simply nodded, turned to Siméon, and clasped his hand.

"Take care of the Oak for me," he said quietly.

The embarkation was a familiar chaos: muskets stacked, cannon lifted by creaking tackle, casks of powder and biscuit rolled up the gangways. The great guns that had thundered across two continents were now lashed securely, silent and obedient for the long voyage. Boston Harbor was alive with masts, merchantmen and privateers mingling with French warships flying the white Bourbon ensign.

As *L'Aigrette* slipped from the harbor on Christmas Eve, 1782, sails taut against a bitter wind, Vincent leaned on the rail and exhaled.

"Homeward. At last."

For men in a land that did not celebrate the day, the act of leaving felt like a Christmas of its own.

But the open Atlantic offered no respite. A violent storm drove the fleet far off course to the north. By December 28th, they were forced into Portsmouth, New Hampshire, for repairs, their decks and gunwales sheathed in ice.

Siméon and Vincent freezing but busy, polishing the ship's guns, helping to secure cargo, scrubbing the decks until they gleamed.

When the fleet finally sailed south, the cold broke slowly into the humid heat of lower latitudes. They put into the great French harbors of Saint-Domingue, Cap Français and Môle Saint-Nicolas, and hovered off the coasts of Spanish possessions like Puerto Cabello and La Guaira. Fresh water, fruit, and salt meat came aboard by lighter, but liberty did not. The temptation of desertion on a Caribbean island was too great, and the officers knew it. The men remained confined to the ships or the guarded wharves, close enough to smell land, sugar fields, charcoal smoke, the wet earth after rain, but never free to walk upon it.

Through the first months of 1783, they swung at anchor in these tropical roads, the air thick with blooms and decay. One night, when the watch changed and the lanterns swayed with the ship's gentle roll in a sheltered bay, Siméon found Vincent and Soriol leaning against the rail, staring toward the lights of a distant town.

"You know," Vincent muttered, "I am starting to think 'returning home' was just a story they told us to keep us quiet."

Soriol snorted. "Speak for yourself. I am fully grown and still fell for it." He kicked lightly at the deck. "Three years of marching, fighting, starving, and now drifting around the islands like a lost fishing boat."

Siméon gave a thin smile. "At least a fishing boat eventually heads for port. We only seem to collect new latitudes."

Vincent shook his head, half amused, half weary. "Face it, brothers, we are never seeing France again. Might as well sprout sugarcane and settle in like the rest of the scenery."

Siméon let the silence settle. "If this is a ruse," he said softly, "it is a very patient one."

Early one morning, as they rode at anchor off La Guaira, Sans Soucy pointed toward a courier vessel cutting through the swell. "News from Europe," he said.

Word spread quickly that dispatches were being ferried to the flagship. The men watched the small boats cross between ships, speculation rippling through the deck. Some muttered about new orders, another campaign. Others dared to hope.

Later that day, Captain Bonnay assembled his men on the main deck as the tropical sun reached high overhead. He stood before them, sweat beading at his temples, his voice thick with emotion.

"Messieurs," he began. "I have just received word from the flagship. On the 30th of November, Preliminaries of Peace were signed in Paris. Britain has recognized American independence. The war has ended. You have served with honor."

Siméon did the arithmetic in his head. November 30th. The peace had been signed before they even sailed from Boston.

For a heartbeat, there was silence but for the creak of the rigging and the lap of waves against the hull. Then came the roar of cheers, laughter, and wild whoops that carried across the water to the other ships at anchor. Caps flew up; men clapped each other on the shoulders.

On April 1, 1783, the order came to ready the fleet, and by that same afternoon they were under sail. But the true homeward crossing did not begin until April 26th, when they departed Cap Français with the French Cape Fleet, their bows finally turned north.

Weeks later, in the gray stillness of early morning on June 17, 1783, Brest rose from the horizon. Siméon stood at the rail, the familiar shape of the harbor stirring something deep and wordless in him. Their boots struck French soil again: real and steady beneath their feet.

Brest, June 17, 1783

The last time Siméon and Vincent had stood on this quay, Louis and Fleur had been beside them, packs heavy, voices light, the Atlantic waiting like a promise. Now the packs were gone, the voices silent.

They had returned just nine days after a volcanic eruption in distant Iceland, though no one yet knew or grasped its scale. For now, the air in Brest was clear enough, and the return was simple: solid earth after six long months of storms, repairs, tropical anchorages, and the slow, almost unbelieving realization that the war was truly over.

The harbor swelled with noise and motion. French warships at anchor blew their salutes as each returning vessel glided into port. Dockworkers and officials moved among the lines of weary men, directing disembarkation, tallying supplies, and shouting orders over the din of gulls. Gun carriages creaked down the gangplanks, their wheels grating on the cobblestones.

As before Yorktown, the artillerymen were called to their guns. Siméon and his comrades joined the crews, easing each piece from the hold, guiding ropes, steadying axles, and locking wheels into place. The work was slow, heavy, and strangely familiar: the same motions that had once prepared them for battle now served only to return the weapons home.

Each thud of timber and clank of iron brought back other sounds: the roar of cannon, the screams in the smoke, Fleur's laughter, Fole's last cry, Louis's cough, all swallowed by the wind. For a moment, the years between seemed to collapse, and Yorktown was again alive in their ears.

Captain Bonnay's company mustered on the rise above the harbor, formally returned to French service. Flags raised. Names read. Bonnay spoke briefly of discipline maintained, steadiness proven at Yorktown. The formalities were spare. Word of the King's commendation followed, naming Colonel d'Aboville and the gunners of Auxonne, whose precision had helped carry the siege.

Before dismissing them, Bonnay remained. The ranks stilled. He unfolded a paper.

"By authority of His Most Christian Majesty," he said, "the following men of the Compagnie Bonnay de la Rouvrelle are granted *congé absolu*, effective the seventh day of July."

He read the names: Sergeant François Le Boeuf, François Berthet, Alexis-Toussaint Gérard, Jean-Joseph Goguillot, Jacques Gouthière, Claude-François Moraux. He paused. "Divertissant." Jean-Louis Varin.

Each man stepped forward and saluted. Their obligation to the King was fulfilled. Their time in uniform was complete.[65]

---

[65] *Congé absolu* (final discharge): The following soldiers of the Compagnie Bonnay de la Rouvrelle received final discharge on July 7, 1783, marking completion of their service obligations: Sergeant François Le Boeuf, known as Sans Soucy (Villers-les-Pots, Burgundy, ten years of service); François Berthet (Pirey, Franche-Comté, eight years); Alexis-Toussaint Gérard (Moncey, Franche-Comté, eight years); Jean-Joseph Goguillot (Besançon, Franche-Comté, nine years); Jacques Gouthière (Villiane-Blésoye, Champagne, eight years); Claude-François Moraux, known as Divertissant (Salins, Franche-Comté, nine years); and Jean-Louis Varin (Besançon, Franche-Comté, eight and a half years). Source: *Les combattants français de la guerre américaine, 1778 – 1783* (Washington: Imprimerie Nationale, 1905), 355.

There were no speeches. No music. No ceremony beyond the words themselves.

To Sans Soucy, Bonnay added a final sentence, thanking him for holding the company together when command weighed heaviest. Sans Soucy met his gaze and saluted one last time. Nothing more.

A quiet passed through the ranks.

As the discharged men gathered their gear, Bonnay called Louis Clément forward. The veteran had served alongside Sans Soucy for years, examining recruits, training crews.

"Clément, you will oversee the gun crews on the march to Auxonne."

Clément saluted. "Yes, sir."

Sans Soucy caught his eye and gave a single nod. "Get them home."

"I will."

As Sans Soucy walked away to gather his papers, Clément turned to face the remaining crews. Siméon watched him square his shoulders despite the weariness. Twenty years of service: he took this new duty seriously, to lead the company home.

They broke formation. Vincent exhaled. "What now? Peace is harder to learn than war."

"Then we will have to teach ourselves," Siméon replied.

Clément wiped his brow and snorted. "Peace is only what the generals declare. The earth has its own notions."

"Then she is in a foul mood," Vincent said, forcing a thin smile.

Siméon did not laugh. His eyes lingered on the strange fog creeping in from the west, thicker by the day.

Orders followed swiftly: six weeks east to Auxonne, through Rennes, Orléans, Dijon. Weary towns and fading milestones, each step deeper into a country familiar but no longer their own.

By Rennes, a dry haze lay heavy over the rooftops. The sun burned dimly, a dull red coin barely piercing the gloom. The air stung their eyes and left a bitter taste. The regiment bivouacked outside the walls while officers arranged provisions.

Men muttered about the fog. Plague, some whispered. Heaven's judgment for blood spilled abroad.

Siméon said nothing.

When an afternoon of leave was granted, he walked into the city alone, finding his way to the grand towers of Saint-Pierre. Even its bells were silent now.

The streets were nearly deserted. Doors closed, windows veiled, fountains dry. The air smelled faintly of ash. The few people out scurried past, heads down, scarves wrapped tight. He turned down her street, each step echoing on the cobbles. Her house looked the same, yet smaller in the stillness. He hesitated, then knocked.

The door opened a crack. Laure's eyes widened. A soft gasp, and the scarf she had been holding dropped to the floor.

"Siméon," she breathed.

He tried to speak but could not. When he reached for her hand, she hesitated, then took it, pressing his fingers between hers.

"Julien is home," she said quietly. "He is very ill. He cannot come to the door."

Siméon inclined his head. "Then I hope he mends soon."

"God willing."

Only then did the tears come, spilling down her cheeks.

"They said you had gone home," she whispered.

"Not yet. We march east tomorrow."

She coughed lightly. "People are ill. The air burns the lungs. They say it comes from the sea, or from God Himself."

"I have heard the same. No one seems certain."

She looked past him toward the colorless sky. "Then may God have mercy on us all."

She pressed his fingers to her cheek, needing proof he stood before her. "I feared I would never see you again."

"You will see me again. I will come back to you."

She leaned closer, as though to memorize his face. "Then I will wait," she said fiercely. "I will wait as long as it takes."

Distant drums beat. He brushed a thumb across her cheek.

"Until I return."

Laure nodded, lips trembling into a smile. "Go, my brave soldier. Come back safe."

"Stay safe, Laure. Keep the shutters closed."

With a final look, he stepped away. The door closed gently, but he could still feel her there, just behind the wood.

When he rejoined the column, no one spoke. Boots scuffed the dust, packs settled into place. The space where Sans Soucy would have stood was empty. Siméon felt it more keenly than he expected.

Vincent bumped his shoulder. "Eyes forward. Franche-Comté's daughters will not wait forever."

Siméon allowed himself a quiet smile. "Well, that is sad for you. Mine is from Brittany, and I know she will."

Vincent groaned. "Romantic to the end. God help us."

On August 18, they bivouacked outside Orléans, a city bound to the memory of Joan of Arc, where armies had passed for centuries. As the regiment settled, the heavens were set ablaze.

Later historians would call it the Great Meteor of 1783, so bright that it lit the ground like daylight and split the sky from west to east. A white fire tore across the night, silent yet brilliant enough to startle the horses and cast every face in pale light.

The Great Meteor of 1783

Men cried out, some praying, others falling to their knees, unsure if miracle or end of days. A murmur rippled through the bivouac. Some whispered that Saint Joan had not forgotten her city, a warning, a summons. No one knew. No one dared say more.

The fire did not vanish but broke into smaller lights that drifted and lingered, their pale trails visible long after the sky went dark. The night air was clear, a blessing in a summer when the sky so often held its breath.

Siméon stood apart, watching. He thought of Laure, wondered if she saw it too, this wandering flame. For one brief instant, the heavens had bridged the distance between them.

The road east became a crucible. Day after day, the heat pressed down, the strange blue-gray fog dimming the world to a copper twilight. No wind. No birds. Livestock stood listless in fields of dying grass.

Soldiers' throats burned, eyes watered. Some wrapped scarves, others tore cloth from their shirts. Siméon did both, tying a strip across his nose and mouth. Someone ahead spat and muttered that if the air meant to kill them, it owes us a sou for every mile.

Vincent coughed, his voice ragged. "The paymaster will die before he parts with a sou."

Siméon managed a half laugh. "That would be right."

Each evening, Clément moved among the gun crews with the same methodical care. But the fog was taking its toll. His cough had deepened, his breathing labored. Siméon watched him wrap a cloth tighter over his face, his shoulders stooped, grey pallor beneath the dust.

Vincent noticed. "You should rest."

Clément shook his head. "We keep moving. This curse will follow us whether we rest or march. We must reach Auxonne."

At first, parish priests spoke only of divine punishment. People fell sick without warning. Crops withered. Children fainted in church. Men muttered of omens and judgment. Officers crossed themselves before each night's rest.

Each step eastward carried the same metallic taste, the same dull ache in his chest. He thought of his parents in Rosières-sur-Mance and of Laure behind her closed shutters in Rennes. The wind that reached them would carry this same poison.

Step after step, they pressed forward through a silence so deep it seemed the world itself had stopped to catch its breath, but could not.

They reached Auxonne in August. The haze still hung on the horizon, a faint red veil above the town. Time had softened into a heat-struck blur. Peace had come wearing the scent of sulfur and smoke.

Clément assembled the gun crews in the parade yard, delivering them to Captain Bonnay with the same brisk efficiency. But standing at attention cost him. His breathing shallow, hand trembling as he saluted.

"Gun crews reporting, sir. All accounted for."

Bonnay's eyes held Clément's a moment, concern flickering, then turned to address the men.

"Reliable veterans may aid their families in the harvest. You remain on the rolls, report weekly. This is leave, not release."

A murmur rippled through the ranks, hoarse, but warm enough to lift the air.

When Siméon stepped forward, Bonnay regarded him with pride. "Your father will need you for the wine-making. You have earned a little earth beneath your feet again."

He signed the papers and added, "Return promptly upon notice." It was not freedom, only borrowed time.

As the men dispersed, Bonnay turned to Clément. "Dismissed. Get some rest."

Clément nodded and turned away. Siméon watched him cross the yard, each step deliberate, like a man walking on the edge of collapse but refusing to fall.

On September 24, word came that Louis Clément had taken a turn for the worse. He had been admitted to the Hôtel-Dieu three days earlier, in the military ward built while the regiment was in America, blessed at the end of 1782, waiting for their return.

That summer, miasmas bred a pernicious epidemic. The Saône had flooded, the haze seemed to rise from the soil itself. The garrison was thick with sick soldiers; the sisters had opened a soup kitchen for those cared for at home. Clément was one of many, but to those who knew him, he was not just a name.[66]

Dr. Bénigne Girault attended him personally. The physician had served the Hôtel-Dieu for over thirty years, long enough to have known Clément when he was still a young artilleryman learning the work of the

---

[66] **Abbé J.-Th. Bizouard**, drawing on hospital archives, recorded that "the land emitted harmful miasmas that engendered a pernicious epidemic" and that "the garrison had numerous sick soldiers" (translated from the French). During this period **Dr. Bénigne Girault** had served as physician for more than thirty years; Mother Renaut had been superior since 1778; and Father Martel served as military chaplain in 1783. Source: *Abbé J.-Th. Bizouard, Histoire de l'Hôpital d'Auxonne (1374 – 1884) (Dijon: H. Grigne, 1884).*

guns. Louis XVI had granted Girault officer rank in recognition of his distinguished service, but no title could help him now. He bled Clément, applied poultices, tried every remedy he knew. The lungs, ravaged by months of breathing the poisoned air, would not heal.

Mother Renaut, the seventy-year-old superior who had come from Salins in 1778 to train the young sisters, looked in on him herself. She remembered the garrison before the regiment sailed, remembered the steady artilleryman who had trained gun crews for as long as anyone could recall. Now he lay in her care, struggling for each breath.

Father Martel, the military chaplain of the Hôtel-Dieu, prayed at his bedside. He had arrived only the year before, but he understood what Clément meant to the regiment. The sisters who tended him spoke of the older soldiers with a particular respect, men who had served so long they had become part of Auxonne itself.

Siméon visited the hospital, standing outside with Vincent and others. They were not allowed in. Through the window, they could see Clément lying still, his chest rising in shallow, labored gasps. A sister moved past the glass, adjusting his blanket, her face composed in the stillness of women who had seen too many soldiers die.

"He got us home," Vincent said quietly.

Siméon nodded.

On September 26, Louis Clément died.[67]

The news reached the barracks in grey morning light. Twenty years, examining recruits, training gunners, crossing oceans, surviving campaigns. He had distinguished himself in the War of Independence and led the company home through the worst summer anyone could remember. Weeks after that final duty, the miasmas claimed him.

They buried him two days later in the cemetery behind the church. Father Martel spoke the Latin rite, commending a soul he had known only days but whose life the whole community had witnessed. Dr. Girault stood among the mourners, his face drawn. Mother Renaut sent two sisters, their white habits bright against the autumn grey.

---

[67] **Louis Clément,** died September 26, 1783, at l'Hôpital d'Auxonne, likely from illness associated with prolonged exposure to the sulfurous haze that blanketed France during the summer and autumn of 1783. Source: *Les combattants français de la guerre américaine, 1778 – 1783* (Washington: Imprimerie Nationale, 1905), 355.

Most of Company Bonnay attended. Captain Bonnay stood at the graveside, his face carved from exhaustion and grief. The coffin descended into French soil, the soil Clément had left four years earlier and fought to see again.

Vincent stood beside Siméon, his jaw set. "Twenty years. He survived everything."

Siméon said nothing. The haze still hung faint on the horizon. What chance did anyone have?

On Thursday, October 2, Siméon set out at first light, heading northeast toward Rosières-sur-Mance. The road followed the Saône through low fields and sleeping villages. His pack held a crust of bread, cheese hardened to stone, and a *flasque* of water that tasted of smoke. By midday the sun vanished behind a gray-blue veil, the world dimming as though a curtain had been drawn.

By evening he reached Pontailler. The tavern stood shuttered, the baker's window bare. A woman sweeping her doorstep told him the grain had spoiled. She pressed a heel of dark bread into his hand. "Pray for rain that smells clean." He slept on the village outskirts and was back on the road before dawn.

The next day he pushed north, his breath shortening as the air thickened. That night he sheltered in a cowshed, the animals coughing softly through the darkness. Before light he rose and continued. As dusk settled short of Gray, he found a copse of trees and gathered hard, bruised apples, their flesh edged with bitterness, as if the poisoned world had soaked into their cores. He ate and slept beneath a sky the color of old bruises.

He woke Saturday, washed in a stream, and set out again. The haze no longer felt like weather but a slow illness settled over the land. He reached Gray as bells tolled for morning prayers. He was among the first to enter the Capuchin convent, its stones damp and darkened by fog. Inside, a single candle burned weakly before Our Lady.

He remembered standing here with Père Charles years ago, warm, bright, alive with whispered prayers. Now a lone flame struggled against the gloom, and the silence was complete.

He knelt, the cold seeping through his breeches, muscles protesting after days of travel. Grit clung to his skin, dust worked into every seam.

"If this is the earth's punishment," he whispered, "spare them at home. Let me bear what is left."

A young friar emerged to tend the altar, not much older than Siméon. Taking in the worn uniform and dust-caked pack, he returned with a cup of water and placed it beside him.

"I am Brother Luc. You have come a long way."

They spoke in low voices. Siméon told him he was returning to Rosières, to his father, mother, and brother Colas.

Brother Luc's expression softened. "God places us on the same road as those who need a companion. I carry herbs to Père Charles at Rosières, my cart has room, if you would share the journey."

"First, we will pray together for good passage."

They knelt side by side, the shared prayer a comfort he had not known he needed.

The day's journey was long but far easier than the road on foot. Half-burned woods slid past, the stinging air softened by shared silence and occasional quiet words. They traveled until light failed, then sheltered at a widow's cottage known to the friar, just outside Membrey.

On Sunday they rose before dawn and reached Rosières as the village came to life, a door closing softly, smoke lifting from a chimney, a family in their best clothes emerging from a narrow lane.

When the cart halted, Siméon turned to Brother Luc. "Thank you, Brother. For the passage, and for the prayer. It was a true gift."

Brother Luc smiled. "Go, my son. Your family is waiting."

With a final nod, his heart pounding, Siméon turned down the lane toward the Gaugien vineyard.

The stone walls still stood, the thatched roof sagged in its familiar way, the dying orchard still leaned toward the millpond. Everything seemed drained of color, as if life itself had thinned.

Colas, October 1783

A figure moved among the vines and turned. Colas. His stride was firm, but his breath came short, and when he drew close, Siméon saw the whites of his eyes streaked with red.

"Mon Dieu," Colas said, gripping his brother's shoulders. "You are thinner than a reed."

Siméon tried to smile. "And you look like you wrestled a sack of peppers."

Colas laughed once, rough and low, brushing his sleeve across his watering eyes. "It is this cursed fog. Stings worse every afternoon. Nothing I cannot handle."

Before more could be said, their father appeared in the doorway, leaning on a cane. He looked at Siméon, his eyes holding the weight of years. "The bell does not wait for reunions. Your mother is already at the church. Come. Let them see you first. The house will still be here."

So, without stepping inside, they turned. Siméon walked with his brother and father through the haze toward the square. The village gathered, faces brightening as they recognized the returning artillerist. Hands reached out, clasping his. No one shouted; joy here had grown quiet.

Inside the church, candles flickered in the red-tinted light. Père Charles turned from the altar and smiled, lifting his hand in blessing. "Welcome home, Siméon Gaugien."

He bowed his head, murmuring thanks, but as he looked across the pews, he faltered. Empty benches marked where families once sat. The fog had left gaps in the village as surely as war had. And then he saw her. His mother, in the family pew, her hand pressed to her mouth, her shoulders shaking with silent sobs.

The prayers rose thinly, the incense heavy and bitter. When the service ended, the family came together in the aisle. His mother reached him first, her composure gone. She gasped at the sight of him and began to weep. Siméon folded her into his arms and held her, solid and real after so many years.

"Let us go home," Colas said softly, and they walked back beneath the dim red sun.

Inside the familiar kitchen, the true homecoming began. His mother fussed, his father poured wine, Colas listened with a tired smile as Siméon spoke of his journey.

That evening, Père Charles stopped at the gate. "I wanted to see that you were truly home. The village has prayed for you."

He refused *souper*, taking wine and news of the regiment before returning to the presbytery.

Jeanne and Nicolas were pleased to have both sons home. Food stores were thin, but tonight they would feast.

Over a simple meal, the conversation turned from war to home. Siméon spoke of the girl from Rennes with a pride he had not known in years. "Her name is Laure. She is clever, and kind. She was born here but has lived in Rennes most of her life. Her cousin writes that she is waiting for me."

Colas managed a weak smile. "A soldier and a romantic. I am happy for you, little brother."

"And what of you? Papa wrote that you have been seen with a cobbler's daughter. I am happy for you too."

Jeanne and Nicolas exchanged a pained glance and looked down at their plates. Colas's smile vanished.

"Élise," he said, the name a whisper. "Her name was Élise. She was so sweet. So gentle. The fog. She was one of the first to be taken. Two months ago."

He pressed a fist against his chest, not coughing, but touching a deep, internal ache. "When she died, I refused to believe it. Some days it still feels like my own heart forgets how to beat."

The silence that followed was heavier than any Siméon had known in the trenches. At twenty-five, Colas carried a broken heart, a weight as crushing as any Siméon had seen.

Furlough granted no rest. Each morning Siméon joined Colas in the fields, harvesting what little they could, turning stubborn earth, mending fences. Michel had fallen ill and could no longer help, but Henri came daily. The chickens were gone. The remaining animals coughed and sickened. Two calves, born early, were already buried behind the barn.

Colas told Pâtre Antoine to keep the animals sheltered. "The air is not right," he said quietly, when he thought no one listened.

At *souper* one evening, Siméon voiced the dread he had carried from the road. "If the harvest fails, what will you do? Bread, grain, feed?"

Their father rubbed his knee. "We will make do. We have survived storms before."

"But this is worse," their mother whispered. "Père Charles says there have been more burials this summer than ever."

"It will pass," Colas said, though his tone carried more hope than certainty. "The fog will lift. We just need strong backs and stubborn hearts." He poked Siméon lightly with his elbow. "And now we have another back to put to work."

Siméon saw how pale his brother had become, the tremor in his hands when he reached for his cup.

He smiled faintly. The fog had not lifted since Brest. If the miasmas could take a man like Clément…

HISTORICAL NOTE: THE LAKI EIGHT-MONTH ERUPTION

On June 8, 1783, a fissure eruption known as Laki (Lakagígar) began in southern Iceland. Unlike a single explosive event, Laki released lava and toxic gases continuously for eight months. Its greatest damage came from the sulfur-rich cloud injected into the atmosphere: a dense haze called the "dry fog" spread across Western Europe within days, blanketing France, dimming sunlight, and irritating eyes, throats, and lungs. Contemporary observers described the air as heavy and poisonous; many feared it signaled divine judgment. An abnormally hot summer gave way to one of the coldest winters in memory. Crops failed, livestock weakened, and food prices soared. Modern estimates suggest tens of thousands died across Europe from disease, famine, and exposure. Source: *Thordarson, T. and Self, S., "Atmospheric and Environmental Effects of the 1783 – 1784 Laki Eruption," Journal of Geophysical Research, 108(D1), 2003.*

Four weeks passed. At Jussey for his pay, he found new orders: return to Auxonne. No certainty when he would see home again.

Before leaving, he pressed every livre into his father's hand. "For the farm. And the winter to come."

His father hesitated, then nodded. Quiet gratitude. Siméon vowed to return as soon as leave allowed.

He found his mother in the kitchen, her hands on the table, steadying herself. She dabbed at her eyes but tried to smile. "I prayed for forty days of peace with you. God gave me twenty-eight. I suppose I should be grateful."

She fussed with his collar, her fingers lingering at his cheek as if memorizing its warmth. "Return to me, *mon cœur.* Do your duty, but come home."

"Of course, Maman. I promise."

They embraced. She kissed his cheek.

Then came the hardest goodbye. Colas waited at the stable, the animals shifting behind him, quiet and subdued.

"Take care of yourself, at least half as well as you take care of everything here. Promise me. No more pretending you are invincible just because you can lift a sack of grain with one hand."

Colas snorted. *"Je suis invincible.* Have you not heard? But I will stay healthy. Because you are coming back. And I want you to see what we have saved."

Siméon's throat tightened. "Just do not let the farm fall apart before I return, grand frère. Would not want to fix all your mistakes twice."

Colas grinned wide, his eyes fierce and proud. "Mistakes or not, you have become a fine man, Siméon. I knew you would make a good soldier. I am proud of you, little brother."

They embraced, strong, wordless, not nearly long enough.

And then, beneath a wounded sky that still smoked with distant fire, Siméon turned toward the road that would carry him back to Auxonne.

The road back felt longer. The air burned eyes and lungs with sulfur; livestock lay where they fell, and everywhere people coughed, eyes red.

The garrison walls of Auxonne rose through the murky haze like a fortress half-swallowed by a skeletal sky. Leave had been restricted. Harvests had failed.

Siméon resumed his duties: repairing caissons, greasing axles, hauling crates until his shoulders ached. He drilled recruits, fresh boys under a sun that dimmed too quickly each day. Supply depots were watched with vigilance now, rumors of theft and riots drifting in from nearby towns.

One evening, after cleaning a cannon's breech until it gleamed, Vincent fell into step beside him.

"You have been staring through walls since you came back. How was it at home?"

Siméon sighed, breath frothing in the cold. "The fog is killing the vines. The calves are already dying. My father can hardly walk. And Colas… he is strong. Stronger than any of us. He will hold the farm together. As long as they do not starve, they will survive."

Vincent tried a small smile. "Your brother sounds like a man who would punch famine in the face."

Siméon managed a short laugh. "He would try."

But each dawn arrived colder. By late November, a brutal winter settled over Franche-Comté, the likes of which no one had seen. Snow buried roads and rooftops. The Saône froze solid. Reports came daily: livestock dying, fodder gone, families burning their last vines and furniture for warmth. The garrison fires burned high, and though the soldiers felt the cold gnaw through uniforms and boots, they knew they suffered less than those outside.

December crept in with a grief Siméon could not outrun.

On the tenth, Captain Bonnay sent for him. The message was brief. Vincent lingered near the doorway, sensing the weight.

Bonnay did not sit. He stood by the window, hands clasped behind his back, the pale winter light flattening his features.

"There is news from Rosières-sur-Mance." He paused, just long enough to draw a breath. "Your brother, Nicolas…"[68]

"Yes, what of him?"

Bonnay turned from the window. When he spoke again, his voice was quieter. "Siméon, I am sorry. He died on the second."

Siméon shook his head violently. "NO. YOU ARE WRONG. Colas is not dead. Colas cannot be dead." He stared at the captain, waiting for the retreat, the correction, the admission of error.

None came.

The room seemed to freeze around them. Outside, breath plumed in the cold. Vincent hesitated at the threshold. Bonnay met his eyes and gave a single nod.

---

[68] **Nicolas Gaugien Jr.**, (referred to as Colas in this book); died on December 2, 1783, in Rosières-sur-Mance, Haute-Saône, France. Source: *Registres paroissiaux et d'état civil, Rosières-sur-Mance, Archives départementales de la Haute-Saône.*

Vincent stepped forward and placed a hand on Siméon's shoulder, a steadying weight against the unreality. Bonnay held his ground, his silence more binding than any written dispatch.

And then the truth, cold and absolute, broke through the barricade of his will.

The strength fled Siméon's legs. His knees buckled. Vincent's grip tightened, the only thing keeping him upright. A sound tore from him, not a sob but the wounded rasp of something breaking from within. Tears came freely now. He covered his face with his hands, his body shaking.

"My brother… my brother is dead."

It was not a question. It was the first, terrible acceptance.

Only then, as grief ebbed into crushing ache, did his mind return to a world that had irrevocably changed.

"I have to go. I have to… Oh God. My mother. My poor mother."

Bonnay answered at once, gently. "You cannot. Travel is forbidden. The roads are buried. No leave is being granted. You would not make it halfway."

Siméon tried to move anyway, a last reflex of defiance, but Vincent stepped in front of him.

"I am sorry, *mon ami*. Too many are dying this winter. You know we would carry you home ourselves if it were allowed."

Something locked inside Siméon then. Not acceptance, but submission to a world governed by frost and duty. He was a soldier, and duty had just become a prison. Grief pressed against his ribs, demanding sound, but he forced it down.

Bonnay's voice softened, only slightly. "Many men receive bad news and must still serve. You are not alone."

"No," Siméon whispered, staring at the snow falling beyond the window. "But my family is."

For a long moment, none of them spoke. The voice of a frozen, failing world, where a brother's death could arrive long before any chance of goodbye.

Siméon bowed his head and mourned in silence, a soldier sealed from the soil that raised him, from the vines and fields that once promised spring would always return. He had known loss before each a stitch pulled from the fabric of his life. But this was not an unraveling. This was the central pillar shattered. This grief did not burn. It pressed down, heavy and immovable, as if the great boulder of the family's land, Colas's land, had come to rest upon him and refused to let him breathe.

When spring came at last and the thaw cracked the ice, Siméon received leave to return home. He set out on foot toward Rosières, boots sinking into mud.

The countryside lay wounded, smelled rotten. Vineyards still lay blackened. Cattle lay bloated and stiff in the fields where they had starved, wells clouded with poison. Even the birds held back. But fear of what he would find kept him walking through the night.

His parents embraced him, relief shadowed by sorrow.

"I can come with you," Nicolas said quietly.

Siméon shook his head. "No, Papa. I need to visit Colas alone."

Nicolas studied him, then nodded. He rested a hand on Siméon's shoulder before turning back with Jeanne.

Colas's grave lay beside those of their grandparents. The earth over him was dark and uneven, winter's hand still visible. There was no stone yet, only a wooden marker bearing his name. He had known it would be painful. Not how overwhelming.

He fell to his knees, wet seeping through his trousers. He remained there in silence until the weight settled into something he could carry.

There was little time for long grief; survival demanded labor.

In the days that followed, Siméon helped rebuild winter's damage: tilling soil, cutting stakes, clearing dead limbs. He hauled carcasses with Michel and Henri to hastily dug pits while Jeanne sprinkled holy water and whispered apologies to each creature.

One afternoon, overwhelmed, he retreated to the wine cellar. The air smelled of old oak and the vinegar breath of casks that had held little more than hope. He sat on an upturned barrel, the weight finally crushing the breath from him.

He did not hear his father's steps on the stone stairs. Nicolas stood there a long moment, leaning on his cane, outlined in the dim light.

"This was his place too," Nicolas said quietly. "Colas knew every cask. He knew which ones to tap first, which ones to let sleep." He limped forward and rested a hand on a massive barrel, as if comforting an old friend. "After you left for the army, he told me this is where you would go when you were thinking too hard. He said, 'If you ever need to find him, Papa, look among the casks first.'"

The shared memory shattered the last of his composure. A sob escaped him, sharp, unbidden, as he let the tears fall for the brother who had known him so completely.

"He was the best of this land," Nicolas said, his own voice thickening. "It loved him, and he loved it back."

Siméon nodded.

"The land does not care for our grief, Siméon. It only knows who tends it. It needed Colas." He took a labored breath. "Now it needs you."

"I know, Papa."

"Do you? You chose the uniform. There is honor in that. But that life is gone. Colas held this land for you. Now you must choose it, not as a soldier on furlough, but as its master. This is your duty now. I am an old man with a bad leg. We will do this together, but you must be here."

Siméon looked at his father, then at the ranks of barrels. He felt the weight of two oaths: the one sworn to His Most Christian Majesty, and the one being asked of him now, in the silence of his ancestral home.

"Papa, my name is on the roll at Auxonne. I pledged eight years to the King. That promise must be fulfilled first."

He saw fear flicker in his father's eyes and braced for argument. But Nicolas's shoulders sagged in a sigh of resignation, not defeat, but understanding. "A promise to the King is a promise before God. It must be honored. I would not have a son of mine be an oath-breaker."

"Then I give you my word, as your son. When my service is complete,

I will return. For good. Until then I will be here as often as furlough allows. I will not leave you again."

Silence settled between them. It was not the solution Nicolas had hoped for, but it was a pledge sealed with the only currency they had: a family's honor. The inheritance had been acknowledged, its acceptance deferred, but no less certain.

When Siméon emerged, the sun felt less harsh. Of the original herd, only one cow and the pig had survived, sickly, ribs showing. Yet he looked at them now not as a visitor, but as a steward. He watched his mother collect water from the fountain, noticing the first grass returning to the pasture.

Encouraged by Père Charles, the village worked as one, neighbors sharing tools, labor, seed. It was resilience by necessity. In rebuilding, the conviction he had found in the cellar took root: communities could rise from ruin, and he would now lead his family's part in that renewal.

Chapter Fifteen: Strong Roots

Summer 1784 – 1799

The worst had passed, though its memory lingered in every hollow-eyed glance. Year by year, the harvests improved; first barely enough to fill granaries, then enough to bring cautious smiles back to the markets and taverns. In Rosières-sur-Mance, green returned to the vineyards that had once looked charred from God's own wrath. Fields were plowed, wells cleansed, and the church bell that had tolled for the dying now rang for marriages and baptisms once more.

Siméon returned to Auxonne, then home again whenever short furloughs allowed. Life found a rhythm between the regiment and the vineyard. At the garrison, he drilled new artillery recruits, teaching them to load and aim with discipline, to respect the terrible weight of a cannon's roar. He saw his own early fears reflected in their eyes and found himself speaking with a steadier voice than he expected.

Letters remained his lifeline. Julien Hudel wrote faithfully, passing along Laure's words: her prayers, her patience, her quiet constancy. Siméon replied with gratitude. What began as affection had matured into certainty.

Colas's death had settled into Siméon's bones and reshaped everything. He was now the inheriting son; the land would one day pass to him. He felt both honored and uneasy beneath the weight of that truth.

There was pride in knowing he could one day offer Laure a life built on solid ground. Yet he feared becoming a man torn in two, duty to France pulling one way, duty to his family's soil pulling the other.

1786

In the summer of 1786, he returned to Rosières on leave, arriving as the village prepared to bless its new church bell. Word had spread that the Marquis de Chappuis and his wife would come from Oricourt to serve as godparents.

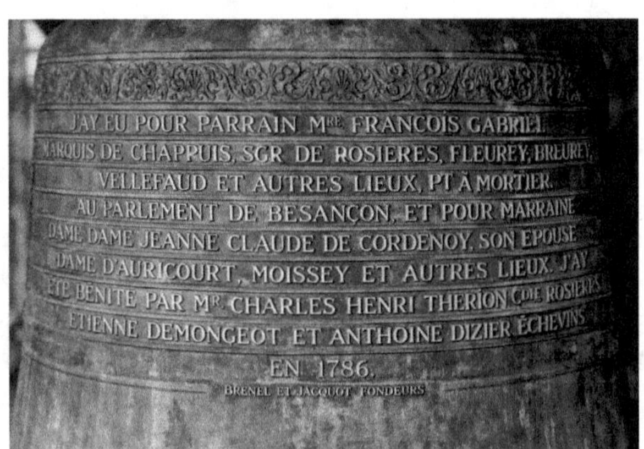

Bell inscription, Église Saint-Siméon le Stylites,
Rosières-sur-Mance, 1786 (digitally restored)

By late afternoon, a procession formed near the square. The seigneur-ial carriage arrived, its lacquered panels catching the light as it halted beside the church. Villagers bowed as the marquis and marquise descended, their quiet formality lending the ceremony a dignity rarely felt in outlying parishes.

Siméon stood with his family as the square tower rose above them. The new bell, cast by Brenel and Jacquot, its bronze still bright, had been given godparents like a child, their names inscribed upon its flank so memory and sound might endure together.

When Père Charles stepped forward, the crowd fell silent. He read the inscription aloud, naming Monsieur François-Gabriel, Marquis de Chappuis, seigneur of Rosières, President of the Parlement of Besançon, and Dame Jeanne-Claude de Cordenoy, his wife, Dame d'Oricourt and Moissey, as godfather and godmother of the bell. The words carried across the square, binding the bell to its patrons before God and village alike.

The curé anointed the bell. The ropes were drawn. The first strike came, and the sound that rolled from atop Église Saint-Siméon le Stylite was deep and confident: a voice meant to outlast wars and harvests, announcing not just the hour but the endurance of the community itself.

Beside him, Nicolas placed a hand on Siméon's shoulder. "Colas would have loved this day."

Nearly three years had passed, yet the memory of the elder brother lived quietly in the family's silences.

For an instant, listening to the bell's clear call, Siméon felt time loosen its grip. Soldier, son, future husband, heir to a plot of stubborn earth. All the roles he carried seemed to settle into place.

***

1787

He remained in uniform until the conclusion of his eight-year enlistment, sworn to His Most Christian Majesty in the cold days of January 1779, when he was still a boy with calloused hands and a heart full of duty. In 1787, he received his *congé absolu*, his honorable discharge, the same year Captain Bonnay concluded his own long service. The notice arrived without ceremony, a simple document bearing the King's seal. When he folded it into his coat, the weight felt like a door closing behind him.

Before leaving Auxonne for the last time, he sought out the two men who had shaped his life in uniform.

Vincent was tightening the straps of a battered travel pack, his eyes bright with the prospect of salt-damp mornings and the family who had taken him in when he was orphaned.

"So, inheriting son," Vincent teased, though his smile wavered. "Try not to fall from any haylofts before I come visit."

"And you," Siméon replied, pulling him into a brief, fierce embrace, "try not to drink the entire port dry before I get there."

They laughed, easier than acknowledging how unlikely those visits would be.

Siméon and Vincent, Auxonne, 1787

They held each other's gaze a long moment, an unspoken vow passing between them. Vincent's smile faltered just enough to show the truth beneath it. Siméon gripped his shoulder once more, memorizing the weight of a friend he might never see again.

Further down the yard, Captain Bonnay stood at a trestle table. Before him lay an open ledger, its pages smudged with years, and beside it a sealed packet Siméon recognized as a captain's *congé*. Bonnay looked up and closed the book without haste.

"So," Bonnay said. "Your service ends."

"Oui, mon capitaine."

Bonnay nodded. "Mine does as well. Not every man leaves by choice, and fewer still leave whole." He paused. "You served well. You learned when to listen, when to act, and when to hold your ground. Those are not small things."

"I owe that to the company. And to you."

Siméon straightened, heels together, and raised his hand in a final salute. Bonnay returned it without hesitation, crisp and exact, as it had been a hundred times before.

For a moment, Bonnay regarded him not as an officer but as one man measuring another. Then he extended his hand. Siméon took it. The captain's grip was firm, unadorned, final.

"Make good use of peace," Bonnay said. "It does not come often, and it never lasts as long as one hopes."

Only when the farewells were finished did the strangeness settle in. With a few handshakes and parting words, he was leaving them behind.

He crossed the garrison gates with the same quiet bearing he had kept while serving within them, a solitary figure moving forward.

From soldier to citizen once more.

Siméon made his way back to Franche-Comté first, to the scents of soil and grape. He stood a long while in the Saint-Siméon churchyard at the graves of his grandfather and brother, then turned west toward Rennes.

Laure still lived with her cousin Julien Hudel, who had raised her since childhood. Their household had endured the famine that followed the strange poison cloud and the growing anger of a people who no longer trusted their king. Rennes felt uneasy, its streets tense with hunger and unrest.

When Siméon stood before Julien, he spoke without ornament, only conviction. Julien had followed his journey through letters, accounts of service that revealed a loyal and unpretending character.

Siméon asked for Laure's hand. Julien measured him with quiet eyes and agreed. The cousin who had raised her would see her settled safely; this union promised not only affection but stability, a refuge from the uncertainty shadowing France.

For Laure, it meant return to the village of her birth, a home she barely remembered, and a future beside a man she had waited eight years to marry. For Siméon, it meant offering her the hills of his own home, where the vines still grew and the earth, for all its scars, remained steady.

January 29, 1788

When Noël arrived in Rennes to escort her home, it was both reunion and farewell. They had not seen each other since Laure was five, sent to live with Julien after their father's death. Now, nearly twenty years later, Noël was bringing her home.

He had married Elisabeth Amiot five years earlier; they had two little ones: Reine, three, and François, one. Elisabeth stayed with the children while Noël made the journey, serving as Laure's chaperone through snow and bitter cold, protective and proud.

They arrived days before the wedding. The vineyards lay bare beneath a thin skin of snow, twisted vines black against white slopes. The Mance River ran sluggish and cold, half frozen where shallows remained in shade. Woodsmoke from winter hearths carried on the air, quiet signs that life, though hard, endured.

France was still, yet beneath the calm, change stirred. Prices had risen, taxes pressed the poor, and talk of reform drifted into the valleys.

That morning, villagers gathered before the church of Saint-Siméon, its stone walls rimmed with ice. Inside, candles flickered against the chill, and cold lingered in the nave like a held breath.

Laure did not wear white; that fashion belonged to another time. She stood in her Sunday best: a pale blue wool skirt brushed clean of travel dust, a fitted bodice, a white linen chemise softening her neckline. Her apron was tied with care, her dark hair drawn back, a small white wedding flower pinned above her ear.

Siméon, solemn and proud, wore his dark brown Sunday coat, woolen breeches, and cleaned, worn boots. In the altar light, his features seemed carved from the same stone as the church, shaped by time as much as strength.

The Wedding of Siméon and Laure

When the moment came, Noël walked his sister down the narrow aisle, her hand resting on his arm. At the altar, he paused, looked once at Siméon with an expression that held both trust and admonition, as though to say, See that you deserve her, and placed Laure's hand gently into his.

Siméon's fingers trembled slightly as he received it.

"You have been my hope through the battles, ma chérie," he whispered.

Laure's eyes shone. "And now, my love, the battles are over."

Père Charles began the Latin rite, his voice low and steady, the sound of an old world still intact. When the vows were spoken and the final blessing given, he smiled. "No musicians, no carriage, no gold," he said gently. "But the angels themselves will remember this day."

The new Chappuis bell rang from high atop Saint-Siméon as they stepped into the pale winter sun. Villagers murmured congratulations, stamping their boots against the cold. No fanfare, only the creak of a cart, the lowing of cows, the smell of fresh-baked bread. It was perfect.

Later, the wedding feast gathered under the Gaugien barn. Barrels of wine were opened, platters of bread, fresh curds, and preserved pears passed hand to hand. Someone found a violoneux, and soon dancing, singing, and laughter filled the space. Even Noël, who had vowed not to dance, was coaxed into a turn with his wife.

Siméon's smile grew wider when his eyes found Laure, cheeks rosy from dancing, a stray curl escaping her coif. The sight of her made his chest feel full and quiet.

He brushed his thumb along her cheek. "I cannot believe I get to come home to you."

Laure's eyes sparkled. "Jamais de ma vie je ne me suis sentie si heureuse." Never in my life have I felt so happy.

As the night deepened, the laughter, the wine, the strings gradually faded. The glow of the hearth replaced the wind, and the crackle of the fire wove the day into a golden memory.

They were together at last. He was home.

The deep winter snows gave way to a slow, muddy spring, then to a summer that felt like his life renewed with Laure. The rhythm of his days was no longer set by the drum but by the sun on the vines and the sound of his wife's voice in their home.

CULTURAL NOTE: HOW FARMING AND THE CHURCH SET THE WEDDING DATE

In pre-industrial rural France, marriage timing followed agricultural necessity. Spring planting, summer tending, and autumn harvest left little time for celebration; late January was one of the few periods when work slowed. The Catholic calendar further narrowed acceptable dates, prohibiting marriages during Advent and Lent and leaving a brief window between Epiphany and February. A winter wedding aligned first births with late autumn, after harvest and before winter scarcity: a safer rhythm for both mother and child. Frozen ground also made rural roads more reliable than spring mud. Sources: *Pierre Goubert, The French Peasantry in the Seventeenth Century (Cambridge: Cambridge University Press, 1986); Jacques Dupâquier et al., Histoire de la population française, Vol. 2 (Paris: PUF, 1988), pp. 124–130.*

1789

That spring, news delayed by the Atlantic finally reached Rosières. A merchant from Jussey brought word to the square: General George Washington had been inaugurated as the first President of the United States.

Siméon stood a long moment, then carried the news home to Laure. He found her in the barn and took her hand.

"I heard something today near the Fountain," he said, warmth in his voice. "General Washington has become the American President."

"Truly? President?" She smiled. "You always said he was different. Quiet. Serious. If they have chosen him, that must be a good thing."

"I saw him in Newport, in Williamsburg, after Yorktown. He never celebrated like a conqueror. He was calm, as though he had only finished a hard day's work. At the last review, he stopped before our regiment and spoke words I have never forgotten."

"Then it is good," she said, more certain now. "If he is as you remember."

"The merchant called it a wonder," Siméon replied softly. "And it is. He is a farmer. To see him chosen to lead again gives me hope."

1790 – 1792

The Gaugien farm, vineyards on the upper slope and communal pasture below, became Laure's daily world. Under Jeanne's patient guidance, she learned to milk the cows, tend the animals, make butter and soft curds, manage fermentation, care for barrels, and read the soil.

She brought knowledge of her own. At the pasture's edge she gathered chamomile to calm a restless cow, comfrey for swollen udders, and thyme to cleanse the milk pails. Jeanne had always found quiet peace in the sweet clover by the fence, its honeyed scent a simple comfort. Laure showed her it was more than a pleasant weed; its flowers, she explained, could be steeped into tea to ease a cough. Jeanne, who knew the land by instinct, respected her learned skill.

In time, Jeanne became more than a mother-in-law. She taught without condescension how to stretch stew through lean winter weeks, salt meat properly, and mend linens so the seams would hold another season. Laure listened with the hunger of one who had lost her own mother too soon, storing each lesson for the years ahead.

Siméon still spoke in a soldier's cadence, *ordre* and *consigne* close to his tongue. He mended fences as if aligning a battery. With Nicolas no longer able to work as before, Noël joined the vineyard, his vintner's heart welcome company during long days among the vines.

Even in the quiet corners of Franche-Comté, signs of strain began to surface. Bread riots flared in nearby towns, the people weary of watching the seigneur claim so much of what little they had. New words crept into the parish records: *citoyen, république, liberté*. In 1790, the church bell rang not for Mass but for the *Fête de la Fédération*, and tricolor cockades appeared even in Rosières. Siméon wore one briefly, more out of solidarity than conviction, though Laure later kept it tucked away with a mixture of pride and unease. Neighbors who once spoke only of weather and vines now argued over the king, the clergy, and the price of freedom.

By 1792, the news from Paris darkened. Word of the King's imprisonment arrived weeks late, yet it struck the village like a sudden storm breaking over familiar ground.

Siméon's stories of America continued to draw the younger men close. They listened to his accounts of campfires and arguments about liberty, of Lafayette's unwavering conviction, of the fierce exhilaration that came from believing one was shaping history itself.

Soon, summons followed. Republican battalions were forming, and Siméon's younger neighbors left their fields behind, muskets replacing plows. Watching them go, he felt an old ghost stir.

Soldiers' wagons began to pass through Vesoul, their wheels grinding over the stones as horses and grain were requisitioned in the name of the nation. Before long, the demand reached Rosières. Père Charles emerged from the presbytery, his face ashen, to surrender the parish keys. The church, a soldier announced, was now national property.

"National property?" Nicolas repeated quietly, as though the words themselves were unmoored. "The house of God belongs to God alone."

The Republic did not hear him. In the days that followed, the crucifix was taken down from above the altar. The painted wooden statues of the Virgin and Saint Joseph were carried out and loaded onto a cart. Jeanne watched from the edge of the square, her hand pressed to her lips.

The worst was the silence. A new law forbade the ringing of the bell for Mass. The great Chappuis bell, which had marked their births, their labors, their prayers, and their deaths, fell mute.

In the Gaugien house, a different kind of quiet took hold. Laure moved through her tasks with new deliberation, one hand often resting on the gentle swell beneath her apron, a private hope taking root as the public world unraveled.

Then Père Charles was gone. Having refused the oath of loyalty to the state, he slipped away one frost-laced dawn, fleeing across the border into Switzerland. There was no farewell.

He had lost his priest, his confessor, the man who had guided him in matters of the soul since boyhood. To a man of such faith, the loss cut deeper even than the King's imprisonment. Nicolas took to sitting for long hours by the cold hearth, while the family moved around him softly, their words hushed.

At home, Nicolas's strength began to fade. He moved more slowly among the rows, leaning on the staff he had carried since injuring his knee the summer before Siméon left to enlist. The land remained generous, yet the air felt different, heavy and expectant. By winter, snow pressed against the shutters, and the ground lay iron-hard beneath the vines. Nicolas grew more weary with each passing day, and when Siméon watched him, he was reminded of the last winter he had shared with his own Grand-père and feared this one might end the same way.

1793

In the last days of January 1793, word from Paris reached even the remote valleys of Franche-Comté. The King was dead. Citizen Louis Capet, formerly King of France, had been beheaded. His queen, Marie-Antoinette, would meet the same fate before the year was out. The decree was read aloud in the square before Saint-Siméon, and the news spread quickly through Rosières.

Nicolas wept openly.

No one in the family had ever seen it before. Not during the famine. Not when Colas died. Not through any of the long seasons of hardship that had tested and shaped him. He stood in the square among his neighbors, an old man who had always been a wall against whatever the world sent, and the tears came without apology or restraint. Those nearest him looked away, to protect his dignity by pretending not to see. Jeanne moved to his side without a word and took his arm in both her hands, steadying him.

To Nicolas, the King remained His Most Christian Majesty, God's anointed, the living emblem of order and faith. "God will punish them," he murmured, "for striking down His chosen one." The shock seemed to break something within him that even prayer could not mend.

For Siméon, the news echoed old vows. He had served eight years beneath the royal standard and carried the memory of that oath as a mark of honor. The King's death left him not only sorrowful but hollow, as if the cause that had once given his life meaning had been erased.

Nicolas was so overcome, one might have thought he had known the late King himself. He told the family he had one reason left to live: to meet his first grandson. The thought of the child's arrival gave him something firm to hold to, at least for a time.

One biting morning in early February, Laure's labor began before sunrise. Jeanne took charge, heating water, gathering linens, and whispering prayers as she moved about the room. The wind rattled the shutters while Laure labored through long, painful hours. Her cries rose and fell, then weakened to quiet gasps. Near midday, the scent of steam and sweat filled the cottage, and at last a thin cry broke through the stillness. It was the sound of renewal, fragile but real. It was a boy; he too would be named Nicolas in honor of his grandfather and late uncle. The elder Nicolas was smiling, visibly happy for the first time since news of the King's death had reached their vineyard.

Laure and her baby boy were both alive, their breaths shallow and uneven. The child's color was pale, his tiny chest laboring with each breath, and Laure lay still, her hair damp against her face. Jeanne wiped her brow, murmuring comfort, but she could see the strain in both mother and child, as if life itself were clinging by the smallest thread. Even in her shattered state, her first thought was for the remedies that might help her son's fragile breathing find its rhythm. "Maman Jeanne," she whispered, her voice a wisp of sound. "My basket… there is lavender… for his chest… and motherwort drops…" It was a desperate, instinctive grasp at the knowledge that had always given her a measure of control in a chaotic world. Jeanne, her own hands shaking, prepared the gentle remedies, but the baby's struggle only seemed to deepen.

As the afternoon light began to fail, the baby's breathing grew fainter, each shallow breath a greater effort than the last. Seeing the life ebb from him, Jeanne fell to her knees beside the bed, her hands shaking as she lifted a small cup of water from the table.

"Siméon," she whispered, her voice barely steady, "his soul… we have no priest now. You must baptize your son."

She took her son's hand and guided it gently to the child's forehead. Together, trembling, they spoke the words they had both known since childhood: "*Je te baptise au nom du Père, du Fils, et du Saint-Esprit.*" The syllables were soft, urgent with a father's love and a grandmother's plea for the baby Nicolas's soul.

As the final syllable faded, the baby's chest fell still and he was gone.

It was so sudden, so shocking, that grief had no time to take shape before silence reclaimed the room.

Laure kept her eyes closed, already knowing the truth as hot tears slid down her cheeks. Siméon enclosed her hand in both of his; no words passed between them, yet everything that mattered was shared.

Only then did Jeanne rise, her legs unsteady, and turn toward the hearth to comfort the boy's grandfather, Nicolas, who had been resting by the fire. "Nicolas," she called softly, thinking he had fallen asleep. He did not move. She took a step closer, then another. The firelight flickered over his face, still and strangely peaceful. "Nicolas," she whispered again, touching his shoulder. He did not stir.

For an instant the room seemed to tilt. The cup she had just used for the *baptême de nécessité* slipped from her hand and struck the floor, water darkened the boards, spreading like a shadow she could not lift. She could not breathe. It could not be true, yet it was. The love of her life, the strong head of her house, the man who had carried their family through every season, was gone.

There are no words to describe that day, which had brought both great joy and unimaginable sorrow to their home.

On February 9, 1793, grief settled heavily over the Gaugien household. Nicolas Gaugien, the venerable *vigneron* who had guided his sons through decades of war and harvest, died at seventy-six. At nearly the same moment, Laure lost her first child, a son named for his grandfather and for his uncle Colas, a loss that fell on a young mother and echoed through an aging matriarch's heart.

Siméon stood heartbroken before the municipal officer with his longtime companion and farmhand Claude Meugnier, whose loyalty to the family reached back to boyhood. Together they recorded the elder Nicolas's death, the officer's quill scratching indifferently while outside the vines slept beneath frost. A second entry was made that same day for the infant Nicolas[69] who bore his name, the clerk simply writing the date once more.

At home, Laure and Jeanne waited in silence, overwhelmed by a grief that struck both wife and new mother in a single cruel day. The patriarch was gone, their newborn son taken, the family line renewed only to be broken at once.

---

[69] **Nicolas Gaugien,** the firstborn son of Siméon Gaugien and Laurence Hudel, was born and died on February 9, 1793, in Rosières-sur-Mance. His birth and death on the same day as his grandfather Nicolas Gaugien are recorded in the *Registres paroissiaux et d'état civil* for *Rosières-sur-Mance,* preserved by the Departmental Archives of Haute-Saône.

That night, the house was restless with grief. Firelight trembled across the beams the elder Nicolas had raised with his own hands. Siméon sat long by the hearth, listening for the echo of his father's voice and the faint cry of the child he would never know. The wisdom of one life and the promise of another had vanished abruptly. No battle had prepared him for this.

Today the soldier was a father burying his firstborn, a husband providing solace, a son in mourning. Outside, the wind pressed hard against the shutters. Within, he was a man who had to make space for the loss he could not fill, and learn to live with the weight he must now shoulder.

Overwhelmed, he drifted down to the cool of the cellar. The scent of earth and old oak settled around him. He found the barrel his father had always called the patient one, the cask that had been sleeping since before Siméon left for Auxonne, and sat with his back against it, his hands loose between his knees. The cold of the stone came up through his boots. He breathed slowly until the weight of the moment loosened just enough to bear. Only then did he climb back up to the world that had so suddenly changed.

1794 – 1797

Life did not pause for grief. The winter of mourning gave way to spring, and the work of the farm resumed. Jeanne still tended the animals with Laure, making curds and churning butter, though her energy waned without her husband. Laure took over the oven trips and more of the household work, while Jeanne supervised from her chair by the hearth.

Spring brought persistent rain and mud, and with it quiet news: President George Washington had been sworn in for a second term. For Siméon, the information landed on a soul already buried. Later, alone by the hearth, the thought returned. While his own world had collapsed, Washington, an ocean away, had again shouldered the burden of leadership. The farmer-soldier he had admired was still standing. The world demanded that men continue.

That autumn, word came from Paris of a new calendar. The Republic had abolished the Christian reckoning of time. No more Sundays, saints' days, Christmas, or Easter. The months were renamed for nature: Vendémiaire for the grape harvest, Brumaire for the fogs, Frimaire for the frost. The seven-day week was replaced by a ten-day décade, with rest only on the tenth day.

In Paris such things might be enforced. In Rosières, the decree arrived like a stone dropped into a well, making a sound before silence closed over it. In December 1793, Christmas was 5 Nivôse, the fifth day of the snow month. The Republic assigned it to a pig. But in Rosières, candles still burned after dark, and prayers, if whispered, were not offered to the Republic.

The villagers did not resist openly. They nodded, said little, and continued as before. The curé, if he remained, said Mass in private homes or barns. The new calendar existed on paper in district offices, but it did not reach the henhouse at dawn or the field at harvest. Siméon and Laure marked time as their parents had, by the length of days, the soil's condition, the swelling of livestock, the turning of leaves. The Republic could rename the months, but it could not change the seasons.

Their animals prospered, a healthy calf born that year. Laure soon became pregnant again, and by autumn 1794 her days were divided between animals, garden, orchard, and home. She tended her body as she did the livestock, brewing raspberry leaf tea to strengthen her womb and ginger infusions to calm her stomach. A patch of lemon balm from the market in Rennes scented the garden each morning. By her third trimester, hope had returned.

Some evenings, Jeanne and Laure shelled beans side by side while Jeanne recounted births and harvests past and Laure felt the baby turn beneath her apron.

On 1 Vendémiaire, Year III, September 22, 1794, Jeanne Richard, Siméon's mother, passed quietly in her sleep. The harvest was at its height, and authorities demanded their quota, so Siméon could not attend the declaration. Claude Meugnier again stood witness in his stead.

Three months later, on December 6, 1794 (16 Frimaire, Year III), joy returned. Laure bore a healthy son, Siméon *fils*[70], a sturdy, bright-eyed boy born just under a year after the loss of both his grandfather and his parents' firstborn.

Under the Directory, the valley adjusted to civic forms and quotas. When the name Bonaparte began to circulate, his exploits quickly became folklore. For Siméon, the stories carried personal weight. Bonaparte had served at Auxonne the year after Siméon's discharge, drilling on the same cold parade ground. The thought that an officer who once walked those ramparts now shaped France's fate spread through the valley with pride and awe. Talk in Rosières shifted from fear to cautious hope that order might finally hold.

HISTORICAL NOTE: BONAPARTE AT AUXONNE

Auxonne played a formative role in the early career of Napoléon Bonaparte. Serving there several times between 1788 and 1791 with the La Fère Artillery Regiment, he studied fortifications, deepened his gunnery training, and earned a reputation for discipline and rigorous study. His letters from Auxonne describe long drills on the parade ground, careful observation of the town's defensive works, and an intense dedication to mathematics and engineering. These years shaped the technical foundation that defined his command style and ultimately remade France. Source: *Correspondance Générale de Napoléon Bonaparte, Vol. 1–2 (Paris: Fayard / Fondation Napoléon).*

The harvest still had to be brought in. Livestock still needed tending. Preparations for the next season could not wait. Yet conversations at the tavern, the fountain, and in the fields grew bolder as news arrived, half understood and hotly debated. Laure held her child a little tighter at the thought of another season of thunder.

She came to see their marriage as a quiet resistance, rooted in labor and love, in the small acts that held families together when governments

---

[70] **Siméon Gaugien, Jr.**, the son of Siméon Gaugien and Laurence Hudel, was born on December 6, 1794, in Rosières-sur-Mance. His birth is recorded in the Registres paroissiaux et d'état civil for Rosières-sur-Mance, preserved by the Departmental Archives of Haute-Saône. He married on January 28, 1817, in Rosières-sur-Mance, and died on January 5, 1865, in Rosiere, Cape Vincent, New York, United States of America. His death is recorded in the civil registers of Jefferson County, New York.

faltered. She also remembered what Siméon had once said: liberty, once seen, could not be forgotten.

The Revolution had promised liberty, yet new burdens quickly replaced the old. As the decade wore on, the weight was war. Requisitions for grain, wine, carts, horses, and oxen pressed hard on villages like Rosières, paid in assignats that lost value by the month. The lords were gone, but the state reached deeper into each harvest than the seigneurs ever had. Liberty had come. Prosperity had not.

In November 1797, Laure bore another son, a strong and healthy boy whom they also named Nicolas[71], in honor of the grandfather they had lost, the brother Siméon had buried long ago, and the tiny firstborn whose life had slipped away before it had fully begun.

Later that winter, during a visit from a merchant with Swiss contacts, Siméon heard a different kind of news from America. It came not as official dispatch but as political gossip, shared with disbelief.

George Washington had relinquished the presidency. That a man would surrender such power struck the merchant as incomprehensible. To Siméon, holding his newborn son, it felt entirely in character.

While Europe tore itself apart for crowns and offices, the man he had admired had shown a rarer strength: the strength to let go.

The Gaugien vineyard had always centered on family and farm. So, it seemed to Siméon, had Washington.

1799

The boys grew, their laughter and restless energy reminding Siméon of his own childhood, running the fields with Colas. His stories of America became bedtime tales, of forests that stretched to the horizon, of bright birds and strange fish, and of men who dared to remake their world.

The prefect's papers demanded wheat and wine for army depots at Vesoul and Gray. War made ordinary goods scarce. The British blockade

---

[71] **Nicolas Gaugien**, the son of Siméon Gaugien and Laurence Hudel, was born on November 27, 1797, and died March 15, 1815. His birth and death are recorded in the *Registres paroissiaux et d'état civil* for *Rosières-sur-Mance, preserved by the Departmental Archives of Haute-Saône.*

tightened around France's ports, driving up prices, while inland merchants, burdened by levies, traveled less each season. Salt, soap, and coarse cloth could still be found, but at a cost that made families measure out each handful as a concession to distant conflict.

For young Siméon Jr., now seven, that weight arrived as a lesson at the village school. Maître Rets dictated figures from a government primer newly issued to replace the old measures. "Un kilomètre égale mille mètres."

The boy came home puzzled. "Papa," he asked, "how far is it to the fountain?"

Siméon paused, hoe in hand. The answer rose instinctively, measured by habit and memory, by the turn in the path and the slope of the ground. He stopped himself. "In the old way," he asked, "or the new way your schoolmaster teaches?"

"The new way."

Siméon crouched so they were eye to eye. "It was always a short walk," he said slowly. "In the new numbers, that would be less than a kilometer." The word felt awkward in his mouth, like a borrowed tool that did not quite fit the hand.

Later, he spoke of it to Laure as she prepared supper. "They are making ghosts of our fathers," he said quietly. "My father knew this land by memory, not by decimals. Now I must account for it in measures that do not belong to it."

Laure wiped her hands, thoughtful rather than bitter. "Then teach them both," she said. "Teach our sons the old measures with your stories, and the new ones with their sums. That way they will know where they come from and still be able to find their way to the fountain."

Chapter Sixteen: Sturdy Vines

1799 – May 1831

The villagers felt the change first: mornings grew quieter, rumors slowed. When word arrived that Bonaparte had swept aside the Directory and installed himself as First Consul, it stirred no debate in Rosières. After a decade of upheaval, it brought relief.

Neighbors saw in him a man who valued discipline and work, the virtues that guided their lives. They recognized order returning.

The Constitution of Year VIII made itself felt: fairer taxes, reopened churches, and the dread that had shadowed whispered opinions began to fade.

Before the spring thaw, distant news crossed the ocean and reached the valley with a different weight. Siméon learned that George Washington had died peacefully at Mount Vernon.

He stood for a long time outside the farmhouse, quiet beneath the shifting light. The memories came unbidden: the general at Newport, at Williamsburg, at Yorktown, and at that last review on the Hudson where he had spoken words Siméon had carried ever since.

The consolidation of power in Paris continued. When Napoléon was named Consul for Life in 1802, then confirmed by national referendum as Emperor of the French in 1804, villagers in Haute-Saône did not see either step as a retreat from the ideals of the Revolution. They saw both as guarantees that the hard-won stability they craved would endure.

Fairer taxes. Returning priests. Roads repaired. The promise of continuity. The Gaugiens, having endured so much upheaval, felt in their vineyard the steadying hand of order. Their vines remained strong, even when the world beyond their valley shifted like sand.

When the drums of Empire sounded, Jean-Claude Petit left his forge to serve. The blacksmith fought at Austerlitz and in Spain, surviving two wounds and carrying home a veteran's quiet pride. He returned to the forge without bravado, reopening his workshop in 1814, a man who served without complaint and returned without ceremony.

A generation after Yorktown, Siméon Gaugien Jr. enlisted at seventeen. On November 29, 1812, he joined the 20th Line Infantry Regiment as a remplaçant, a paid volunteer taking the place of a conscript. The payment would serve the family well.

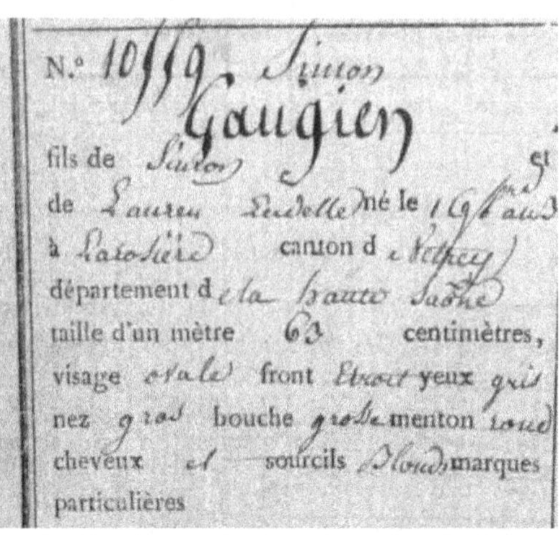

Napoleonic Army Enrollment Record for Siméon Gaugien Jr., Soldier No. 10559, November 1812

The clerk recorded entry number 10559: Siméon Gaugien, son of Siméon and Laurence Hudel, of Rosières-sur-Mance.

He replaced the conscript who had drawn unlucky number 7. In Rosières, only one family had both the motive and the two thousand francs to pay for a substitute: the family of their former seigneur, the Marquis de Chappuis, old and ailing, securing his lineage. For Siméon, it was a chance to serve and to earn the capital his family needed, money that would also secure his future and his hope to marry his sweetheart, Jeanne-Baptiste Thierat. It was duty, opportunity, and hope woven into a single decision.

By 1813, his regiment was in northern Italy, garrisoned along the Po Valley. Rearguard skirmishes, collapsing supply lines, the slow retreat of French influence: the young soldiers endured it all. The front settled into grim stasis. Days passed in watchfulness, men measuring time by rations and river levels.

Siméon Gaugien Jr. during the Italian
Campaigns of the Napoleonic Wars

In those months, he recalled his father's words: the hardest part of America had not been the guns or the marches, but the waiting, the not knowing whether home would still exist.

When news of Napoléon's abdication reached the garrisons in April 1814, some wept, others cursed. Siméon Jr. felt only hollow relief. He had survived.

After the Armistice of Schiarino-Rizzino, he returned home honorably released, barely nineteen, with savings in his pocket and the weight of experience on his shoulders. Like his father after Yorktown, he returned changed.

No one greeted him with more joy than his younger brother, Nicolas. Three years his junior, full of restless admiration, Nicolas clung to every word, turning marches into legend, discipline into honor, endurance into proof of France's greatness.

For a brief time, peace seemed possible. Then, in the spring of 1815, everything changed. Napoléon escaped from Elba and reclaimed the throne. The news reached the valley like thunder. Tricolor ribbons reappeared in windows, voices grew bolder, and old loyalties surged back to life.

Barely seventeen, Nicolas wore the tricolor cockade openly and spoke of honor and renewal with the fierce confidence of youth. Siméon Jr., newly returned from Italy, listened in silence. He had seen that same brightness before, not in words but in faces, among boys who believed courage could outrun fate.

Even quiet roads that had long known only routine and silence could now carry a threat of sudden violence.

Then on March 15, 1815, Nicolas Gaugien died at the age of seventeen.

The parish register offers no explanation, only the facts: his death at four in the afternoon, declared the next morning by his father, then fifty-four, and witnessed by his uncle Noël Hudel. He had buried one son already. Now he buried another.

The timing carried its own weight. France was once again divided and Nicolas had worn his loyalties openly. Just two weeks earlier, Napoléon had landed at Antibes after escaping from Elba; at Paris he would reclaim his throne. In such moments, even quiet valleys could turn dangerous for those who declared themselves too loudly.

Whether from caution, grief, or custom, Siméon Sr. reported the death without elaboration. Within three months, whatever cause Nicolas might have believed in collapsed at Waterloo. Napoléon was defeated and exiled once more.

The summer of 1816 brought destruction to the vines: hard frosts, sleet, icy rains. Wheat blackened; swollen rivers spread floods. Bread became scarcer than wine across eastern France, *l'année sans été*, the year without a summer.

The Gaugiens watched their vines yield a small, bitter harvest. Families slaughtered livestock early to stretch dwindling stores. Through these months, the sum Siméon Jr. had earned as a replacement soldier became their bulwark: chestnut meal to stretch flour, salt to preserve meat, seed for the next planting. Many neighbors had nothing left for spring. The Gaugiens did not starve, but they knew hunger's edge.

The mill and press had passed into private hands, but grain still had to be ground, grapes pressed. What had once been payments to the seigneur were now fees to private interests. The names on the ledgers changed; the coins left the same pockets.

HISTORICAL NOTE: ERUPTION OF MOUNT TAMBORA: YEAR WITHOUT A SUMMER

In April 1815, Mount Tambora erupted in the Dutch East Indies, casting ash and sulfur into the upper atmosphere, dimming sunlight across Europe and North America. The summer of 1816, l'année sans été, brought cold rains and unseasonal frosts to regions like Franche-Comté and Haute-Saône, destroying crops and vineyards. Wheat failed to ripen, grapes shriveled, livestock faced starvation, and bread prices soared. The famine of 1816 and 1817 left lasting scars on rural life. Source: *William K. Klingaman and Nicholas P. Klingaman, The Year Without Summer: 1816 and the Volcano That Darkened the World and Changed History (New York: St. Martin's Press, 2013).*

Siméon Gaugien Jr. took a bride. Steady in manner and shaped by hardship, he married Jeanne-Baptiste Thierat on January 28, 1817, as his father had married Laure on nearly the same winter days twenty-nine years earlier.

She came from a neighboring village, known for her bright laugh and capable hands, the kind of woman who could soothe a fretful child while tending dough with perfect instinct. Her family were humble farming folk.

When Jeanne entered the Gaugien farmhouse as a new wife, Laure welcomed her with open arms. She remembered her own early steps into this home decades earlier, frightened and missing the mother she had lost too young. She knew what it meant to arrive unsure of one's place and determined that Jeanne would feel as welcomed as she had been. She guided her through the rhythms of the household, sharing with her the names and temperaments of the cows, the spot above the hearth where herbs dried best, the feel of dough ready to rise, and which pear tree offered the first fruits of summer. She pointed to the sweet clover near the garden gate, its scent a promise that joy still returned each year. Every remedy, recipe, and secret to keeping family and farm alive was offered freely from one woman to the next. The thread of love and labor that had begun with the elder Jeanne seemed now to stitch itself into the hands of her young namesake.

Both Siméon Sr. and his son watched the easy bond forming between the two women with quiet gratitude. Through that long gray year, the farmhouse became their refuge. Prayers lengthened, and laughter faded as hunger and worry pressed in. When the thaw came at last in 1817, and the soil softened beneath their feet, the family returned to their fields.

Fortunes slowly shifted. In January 1818, Jeanne gave birth to their first son, Charles André[72], a lively child whose arrival lifted the spirits of the entire household. For a time, hope felt steady again. Two years later, on the first day of 1820, Jacques Antoine was born, spirited and strong.

---

[72] **Charles André Gaugien (Gosier)**, eldest son of Siméon Gaugien, Jr. and Jeanne-Baptiste Thierat, was born on January 20, 1818, in Rosières-sur-Mance, Haute-Saône. He immigrated to the United States, arriving in New York, married Geneviève Branche, and died in 1898 in Rosiere, Cape Vincent, New York. His birth is recorded in the *Registres paroissiaux et d'état civil for Rosières-sur-Mance, preserved by the Departmental Archives of Haute-Saône. His death is recorded in the civil registers of Jefferson County, New York.*

Then came another son, Nicolas, in the autumn of 1821. Fragile from birth, he was gone by the following summer.

When told of his passing, his grand-père Siméon only closed his eyes. He prayed for his brother Colas, his own firstborn son Nicolas, his son Nicolas in 1815, and now this child, his grandson Nicolas. Only the patriarch Nicolas had lived to old age.

In August 1824, Jeanne bore another son, Jean Baptiste, a healthy child whose curious gaze brought laughter back to the farmhouse. In December 1829, a daughter, little Marie, survived only moments after birth.

In late 1830, as preparations began for the feast of Saint Siméon, a stranger arrived: Abbé François Lesueur, sent by the French-American landowner James Le Ray de Chaumont to speak with families.

In a valley where faith shaped every season, a priest's voice carried weight. Lesueur spoke calmly of America: land plentiful, faith respected, French-speaking communities forming along the St. Lawrence. Every veteran understood: Joseph Bonaparte[73] himself had chosen the North Country as a refuge. For men still carrying wounds from the Napoleonic wars, his message felt like permission to hope.

For the people of Rosières, this was a rare convergence of opportunity and trust: a compelling vision of a better future, a respected cleric delivering it, and, perhaps for the first time in years, a genuine chance to thrive.

After Mass, families gathered in the square, huddling around spiced wine, speaking in low voices. The Petits, the Vauthrins, the Simards, the Pioches; they compared what they had heard, what they feared, what they hoped. They had endured wars and revolutions together; the thought of crossing an ocean alone was unthinkable. If they left, they would leave together.[74]

---

[73]**Joseph Bonaparte**, Napoléon's elder brother and former King of Spain, lived in the United States from 1815 to 1832, primarily at his estate "Point Breeze" in Bordentown, New Jersey. He also acquired extensive property in upstate New York, including land in the Adirondack region where Lake Bonaparte bears his name. Local tradition in Cape Vincent holds that he commissioned the octagonal Cup and Saucer House as a hunting and fishing lodge on the St. Lawrence River in the 1820s; though primary documentation of the commission remains elusive, the house appears in period descriptions and an 1850 sketch by Mrs. Fort. Sources: *Patricia Tyson Stroud, The Man Who Had Been King: The American Exile of Napoléon's Brother Joseph (Philadelphia: University of Pennsylvania Press, 2005); Roswell P. Flower Memorial Library, "Artwork in the Napoléon Room,"https://www.flowermemoriallibrary.org/napoleon-room/; Nelie Horton Casler, Cape Vincent and Its History (Watertown, NY: Hungerford-Holbrook Co., 1906).*

[74] Rosières-sur-Mance, where Siméon's story began, is home today to an estimated fifty people.

Siméon Sr. and his son met with Lesueur. He spoke of the region along the St. Lawrence where Joseph Bonaparte had commissioned a hunting lodge called the Cup and Saucer House. Rumor or truth, the Emperor's brother carried weight. For veterans, building a life where he had made his refuge felt like providence.

Over weeks, they gathered information, weighing the decision. The valley had grown harsher, the vineyards unpredictable. Winters colder. Harvests unreliable. Among those who had served under Napoléon, his name had become a lost identity. The thought of a land where their children might find stability pulled hard. America became a plan.

Both father and son intended to leave. Several neighbors hoped to travel together. But delays came: livestock to sell, debts to settle, ground to thaw. For the Gaugiens, the obstacles were personal: Siméon Sr.'s health declined; Jeanne Thierat was expecting another child. Though the plans moved forward with his blessing, they all understood he would not live to see the journey completed. The weight pressed on every conversation, every whispered plan.

HISTORICAL NOTE:
JAMES DONATIEN AND JACQUES-DONATIEN LE RAY DE CHAUMONT

James Donatien Le Ray de Chaumont, known in America as James Le Ray, arrived in the United States in 1785 and became the primary developer of French Catholic settlement in northern New York. His land holdings, financial backing, and encouragement of French community life shaped the region for generations. His father, Jacques-Donatien Le Ray de Chaumont, was among the most consequential private supporters of the American Revolution. Known as the "French Father of the American Revolution," he served as Governor of Les Invalides, hosted Benjamin Franklin at his estate in Passy during the crucial years of Franco-American negotiations, and supplied funds, clothing, weapons, and naval support to the Continental cause. He refitted and gifted the warship *Bonhomme Richard*, named in tribute to Franklin's *Poor Richard's Almanack*, and placed it under Captain John Paul Jones, who declared from its deck: "I have not yet begun to fight." Sources: Thomas Jefferson to James Le Ray de Chaumont, May 29, 1818, Founders Online; Samuel Eliot Morison, *John Paul Jones: A Sailor's Biography* (Boston: Little, Brown, 1959).

When Siméon Gaugien died on May 30, 1831, he left no monument of stone, only the traces of a life shaped by integrity and the quiet persistence of vines stretching across the slopes above Rosières-sur-Mance. Time had lined his face and silvered his hair, yet neighbors still knew him as the steady artilleryman who had returned home decades earlier and rebuilt his life among seasons and soil.

In his final days, Siméon asked for the shutters to be left open so he could see the vineyard, his vineyard, lit by the shifting light of late spring. Rows of promise stretching toward June. He watched them the way a father watches his children, with love, worry, and pride woven tightly together.

His breath came more slowly now, but his mind wandered clearly across the years. He saw the cannon smoke of his youth, the biting cold of winter marches, and the steadfast faces of Fleur, Louis, Alexis, and so many others, who had not lived to grow old as he had. The artillery had been a harsh teacher, yet it had given him purpose when he was a young man with little more than a uniform and a name. He could still recall laughter shared around meager fires, songs to chase off fear, and the strange comfort of camaraderie in the midst of chaos. Those memories, once sharp, now softened into something like gratitude.

A shallow catch in his breathing made Laure rise. Quietly she stepped to the doorway, where their son stood. "Go," she said softly. "Bring the abbé."

Siméon Jr. hurried toward the village. Not long after, Laure guided Abbé Jean-François Ignace Bergier into the room. The young priest carried his stole, a small ritual book, and the holy oils. His expression was solemn but gentle.

Laure moved aside so he could draw near. The abbé placed a steady hand on Siméon's shoulder. "My son," he said quietly. "I am here."

Siméon's eyes lifted at the familiar voice.

The priest prepared the oils and opened his ritual book. In the ancient Latin of the Church, he spoke the prayers of *Extreme Unction*, anointing each sense in turn, absolving the sins committed through sight, through hearing, through smell, through taste and speech, through touch. When he came to Siméon's hands, the same hands that had guided cannons, tended vines, and held his family, the abbé's voice softened with particular tenderness.

"*Per istam sanctam unctionem et suam piissimam misericordiam, indulgeat tibi Dominus quidquid per manus deliquisti.*"

He anointed Siméon's feet last, marking the sign of the cross upon them.

Then the abbé placed his hand lightly upon Siméon's shoulder and prayed the final commendation.

"*Proficiscere, anima Christiana.* Go forth, Christian soul. May our Lord Jesus Christ, who suffered for you and redeemed you with His precious blood, receive you in peace. May the holy angels lead you into paradise. May the saints of God come to meet you, and may you have eternal rest."

He made the sign of the cross over Siméon. "And may the blessing of Almighty God, Father, Son, and Holy Spirit, descend upon you and remain with you."

Laure wiped a quiet tear from her cheek and returned to her place beside him. Her fingers slipped into his, steady and warm, her touch a wordless promise that she would not leave him.

He looked toward the doorway, where their son stood with Jeanne and the children nearby. Siméon Jr., tall and sure-footed, carried his father's patience and his mother's quiet steadiness.

From her place at the bedside, Laure lifted her eyes toward their son and gave a small, urging nod. The gesture was enough. He crossed the room at once and knelt beside his father so he could hear the softened voice.

"I worried, son," Siméon whispered, each word a fragile offering. "For so long … that I had not given you enough. Or prepared you enough." He managed a faint smile. "But you have done better than I ever hoped, mon garçon. You honor my name, not with medals or grandness, but with how you love our family."

Siméon Jr. bowed his head, his voice thick with emotion. "Everything I know that matters, you taught me."

Siméon Gaugien, 1761–1831

Siméon's eyes glistened. "Then I can rest."

Outside, the church bell sounded the Angelus, calling the villagers to prayer. It was the same bell that had rung for his wedding, for baptisms, funerals, and every harvest blessing, silent only during the Revolution before its voice returned to the valley. Its steady chime stitched the moments of his life together, blending the smell of gunpowder and grapevines, the thunder of artillery and the quiet trickle of the millstream, the loneliness of battle and the warmth of family meals.

He could feel Laure's thumb gently tracing circles over his knuckles. "Stay with me," she murmured.

"I will," he breathed. "Just … not as I have."

The room blurred into shapes of light and shadow. His chest rose shallowly once more. He imagined the distant echo of cannon fire, yet now it carried no thrill. It sounded almost like a salute, as though old comrades were welcoming him home.

With his last strength, he squeezed Laure's hand, his eyes fixed on hers, full of love and gratitude. *"À bientôt, ma chérie,"* he whispered. Until we meet again.

As a soft breeze stirred the vines outside, Siméon Gaugien slipped quietly away.

Abbé Jean-François Ignace Bergier led the prayers with steady calm as he commended Siméon's soul to God. When the final blessing was complete, he quietly noted the hour, six o'clock in the evening, before closing the ritual book. Neighbors filled the small nave to honor a man known in the village for his humility and care. Women dabbed their eyes, and men bowed their heads, recalling a life marked by small, steady kindnesses: tools mended without fuss, quarrels eased rather than inflamed, a greeting offered with a nod of quiet respect.

Afterward, the procession moved to the cemetery behind the church, where Siméon was laid to rest among generations of Gaugiens. Laure, now a widow, guided her family home through a soft spring rain, her steps measured, her posture unbroken. In the Gaugien home, Siméon Jr. and his wife, Jeanne-Baptiste, awaited the birth of another child, their daily routines continuing even as mourning settled gently around them.

CHAPTER SEVENTEEN:
WEATHER ANY STORM

Autumn 1831 – Present

By harvest, the rhythm of work had reclaimed the household. Taxes rose, harvests faltered, and the burdens on small landholders grew heavier. What pressed most heavily now was the work of making a life in narrowing circumstances.

For Siméon Jr., the uniform no longer felt like a badge of honor. It had become a reminder of how quickly the ground beneath a man's feet could shift.

It was Jeanne and Laure who held the pieces together. One steady with experience, the other quick with resolve, they spent long evenings at the table with Siméon Jr., weighing their fears against their hopes for the future. They had no illusions. The land that had sustained the Gaugien family for generations could no longer guarantee a livelihood for those yet to come. Their children, they believed, deserved the chance to stand on soil that did not shift beneath them with every decree from Paris. Together, they prayed.

On November 19, 1831, their prayers were answered with the birth of a healthy daughter, Claire, small but strong-lunged, with her grandfather's dark eyes. She was their sixth child and second daughter, their living children now numbering four. The year that had taken one life also brought another, and the Gaugiens, deeply rooted in the soil of Rosières-sur-Mance, continued to endure, growing like the vines that never stopped climbing toward the light.

With Claire's birth and Laure's quiet encouragement, Siméon Jr. and his wife renewed their decision to leave. They would join other families from Franche-Comté preparing for the long voyage across the ocean. Their roots would now be transplanted, but not without Papa Gaugien's blessing. America became not just a distant dream whispered by a hopeful husband, but a promise carried forward by the women who refused to let his hopes die with his father. In their resolve, grief became purpose.

Their departure would follow the path already opened by Jean Branche, the first from Rosières-sur-Mance to settle on Le Ray's lands, whose letters and example had made the journey conceivable. Their new hamlet would be named Rosiere, a remembrance of the home they had left behind. The idea of a parish in the wilderness gave shape to their hopes, anchoring their future in faith.

When Laure, Siméon Jr., and Jeanne set sail, they did not travel alone. They were part of the wave of families from Rosières-sur-Mance and the nearby villages of Saint-Marcel, Bougey, Arbecey, Vitrey-sur-Mance, and Blondefontaine who left their ancestral valley and carried its name to northern New York. Emigration from eastern France to America was a daring and costly undertaking. Passage on ships like the transatlantic brig *Larpool* from Le Havre to New York often cost between 120 and 150 francs per adult, with reduced fares for older children: for a family of seven, an expense requiring careful collective preparation rather than impulse. And beyond the cost of passage were the funds needed to begin again: land from James Le Ray de Chaumont, livestock, tools, seed, and the raw materials of a life rebuilt from the soil up.

Before they could depart, official permission was required. Under the rule of King Louis-Philippe I, every French citizen leaving the country had to obtain a passport from the local prefecture. On April 6, 1832, the Préfecture de la Haute-Saône in Vesoul issued one to Siméon Gaugien Jr., describing him as thirty-eight years old, of ruddy complexion, with chestnut hair, an oval face, and a height of five feet eight inches. Signed and sealed by the prefect, the document authorized his travel to New York (Amérique). It marked his final legal act as a French citizen and the first as an emigrant bound for a new continent.

On March 18, 1832, the family's lands were sold, the transaction recorded before a notary and executed through their appointed agent, Claude-Charles Bouyer. The sale encompassed the properties accumulated across generations: fields, vineyards, and holdings long worked by Gaugien and Hudel hands. From the proceeds, the pooled households realized approximately nineteen hundred francs, intended not as profit but as provision. It would fund passage, purchase land, and sustain the family through the uncertainty of beginning again.

The house itself, long held by the family, passed to a local buyer, closing the last material tie to the village. What could be carried was packed. What could not was entrusted to memory.

They delayed their departure so they could celebrate one final Palm Sunday with their community at the Church of Saint-Siméon. On that morning April 8, 1832, the bell rang over the valley. For the Gaugiens, the Mass served as both farewell and blessing.

With their affairs settled, they set out toward the sea. The rail line between Paris and the east would not open for another generation, so they traveled as emigrants of their time did, by ox cart and carriage. The road carried them north and west through Langres, toward Paris, and onward to the coast, following the same route countless families from Franche-Comté would take in the years to come.

They reached Le Havre on April 20, 1832. Siméon Jr. stood on the same coast where his father had stood fifty-three years before.

On April 23, they boarded the brig *Larpool*. When Laure Hudel Gaugien, Siméon Gaugien Jr., and Jeanne-Baptiste Thierat Gaugien set sail, traveling with them were several families from Rosières-sur-Mance and its neighboring villages, many of whom would later appear in the records of northern New York. Among their companions were Jean-Claude Petit, the maréchal-ferrant and a veteran of Napoléon's campaigns, with his wife and two children; Jean-Claude Vauthrin and his wife Gabrielle Testevuide with their three daughters, also of Rosières; and Pierre Vauthrin and Françoise Testevuide, likely close relations of the same family. From nearby Betoncourt-sur-Mance came Jean-Baptiste Simard, with his wife and their four children, Jean-Baptiste Pioche, his wife, and their daughter Élisabeth, from Vitrey-sur-Mance. The manifest read like a roll call of the Mance Valley.

The brig *Larpool* crossing the Atlantic from Le Havre to New York, 1832

When the *Larpool* docked in New York on June 5, 1832, more than half a century before Ellis Island opened and the Statue of Liberty rose in the harbor, the Gaugiens and their fellow countrymen stepped into a young republic still defining itself, carrying the hopes of their village and the weight of all they had left behind.

The families made their way to the New York office used by Le Ray's agents, a narrow building tucked among warehouses facing the river, where French-speaking clerks assisted newly arrived settlers from France. A clerk greeted them with easy familiarity: Monsieur James Le Ray de Chaumont maintained land offices for French families from Franche-Comté, and several from Rosières-sur-Mance were already established on his northern estates.

As the clerk spoke of the route north, of Cape Vincent and the settlements along the river, Siméon Jr. said carefully, "My family and I take comfort in knowing we are traveling north, near the lands held by the brother of our late Emperor. Along the Saint Lawrence."

The clerk's expression shifted. He hesitated, then nodded once.

"Monsieur Bonaparte departed for Europe this very month," he said. "After seventeen years in America. You have crossed paths in opposite directions."

The words fell between them and remained there. Siméon Jr. did not respond at once. He had carried that thought across the ocean: that he was moving toward a place where the Emperor's family still stood, where the world he had served had not yet vanished.

After a moment, the clerk spoke again, more quietly. "The community he knew remains. Many who served the Emperor have found their place there."

Siméon Jr. nodded. The assurance was real, but it did little to ease the ache of timing. Unrolling a worn map, the agent outlined the journey ahead.

They would travel by steamboat up the Hudson River to Albany, then follow the Erie Canal west toward Syracuse, the great waterway that had opened only seven years earlier. From there, overland in wagons and small caravans north along the eastern shore of Lake Ontario toward Cape Vincent: a village named for Vincent Le Ray, the son of the proprietor who had championed this French settlement in the North Country. These were lands once held by the great Iroquois Confederacy, still being settled, still carrying their own deep history. The clerk prepared a brief note of introduction for the official Le Ray Land Office in Cape Vincent, where deeds were issued and parcels assigned. "It is wild country," he said, "but rich land for those strong enough to make it theirs."

The days that followed were long and dusty, the nights alive with insects and the scent of pine. Their journey carried them from the stone lanes of Rosières-sur-Mance to the raw northern edge of America, where the forests seemed without end. Oak, maple, beech, ash, and poplar crowded the shoreline, rising behind stands of white pine, spruce, and fir. The trees were older and taller than anything they had known at home, their shadows deep even at midday. At night, deer moved cautiously through the underbrush, foxes barked from distant thickets, and the occasional crack of branches hinted at larger animals passing between the trees. It was a world vast and alive, both strange and beautiful.

Emigrants Traveling Along Lake Ontario, 1832.

Yet amid all this newness, it was the sweet clover along the towpaths that comforted Laure most. Its scent was exactly the same as the sweet clover in her garden in France. Memory and hope folded together as the family traveled inland.

Illustration of Early Family Cabin

In the weeks after their arrival, the Gaugiens purchased twenty-five acres. Their first dwelling was a single-room cabin of rough-hewn timber, with a loft above and a hearth below, a humble reminder of the stone houses they had known in France. Around them, smoke rose from other cabins as neighbors cleared their parcels, the steady ring of axes carrying through the woods. As families from the Mance Valley had always done, they worked side by side to carve a livelihood from a land that held its own deep history long before they arrived.

In time, they helped establish the settlement that came to be known as Rosiere, New York. Originally called the French Settlement, it was first part of the Town of Lyme and later of Cape Vincent, a small colony where families from the Mance Valley rebuilt their lives far from home.

Artist rendering based on a 19th-century illustration of the original 1832 Saint Vincent de Paul Catholic Church, erected by French settlers in Rosiere, New York, lost to fire 1870s.

The cornerstone of what would become St. Vincent de Paul Church, known locally as the old French church, was laid in the summer of 1832. The parish traced its origins to Bishop John Dubois, a fellow Frenchman who had fled the Revolution four decades earlier and remade his life in America. He had found support through figures such as Lafayette and risen to become the third Bishop of New York. He traveled north to bless this frontier community, offering encouragement to settlers who shared his language and faith. To them, his arrival was more than ceremony: it felt like confirmation that their long journey had purpose.

John Dubois, Third Bishop of New York

Mr. Le Ray donated a tract of land whose rents provided steady support for the parish, one of several endowments he created to sustain Catholic worship in the North Country. The first Mass was celebrated by Father Simon, assisted by an altar boy, Charles André Gaugien, the eldest son of Siméon Gaugien Jr. and my third great-grandfather.

In the years that followed, the settlers were served by priests from St. Mary's Cathedral in Kingston, Ontario, who crossed the St. Lawrence by boat in summer and by sleigh in winter, along with itinerant missionaries who came at intervals to celebrate Mass and hear confessions. Through these visits, and through their own labor, the people of Rosiere preserved the language, faith, and fellowship they had carried from the valleys of Franche-Comté to the forests of northern New York.

Winters were brutal in the new land. In 1835, the Black River flooded, cutting off supplies to the frontier. The small community pulled together, their strength drawn from a shared history that now spanned two continents.

1842 brought frost and famine, a killing freeze in June. The winter of 1843 tested the community more than any season since the crossing.

Snow fell early and lingered, burying cabins and thinning stores. At night, Siméon Jr. fed the hearth carefully while Jeanne-Baptiste kept the children close. When wood ran low and the wind howled off the lake, he spoke to them of France, of vineyards and bells and the long road that had brought them here, offering memory as comfort when fuel failed.

Yet the farms endured. The French families of Rosiere pooled labor, shared seed and meals, and took solace in parish life.

Grief returned in the summer of 1847. Laure Hudel had crossed the ocean when most women of her generation would not have dared it. She had watched the forests of the North Country replace the vineyards of Franche-Comté, had learned to make do with what the new land offered, and had found in the scent of sweet clover along the canal towpaths something that still smelled like home. She died at Rosiere that summer and was buried in the churchyard of the community she had helped establish. Hers was the first family grave in American soil. The stone stood at the edge of a clearing that had been wilderness when she arrived.

In 1852, a gale smashed docks at Cape Vincent and crippled ships in the harbor. Yet that same year, Rosiere saw signs of modern change when the first train steamed into Cape Vincent, linking the village by rail to Watertown and Rome. The line would later become part of the Rome, Watertown and Ogdensburg Railroad, known across northern New York as the "Hojack."

Rosiere Depot, On The Rome, Watertown, Ogdensburg R.R.

The nickname's origin is debated. Some say it came from a trackside worker shouting "Whoa, Jack!" to signal an engineer. Others trace it to railroad slang. Whatever its beginnings, the name endured. By the late nineteenth century, the Hojack had become an artery of commerce along

Lake Ontario's southern shore. Its rails stitched together fishing ports, dairy farms, and immigrant settlements, carrying milk, hay, timber, and limestone to markets in Watertown, Syracuse, and beyond.

For immigrant families, the railway promised more than goods and travel. It offered connection, opportunity, and the sense that their settlement might endure. Where lake traffic once froze solid each winter, the iron road kept moving. Even in snowbound months, trains pressed through drifts, binding Cape Vincent and its hamlets to the wider world.

By 1861, the nation had fractured, and the Civil War carried uncertainty into even the quietest households. Though Cape Vincent lay far from the fighting, the war reached it nonetheless through enlistments, anxious waiting, rising prices, and the steady presence of loss.

The Fourth of July 1861 dawned clear and mild in Cape Vincent. A steady breeze off Lake Ontario kept the heat at bay, stirring long grass and lifting Union flags from porches along the village streets. Beneath the summer calm lay the knowledge that the nation was at war and that the inheritance forged at Yorktown was once again being tested.

Siméon Jr. brought the family to the annual Fourth of July picnic and oration. Among them stood his son Charles André. The orator was Louis C. Thierry, Esq., an educator from nearby Watertown invited to speak at a moment of national peril.

Nearly three months into the Civil War, the picnic oration moved from memory to urgency. As reported in *The Cape Vincent Gazette*, Thierry contrasted British caution with France's reluctance to recognize the Confederacy, invoking the Marquis de Lafayette, the Comte de Rochambeau, and Admiral de Grasse. He affirmed the supremacy of American law and argued that the Revolution's legacy was a trust still to be defended. For families like the Gaugiens, whose family history was bound to that earlier struggle, the words brought a moment of pride in their former country and their new.

Within three weeks, nine men from Cape Vincent stepped forward, the first of what would become 108. They entered service that would become known as the Black River Artillery, a locally raised unit that later consolidated into the 10th New York Heavy Artillery, known as the

Jefferson County Regiment. Recruited from towns all along the Black River and the upper St. Lawrence, including Cape Vincent, Clayton, and Watertown, the regiment carried the war far from home, from the defenses of Washington to the brutal siege of Petersburg.

Over the course of its service, the regiment lost 26 enlisted men killed in action, 21 mortally wounded, and more than 220 to disease and other causes.

By the winter of 1864, the war no longer arrived in Cape Vincent as headlines. It settled instead into absence. Empty chairs at supper. Fields tended by boys and aging fathers. Victory seemed nearer now, but even the hopeful understood what victory would not return every son.

In November, word came that Abraham Lincoln had been re-elected. The message carried north by rail and river confirmed what most already sensed: the struggle would continue to its full measure. There would be no negotiated peace, no turning back. In the North Country, that certainty brought a tightening of resolve.

On January 5, 1865, Siméon Gaugien Jr. died at age seventy, only months before the conflict's end. His photograph survives, a rare image of one of the earliest French settlers of Rosiere. He rests in the cemetery behind St. Vincent de Paul Church in Cape Vincent, his headstone and family monument standing as quiet witnesses to the North Country's French roots.

Siméon Gaugien, Jr. c. 1863

Twelve days after President Lincoln was assassinated at Ford's Theatre in Washington, the *Northern N.Y. Journal* out of Watertown ran the headline "THE NATIONAL CALAMITY: Further Interesting Particulars." The front page carried eyewitness testimony from inside the theatre and the account of the Army surgeon who found Lincoln in his chair; the simultaneous attack on Secretary of State Seward; and the quiet inauguration of Andrew Johnson as president. For readers in Jefferson County, whose sons had stood in the very defenses of Washington, the particulars were not distant history. They were the final passage of a war that had already taken everything.

The war was over. The men who came home came home changed. Those who did not come home left behind the particular silence of unfinished lives. In time, the village found its footing again; the rhythms of dairy and harvest and parish are patient, and they do not wait for grief to finish. But the decade that followed the war asked more of the North Country. In the autumn of 1873, financial panic swept the North

Gaugien family monument,
Cape Vincent, New York

Country again. By November, Jeanne-Baptiste, eight years a widow, could read the first signs in the pages of *The Cape Vincent Eagle*:

"Machine shops and cotton mills in various parts of the country are discontinuing work, and thousands of people are thus thrown out of employment. These are the saddest features of the panic."

Why are Bushnell &
Kelsey slaughtering prices
as they are now doing?
Because they want the
CASH!

You say times are
hard and money scarce,
Then trade with Bushnell & Kelsey, where a LITTLE MONEY will buy A
GOOD DEAL of goods.

November 6, 1873 Advertisement
in the *Cape Vincent Eagle*

Local merchants, pressed for cash, slashed prices and appealed directly to their neighbors. In the same issue, Bushnell & Kelsey asked: *"Why are Bushnell & Kelsey slaughtering prices as they are now doing? Because they want the CASH! You say times are hard and money scarce, then trade with Bushnell & Kelsey, where a LITTLE MONEY will buy A GOOD DEAL of goods."*

Fifty-five railroads across the nation had failed by November. Within a year, sixty more had collapsed. The depression that followed endured until 1879 and was deep and widespread across both Europe and North America.

Siméon Jr.'s widow, Jeanne-Baptiste Thierat Gaugien, lived until September 13, 1878. Her life spanned the distance from the rough-hewn cabins of the 1830s to the settled fields of the late nineteenth century. By the 1870s, some of those first log homes still stood, weathered but upright, relics of endurance, not defeat.

In 1881, Charles André Gaugien, later Gosier[75], purchased a limestone farmhouse near Rosiere. Solid and enduring, its thick walls marked how far the family had traveled since their arrival. His daughter, Mary C. Gosier[76], later Aubertine,

Jeanne-Baptiste Thierat Gaugien c. 1863

had been raised in a log cabin. The stone house signaled permanence. The roots planted in uncertain soil had taken hold.

Rosiere Station (Depot) 1908

The memory of Charles André and his wife, Geneviève Branche Gosier, was honored in a stained-glass window at St. Vincent de Paul Church in Cape Vincent, New York. The glass still glows in the morning light, casting color across the sanctuary where they once knelt. By 1898,

---

[75] **French immigrant surnames** were often anglicized in nineteenth-century New York through phonetic record keeping and deliberate simplification; "Gaugien" appears frequently as "Gosier" in local records. See S. Baird, "Anglicizing Ethnic Surnames," *Names: A Journal of Onomastics 54*, no. 2 (2006).

[76] **Mary Gaugien**, also recorded as Gosier, later Mary Aubertine; born 1858 in Rosiere, town of Cape Vincent, Jefferson County, New York, daughter of Charles André Gaugien and Geneviève Branche; married Nicholas Aubertine on November 11, 1879, in Rosiere, Cape Vincent; died there March 11, 1933. Civil registers, Jefferson County, New York.

the hamlet of Rosiere held roughly one hundred inhabitants, its farms averaging twenty-five acres.

Rosiere House circa 1915, R. Mallaby, Proprietor

Through their granddaughter, Grace Sarah Aubertine[77], who married Walter Hollenbeck, my great-grandparents, in June 1912, they carried that legacy into the twentieth century.

At the Hollenbeck homestead known as Sunnyside Farm, a fifty-acre dairy and hay operation near Cape Vincent, they continued the constancy that had begun centuries earlier beside the millstream of Rosières-sur-Mance. The new train depot, a modest wooden structure set close to the tracks, its platform crowded with milk cans at dawn and trunks in summer, stood not as a monument but as a threshold. Life in Jefferson County was still set by the land, the turning of seasons, and the milking of cows, but it was now timed to the railroad whistle and the printed schedule in *The Cape Vincent Eagle*. Three trains left the village depot each day at 7:10 a.m., 11:50 a.m., and 5:00 p.m., stitching farms like Sunnyside to markets and to the new century's economy.

When the stock market collapsed in October 1929, the shock did not immediately register in the North Country. On the front page of *The Cape Vincent Eagle* there were no banner headlines announcing catastrophe, no warnings of panic, no language of collapse. Not until 1932, nearly three

---

[77] **Grace Sarah Aubertine Hollenbeck**; born June 1, 1891, in Rosiere, town of Cape Vincent, Jefferson County, New York, daughter of Mary Gaugien, also recorded as Gosier, and Nicholas Aubertine; married Walter Andrew Hollenbeck; died January 4, 1983, in Watertown, Jefferson County, New York. Civil registers, Jefferson County, New York.

years after Black Tuesday, was local hardship unmistakable. Reports of hundreds of Jefferson County families receiving relief, discussions of tax delinquencies, and explicit references to "times of depression" entered the public record. The North Country had not escaped the Depression. It had experienced it on delay. Over the following years it became institutional: relief administrations, bond issues, public works programs. By 1936 employment figures and political debates dominated local reporting.

Sunnyside Farm, Cape Vincent, NY

Recovery did not come through markets. It marched in through Pine Camp, when in October 1938 the Federal government announced its expansion under a national defense program. By October 1940 the shift was unmistakable: millions of dollars appropriated, hundreds of buildings planned, thousands of workers employed.

By 1942, the North Country lived under WWII wartime directives: tire surrenders, scrap drives, ration enforcement, and casualty lists. Federal authority became ordinary, embedded in the language of daily life. The vocabulary of "depression" vanished, replaced by "emergency" and "national defense." Labor shortages replaced unemployment. By 1943, *The Cape Vincent Eagle* printed War Fund quotas, manpower statistics, and the names of local men and women in uniform. War no longer approached. It had become a new order to daily life.

The Hollenbeck, Aubertine and many other farming families were strong supporters of the Grange[78]. In 1948 alone Grace was honored for nine years as a lecturer, carrying the membership through depression, war, and the uncertain years between. That same year she led a program posing the question the age itself was asking: "Will the Radio Ever Take the Place of Newspapers?" Walter served alongside her in the Grange's formal leadership, as did Walton Aubertine and his wife, Grace's own kin, two families rooted together in the Grange for a decade.

By 1952, the great surge of World War II had long since receded. Dairy prices and ferry crossings again marked the rhythm of village life. The Korean War, though ongoing, did not command the local front page as WWII had. There was no sweeping economic conversion, no vast expansion of Pine Camp, no flood of construction crews. Life in Cape Vincent moved in its accustomed steadiness.

Then, before spring, the war entered their home.

Walter and Grace's son, Chief Warrant Officer Richard Walter Hollenbeck, was serving in Korea with the 55th Military Police Criminal Investigation Detachment when on March 15, 1952, he was killed.

The loss was not geopolitical. It was personal. He had served in both World War II and Korea. For leadership and valor, he was awarded the Silver Star, the Purple Heart with two Oak Leaf Clusters. Honors follow sacrifice. They do not prevent it.

My given middle name, Richard, carries his.

The Wolfe Island ferry continued its crossing. Dairy herds were milked before sunrise. In the village, the printed columns recorded prices and meetings, as they had for generations. Yet for the Hollenbeck family, time divided cleanly: before the telegram and after.

By now the Saint Lawrence Seaway was reshaping the river. Freighters now moved where wooden fishing boats once dominated. Federal presence increased again as Pine Camp[79] continued to grow. Local families

---

[78]**The National Grange of the Order of Patrons of Husbandry**, founded in 1867, was the largest agricultural organization in the United States. Local chapters served as farmers' advocacy organizations, mutual aid societies, and civic institutions. One of the first American fraternal organizations to admit women as full members on equal terms with men, the Grange reached its postwar peak in the late 1940s with membership exceeding eight hundred thousand families nationwide.

[79] In 1974 **Pine Camp** was redesignated Fort Drum, reflecting its expanded mission and

remained as they had been: resilient and river-bound.

After his seventy-fifth birthday, Walter Hollenbeck began telling the family he had only one wish left: to live long enough to meet his first great-grand-son. I was born in April 1964. He died that June. We did meet.

Nearly two centuries earlier, Nicolas Gaugien had voiced the same hope, to see his first grandson. He held that child for a fleeting moment before both died the same day. Walter, generations later, was granted what Nicolas was not. He saw the next branch of the family take root and then, at peace, released his hold on this life.

Their daughter, Mary Hollenbeck Ransier[80], my Granny, was raised in that same tradition, a bridge between worlds. She was the first to leave the farm, moving to Watertown to enroll in the Watertown School of Commerce; for a farm girl of her generation, this was no small thing. She preserved their stories in quiet ways, passing them forward without ever knowing how far they would travel.

And so the story comes full circle.

It began with Siméon Gaugien, tending vines beside a French mill-stream, learning that strong roots make a sturdy vine. His life proved that truth, from the vineyards of Franche-Comté to the battlefield of Yorktown, and in the steadfast resolve that carried his family across an ocean. Their new home in New York's North Country grew from the roots he helped plant.

The victory was not only in arms, but in endurance. Survival over war. Harvest over hunger. Resilience over despair. From snowdrifts and rough cabins grew a rooted community.

The truest victory is forged not in a single battle, but across generations.

---

reinforcing its role as a major military installation and economic anchor in northern New York.
[80] **Mary Hollenbeck Ransier**, known as Granny; born March 13, 1917, in Cape Vincent, Jefferson County, New York, daughter of Grace Sarah Aubertine Hollenbeck and Walter Andrew Hollenbeck; married Kenneth Ransier on May 27, 1942; died August 7, 2007, in Rodman, Jefferson County, New York. Civil registers, Jefferson County, New York.

BIBLIOGRAPHY

Primary Sources

Archives Diocésaines de Besançon. *Registres paroissiaux et d'état civil: Charles Henri Thérion; Lécourt and Rosières-sur-Mance.*

Bizouard, J.-Th. (Abbé). *Histoire de l'hôpital d'Auxonne (1374 – 1884).* Dijon: H. Grigne, Libraire-Éditeur, 1884.

Blanchard, Claude. *The Journal of Claude Blanchard: Commissary of the French Auxiliary Army Sent to the United States During the American Revolution, 1780 – 1783.* Translated by William Duane, edited by Thomas Balch. Albany: J. Munsell, 1876.

Bonaparte, Napoléon. *Correspondance générale.* Vols. 1–2. Paris: Fayard / Fondation Napoléon, 2004.

Cape Vincent Eagle (Cape Vincent, NY). Weekly. 1872 – 1879. Ames & Hart. Available online via Northern New York Library Network and Chronicling America.

The Cape-Vincent Gazette. Cape Vincent, N.Y.: Paul A. Leach, 1858 – 1862. Weekly. Available online via Chronicling America, Northern New York Library Network (15 May 1858 – 14 September 1861; 112 issues).

Chaignay (Côte-d'Or, France). *Contract of the Communal Herdsman,* 1791.

Clermont-Crèvecoeur, Jean-François-Louis de. "Journal of the War in America During the Years 1780, 1781, 1782, 1783." In *The American Campaigns of Rochambeau's Army,* edited by Howard C. Rice Jr. and Anne S. K. Brown. Princeton: Princeton University Press, 1972.

Cornwallis, Charles, 1st Marquess Cornwallis. "Letter to Sir Henry Clinton, October 20, 1781." *Teaching American History.* https:// teachingamericanhistory.org/document/cornwallis-to-clinton/.

Departmental Archives of Haute-Saône. *Notarial and civil registers, Rosières-sur-Mance (1790 – 1814).*

FamilySearch. "Schweiz, Katholische und Reformierte Kirchenbücher, 1418 – 1996," Carolus Heinricus Thérion.

Great Britain. House of Commons. *Journals of the House of Commons.* Vol.

37. London: His Majesty's Stationery Office, 1779.

Huggins, Benjamin L., ed. *The Papers of George Washington, Revolutionary War Series*. Vol. 27. Charlottesville: University of Virginia Press, 2019.

Idzerda, Stanley J., ed. *Lafayette in the Age of the American Revolution: Selected Letters and Papers, 1776 – 1790*. Vol. 2. Ithaca: Cornell University Press, 1977.

Jefferson, Thomas. "To George Washington, January 10, 1781." *Founders Online*, National Archives.

Jefferson, Thomas. "To James Le Ray de Chaumont, 29 May 1818." *Founders Online*, National Archives.

Les combattants français de la guerre américaine, 1778 – 1783. Washington: Imprimerie Nationale, 1905.

Marins et soldats français en Amérique. Vol. 1, *Armée de Rochambeau*, 1780. Paris: Imprimerie Nationale, 1903.

Martin, Joseph Plumb. *A Narrative of a Revolutionary Soldier*. 1830.

Massachusetts Bay Colony. *Law of 1659*.

Moré, Charles-Albert de Pontgibaud. *A French Volunteer of the War of Independence*. Translated and edited by Robert B. Douglas. New York: G. P. Putnam's Sons, 1898.

National Archives. *Treaty of Alliance with France (1778)*. https://www.archives.gov/milestone-documents/treaty-of-alliance-with-france.

Nelson, Thomas, Jr. *Letters of Thomas Nelson, Jr., Governor of Virginia*. Richmond: Virginia Historical Society Publications, New Series, no. 1, 1874.

Pickering, Timothy. "To George Washington, 5 October 1781." *Founders Online*, National Archives.

Ramsay, David. *The History of the American Revolution*. Lexington, KY: Downing and Phillips, 1815.

Rosières-sur-Mance (Haute-Saône, France). *Registres d'état civil (1790 – 1814)*. Accessed via Geneanet Family Archives.

Service historique de la Défense (Vincennes). *Sous-série Yb (Régiment d'Auxonne)*.

Shaw, Samuel. *The Journals of Major Samuel Shaw*, The First American Consul at Canton. Boston: Wm. Crosby and H. P. Nichols, 1847.

Smith, Isaac, Sr. "To John Adams, September 13, 1781." *Adams Family Correspondence*, 4:211–212. *Founders Online*, National Archives.

Susane, Louis. *Histoire de l'artillerie française*, Tome I. Paris: J. Dumaine, 1874.

United States Congress. Senate. *The Siege of Yorktown*. Senate Document no. 234, Serial Set no. 9347. Washington, DC: Government Printing Office, 1976.

von Closen, Ludwig, Baron. *The Revolutionary Journal of Baron Ludwig von Closen*, 1780 – 1783. Edited by Evelyn M. Acomb. Chapel Hill: University of North Carolina Press, 1958.

von Steuben, Friedrich Wilhelm. *Regulations for the Order and Discipline of the Troops of the United States*. Philadelphia, 1779.

Washington, George. *The Diaries of George Washington*, Vol. 3. Charlottesville: University Press of Virginia, 1978.

Washington, George. "General Orders, September 13, 1782." *Orderly Book, September 6 – November 19, 1782*, Verplanck's Point. SNAC Resource ID: 7770115.

Washington, George. "To Benjamin Franklin, October 18, 1782." *Founders Online*, National Archives. https://founders.archives.gov/documents/Washington/99-01-02-09754.

Washington, George. "To Major General Lafayette, March 8, 1781." *The Papers of George Washington. Founders Online*, National Archives.

Washington, George. "To Major General Lafayette, March 11, 1781." *The Papers of George Washington. Founders Online*, National Archives.

Washington, George. "To Samuel Huntington, March 11, 1781." *The Papers of George Washington. Founders Online*, National Archives.

Secondary Sources

Afkham, Emad. "Peasant Revolts During the French Wars." MA thesis, Central European University, 2016. https://www.etd.ceu.edu/2017/afkham_emad.pdf.

Anderson, Fred. *Crucible of War: The Seven Years' War and the Fate of Empire in British North America, 1754 – 1766*. New York: Knopf, 2000.

Andress, David. *The Terror: The Merciless War for Freedom in Revolutionary France*. New York: Farrar, Straus and Giroux, 2005.

Baird, Scott. "Anglicizing Ethnic Surnames." *Names: A Journal of Onomastics* 54, no. 2 (2006).

Blaufarb, Rafe. *The French Army 1750 – 1820: Careers, Talent, Merit*. New York: Palgrave Macmillan, 2002.

Boatner, Mark M., III, ed. "Aboville, François Marie, Comte d'." *In Encyclopedia of the American Revolution*. New York: David McKay Company, 1966. Accessed via Encyclopedia.com.

Callaway, Hannah. "A Contested Inheritance: The Family and the Law from the Enlightenment to the French Revolution." *Law and History Review* 37 (2018): 61–87.

Calloway, Colin G. *The Scratch of a Pen: 1763 and the Transformation of North America*. New York: Oxford University Press, 2006.

Casler, Nelie Horton. *Cape Vincent and Its History*. Watertown, NY: Hungerford-Holbrook Co., 1906.

Chaline, Olivier. *Naval Leadership in the Atlantic World*. Edited by Richard Harding and Agustín Guimerá. London: University of Westminster Press, 2017.

Chandler, David G. *The Campaigns of Napoléon*. New York: Scribner, 1973.

Chartrand, René. *The French Army in the American War of Independence*. Men-at-Arms Series No. 244. London: Osprey Publishing, 1991.

Claerr, Christiane. "Statuette de pèlerinage: Vierge à l'Enfant dite Notre-Dame de Gray." *Inventaire du patrimoine culturel de Bourgogne–Franche-Comté*, 1991.

Corvisier, André. *L'Armée française de la fin du XVIIe siècle au ministère de Choiseul: Le soldat.* Paris: Presses Universitaires de France, 1964.

Dictionary of National Biography. London: Smith, Elder & Co., 1885 – 1900. S.v. "Dundas, Thomas" and "Ross, Alexander (1742–1827)."

Doyle, William. *Origins of the French Revolution.* Oxford: Oxford University Press, 1980.

Dull, Jonathan R. *The French Navy and American Independence: A Study of Arms and Diplomacy, 1774 – 1787.* Princeton: Princeton University Press, 1975.

Dupâquier, Jacques, et al., eds. *Histoire de la population française.* Vol. 2. Paris: Presses Universitaires de France, 1988.

Fagan, Brian. *The Little Ice Age: How Climate Made History, 1300 – 1850.* New York: Basic Books, 2000.

Faber, Eli. "Haym Salomon." *Immigrant Entrepreneurship: German-American Business Biographies,* 1720–1920. German Historical Institute. Last modified 2014. https://www.immigrantentrepreneurship.org/entries/haym-salomon/.

Ferreiro, Larrie D. *Brothers at Arms: American Independence and the Men of France and Spain Who Saved It.* New York: Knopf, 2016.

Fraser, Antonia. *Marie Antoinette: The Journey.* New York: Doubleday, 2001.

Frey, Sylvia R. *Water from the Rock: Black Resistance in a Revolutionary Age.* Princeton: Princeton University Press, 1991.

Giesler, James. "Francisco de Saavedra's Role in Securing the Independence of the United States." Queen Sofía Spanish Institute, 2022.

Gottschalk, Louis. *Lafayette and the Close of the American Revolution.* Chicago: University of Chicago Press, 1942.

Goubert, Pierre. *The French Peasantry in the Seventeenth Century.* Cambridge: Cambridge University Press, 1986.

Greene, Jerome A. *The Guns of Independence: The Siege of Yorktown, 1781.* New York: Savas Beatie, 2005.

Jannin, Marie-Christine. "Verreries d'Argonne, quoi de neuf? Dynamique d'une exposition." *Bulletin de l'AFAV* (2020): 132–136.

Kennett, Lee. *The French Forces in America, 1780 – 1783.* Westport, CT: Greenwood Press, 1977.

Klingaman, William K., and Nicholas P. Klingaman. *The Year Without Summer: 1816 and the Volcano That Darkened the World and Changed History.* New York: St. Martin's Press, 2013.

Kranish, Michael. *Flight from Monticello: Thomas Jefferson at War.* New York: Oxford University Press, 2010.

Kwass, Michael. *Privilege and the Politics of Taxation in Eighteenth-Century France.* Cambridge: Harvard University Press, 2000.

Larrabee, Harold A. *Decision at the Chesapeake.* New York: Clarkson N. Potter, 1964.

Linÿer de La Barbée, Maurice. *Le chevalier de Ternay: Vie de Charles Henry Louis d'Arsac de Ternay, chef d'escadre des armées navales, 1723 – 1780.* 2 vols. Grenoble: Éditions des 4 Seigneurs, 1972.

Lockhart, Paul. *The Drillmaster of Valley Forge: The Baron de Steuben and the Making of the American Army.* New York: HarperCollins, 2008.

Lynn, John A. *Giant of the Grand Siècle: The French Army, 1610 – 1715.* Cambridge: Cambridge University Press, 1997.

Lynn, John A. *The Wars of Louis XIV, 1667 – 1714.* London: Longman, 1999.

McPhee, Peter. *Liberty or Death: The French Revolution.* New Haven: Yale University Press, 2016.

Merriman, John M. *A History of Modern Europe: From the Renaissance to the Present.* 3rd ed. New York: W. W. Norton, 2010.

Morison, Samuel Eliot. *John Paul Jones: A Sailor's Biography.* Boston: Little, Brown, 1959.

Phillips, Rod. "The Very Long and Very Short History of Barrel-Aged Wine." *World of Fine Wine*, January 5, 2026. Accessed February 19, 2026. https://www.worldoffinewine.com.

Picard, Ernest, and Louis Jouan. *L'artillerie française au XVIIIe siècle.* Paris: Berger-Levrault, 1906.

Pichichero, Christy. *The Military Enlightenment: War and Culture in the French Empire from Louis XIV to Napoléon*. Ithaca: Cornell University Press, 2017.

Popkin, Jeremy D. *A New World Begins: The History of the French Revolution*. New York: Basic Books, 2019.

Pybus, Cassandra. *Epic Journeys of Freedom: Runaway Slaves of the American Revolution and Their Global Quest for Liberty*. Boston: Beacon Press, 2006.

Rees, Dylan, and Duncan Townson. *France in Revolution*. 4th ed. London: Hodder Education, 2012.

Roche, Daniel. *France in the Enlightenment*. Cambridge, MA: Harvard University Press, 2000.

Roswell P. Flower Memorial Library. "Artwork in the Napoléon Room." Accessed February 7, 2026. https://www.flowermemoriallibrary.org/napoleon-room/.

Ruppert, Bob. "France and Spain Invade England—Almost." *Journal of the American Revolution*, January 30, 2020. https://allthingsliberty.com/2020/01/france-and-spain-invade-england-almost/.

Schama, Simon. *Citizens: A Chronicle of the French Revolution*. New York: Vintage Books, 1989.

Schama, Simon. *Rough Crossings: Britain, the Slaves, and the American Revolution*. New York: Ecco, 2006.

Sée, Henri. *Economic and Social Conditions in France During the Eighteenth Century*. Translated by Edwin H. Zeydel. Kitchener, ON: Batoche Books, 2004.

Segalen, Martine. *Love and Power in the Peasant Family: Rural France in the Nineteenth Century*. Chicago: University of Chicago Press, 1983.

Selig, Robert A. *March to Victory: Washington, Rochambeau, and the Yorktown Campaign of 1781*. Washington, DC: U.S. Army Center of Military History, 2007.

Smith, David G. *The Siege of Savannah: A Pivotal Battle in the American Revolution*. Columbia: University of South Carolina Press, 2005.

Stroud, Patricia Tyson. *The Man Who Had Been King: The American Exile of Napoléon's Brother Joseph*. Philadelphia: University of Pennsylvania Press, 2005.

Swinton, William. *First Lessons in Our Country's History: Bringing Out Its Salient Points, and Aiming to Combine Simplicity with Sense; with Numerous Illustrations*. New York: Ivison, Blakeman, Taylor, 1872.

Thordarson, Thorvaldur, and Stephen Self. "Atmospheric and Environmental Effects of the 1783 – 1784 Laki Eruption." *Journal of Geophysical Research* 108, no. D1 (2003).

Tilley, John A. *The British Navy and the American Revolution*. Columbia: University of South Carolina Press, 1987.

Unger, Harlow Giles. *Lafayette*. New York: Wiley, 2002.

Van Buskirk, Judith L. *Standing in Their Own Light: African American Patriots in the American Revolution*. Norman: University of Oklahoma Press, 2017.

Verdier, Nicolas, et al. "Postal Horse Relays and Roads in France, from the 17th to the 19th Centuries." *Cybergeo: European Journal of Geography* (2025). https://doi.org/10.4000/13gxr.

Weiser, Francis X. *Handbook of Christian Feasts and Customs: The Year of the Lord in Liturgy and Folklore*. New York: Harcourt, Brace and Company, 1958.

Wheaton, Barbara Ketcham. *Savoring the Past: The French Kitchen and Table from 1300 to 1789*. Philadelphia: University of Pennsylvania Press, 1983.

Willis, Sam. *The Struggle for Sea Power: A Naval History of the American Revolution*. New York: W. W. Norton & Company, 2016.

Winfield, Rif. *British Warships in the Age of Sail: 1714 – 1792*. Barnsley, UK: Seaforth Publishing, 2007.

Index

A

Aboville, François-Marie d' (Colonel) artillery command at Yorktown 133, 150, 154, 166, 178, 194, 205, 261, 282, 290, 306
Artillery Gribeauval system at Yorktown see also Régiment d'Auxonne X, 24, 27, 29, 30, 42, 43, 67, 70, 86, 90, 99, 103, 105, 108, 109, 111, 112, 113, 114, 119, 128, 132, 133, 134, 135, 137, 149, 150, 154, 155, 157, 158, 162, 167, 171, 172, 178, 180, 185, 189, 204, 205, 206, 218, 232, 237, 238, 246, 248, 251, 252, 258, 259, 269, 274, 275, 276, 279, 281, 282, 290, 292, 293, 299, 327, 355, 357
Auxonne (city) see also Régiment d'Auxonne X, XII, 21, 27, 68, 85, 86, 87, 93, 97, 98, 99, 100, 101, 105, 106, 107, 108, 109, 111, 112, 113, 115, 116, 117, 118, 129, 132, 133, 135, 137, 147, 149, 150, 151, 155, 157, 166, 170, 171, 172, 173, 177, 178, 179, 184, 185, 187, 191, 203, 205, 207, 220, 226, 234, 242, 244, 246, 247, 257, 258, 260, 262, 282, 290, 293, 294, 295, 297, 298, 299, 302, 306, 307, 311, 312, 313, 319, 320, 324, 327, 329, 330, 341, 343

B

Barras, Jacques-Melchior, Comte de (Admiral) 233, 239, 242, 243, 246
Black soldiers 268, 269
Blanchard, Claude (commissary officer) 202, 254, 255, 282
Bourbon dynasty see also Louis XVI 276, 302
Brandywine, Battle of 135, 136
Brest 82, 157, 166, 178, 179, 184, 185, 187, 189, 190, 191, 197, 304, 305, 318

C

Cape Vincent, New York XII, 181, 343, 352, 353, 362, 363, 365, 367, 368, 369, 370, 371, 372, 373, 374, 375
Carhaix (Carhaix-Plouguer) 184
Channel Coast strategy (1779) 82, 149, 151, 156, 158, 159, 160, 161, 173, 174, 185, 189, 190, 195, 208, 238, 254
Chesapeake Bay see also Virginia Capes, Battle of 200, 205, 223, 225, 230, 231, 232, 243, 244, 245, 246, 279, 289, 290, 292, 296, 299
Colas (see Gaugien, Nicolas, brother) 20, 21, 22, 23, 24, 25, 26, 29, 31, 32, 33, 34, 35, 39, 40, 41, 43, 47, 48, 50, 51, 52, 55, 56, 57, 58, 59, 60, 69, 70, 71, 72, 74, 75, 76, 77, 78, 82, 87, 88, 90, 91, 92, 94, 142, 146, 174, 175, 176, 177, 181, 222, 224, 240, 288, 315, 316, 317, 318, 319, 320, 321, 323, 324, 328, 329, 338, 340, 344, 353
Conquérant (ship) 188, 189, 190, 194, 202, 228, 229, 230, 231
Continental Army 136, 137, 197, 245, 354